KICKING OFF AGAIN

The PITCH Report

Love great sportswriting? So do we.

Every month, Pitch Publishing brings together the best of our world through our monthly newsletter — a space for readers, writers and fans to connect over the books, people and moments that make sport so captivating.

You'll find previews of new releases, extracts from our latest titles, behind-the-scenes interviews with authors and the occasional giveaway or competition thrown in for good measure.

We also dip into our back catalogue to unearth forgotten gems and celebrate timeless tales that shaped sporting culture.

Scan the QR code and join the growing Pitch Publishing reader community today.

KICKING OFF AGAIN

Football's Greatest Season

Brian Halford

pitch

First published by Pitch Publishing, 2026
1

Pitch Publishing
9 Donnington Park, 85 Birdham Road
Chichester, West Sussex, PO20 7AJ
www.pitchpublishing.co.uk
info@pitchpublishing.co.uk

Set in Adobe Caslon Pro

Typeset by Pitch Publishing

Cover design by Olner Design

Printed and bound in India by Thomson Press India Private Limited

The authorised representative in the EEA is Easy Access System Europe OÜ, Mustamäe tee 50, 10621 Tallinn, Estonia gpsr.requests@easproject.com

A CIP catalogue record for this book is available from the British Library

ISBN 978-1-83680-420-8

Papers used by Pitch Publishing are from well-managed forests and other responsible sources

MIX
Paper | Supporting responsible forestry
FSC® C010615

For Anele

Contents

Introduction

SATURDAY, 31 August 1946 was a unique and momentous day for English football but also resonated far beyond the insular bubble in which sport often exists. After seven incredibly difficult years, people in the UK were craving a return to normality and familiarity. The return of the Football League offered a huge measure of those.

There was football during the war but, like every aspect of life, it was hugely affected and compromised by the conflict. Travelling was restricted, so leagues became regional, removing the appeal of meeting opponents from other parts of the country. Many players were called up by the armed forces, so clubs were allowed to field guest players. This sometimes offered supporters an unexpected glimpse of a star they would otherwise never have seen, but the overall effect was to diminish the identity of clubs.

The large attendances, especially later in the war, showed that in the midst of a deeply troubling big picture – the anxiety, fear, sadness and hardships caused by the conflict – the national love of football was as high as, if not higher than, ever. And the longer the 'ersatz' temporary leagues went on, the more a return to 'proper' football was desired.

The FA Cup returned in the 1945/46 season, starting with four ties in the extra preliminary round – Aylesbury United 5 Chesham United 0, Banbury Spencer 8 Headington United 1, Pressed Steel 1 Morris Motors 0 and Uxbridge 11 Lyons Club 1 – and ending with the Wembley final, Derby County 4 Charlton Athletic 1 on 27 April 1946. The following four months gave clubs the chance to prepare for the precious resumption of the Football League. On 31 August, with the same 44 fixtures with which it had started the aborted 1939/40 season, it was back.

1

Football League Division One
Everton 0 Brentford 2 (HT: 0-1)
Scorers – Brentford: Wilkins, McAloon
Attendance: 55,338

'Brentford, with their liberal sprinkling of bald heads, were as lively as a bunch of spring lambs.'

ON SATURDAY, 31 August 1946, readers of the *Liverpool Daily Post* had a strange story to digest along with their heavily rationing-affected breakfasts. The paper's front page carried the headline, 'ODDEST STORY OF THE WAR – SOLDIER WHO DIDN'T KNOW IT WAS OVER'.

The soldier in question was Private Clarence Paxton. The 30-year-old Canadian had appeared before a court martial at Tweedsmuir Repatriation Camp in Thursley, Surrey. He faced a charge of absence without leave for 393 days.

Private Paxton's story was indeed odd. The Second World War had concluded on 2 September 1945, but the defendant told the court that he had not found that out until 18 January 1946. It was on that wintry day, he claimed, that, residing in the remote Italian mountain village of Vinchiaturo, he suddenly recovered the memory which he had lost ten months earlier.

Curiously, for someone whose memory deserted him for almost a year, Paxton could pinpoint the very moment that it went.

'He said his unit was moving out of the Italian village at 4am on 12 March 1945,' reported the *Daily Post*. 'He'd been out drinking with some British soldiers the previous night and woke up at five to four, rushed out to join the convoy, grabbed hold of the tailboard of a lorry and from that moment his mind went blank until 18 January 1946.'

When Paxton's memory suddenly returned (what occurred on 18 January to restore it was not reported) and he was informed that the war had ended some months earlier, he 'could not believe it', the court heard.

Paxton's story was supported by Major R.J.F. Cawthorpe, a neuropsychiatrist, who was convinced after administering to the soldier a quantity of sodium amytal, a truth drug. 'In my opinion,' Cawthorpe testified, 'when he tried to get in the lorry, Paxton was filled with terror and fright and had suffered from genuine hysterical amnesia.'

Paxton was acquitted. It was a good result for him and no doubt intrigued the readers of the *Daily Post*, though on that particular Saturday morning it's safe to say the vast majority of them were more interested in another kind of result. The sort generated by blokes in shorts on a grassy oblong rather than chaps in suits in a windowless courtroom.

On 31 August 1946, after seven years in abeyance following Britain's declaration of war on Germany on 3 September 1939, the Football League returned. After seven seasons of regional and makeshift competition, travelling restrictions, teams full of guests and matches truncated by air raids, the nation welcomed back 'proper' football. It began with the full fixture list that had already been fulfilled once as the Football League stuck with the schedule from the 1939/40 season which was abandoned after three games. The attention of Merseyside's footy fans was, therefore, divided between Bramall Lane, where Liverpool visited Sheffield United, Prenton Park, where Tranmere Rovers faced bogey side Rotherham United, The Racecourse, where New Brighton visited Wrexham, and Goodison Park, home of the reigning champions. Could Everton open their long-delayed title defence with a win at home to Brentford?

The Toffees had been champs for seven years, having been crowned in the spring of 1939, four months before war broke out. It was not the first time that the Blues of Merseyside had retained the title due to global conflict; they were the champions in 1914. Everton winning the First Division did not augur well for world peace.

In August 1946, 11 months on from the end of the war, life in the UK was still massively dictated by the conflict and its consequences. Many basic components of daily life often taken for granted – safety, food and drink, clothing, transport, leisure – were reduced or compromised. Life remained complex and difficult so every tiny step back towards normality was a lift for national morale. The return of the Football League was a huge step.

'Facing what is likely to be the greatest season in its 60-year history, English league football opens its first full-scale, back-to-normal campaign,' reported the *Daily Post*. 'On Merseyside the chief attraction is at Goodison Park where Everton receive Brentford.'

The joy at football's return was widespread but not unanimous. Rather than joining the excitement at the potential 'greatest season', the Churches Committee on Gambling took a portentous tone. The committee chose the eve of the long-awaited day to point out that more than £25m had been spent on football pools during the 1945/46 season. That the pastime offered an avenue of pleasure to a bruised, bombed and bereaved nation cut no ice with the committee.

'Everything points to the conclusion that the country is heading for the biggest pools deluge ever known,' it moaned. 'In spite of postwar restrictions and national requirements, the shameful prewar records are likely to be broken this season.'

The grave warning evidently fell on a lot of deaf ears, judging by the following Monday's *London Daily News*. 'Heavy rain in places could not damp the ardour of football enthusiasts for the opening on Saturday when nearly a million people turned up at the 43 league games [one of the scheduled 44 did not take place – more in Chapter 28],' the paper reported. The biggest crowd was 61,464 for Chelsea v Bolton Wanderers at Stamford Bridge. Five others also exceeded 50,000: Aston Villa v Middlesbrough, Sunderland v Derby County, Tottenham Hotspur v Birmingham City, Wolverhampton Wanderers v Arsenal and Everton v Brentford, where 55,338 gathered at Goodison.

Since it last hosted a Football League match, Brentford's visit on 26 August 1939, Goodison Park had been battered by bombing. Its proximity to Liverpool's docks put it literally in the firing line and while club employees living locally organised a rota of watchers, scanning the skies for enemy aircraft, they could do little but seek shelter when the bombers came. The Gwladys Street End, completed in 1938 at a cost of £50,000, was damaged. So was the Bullens Road stand. Both incidents were kept out of the press at the time to protect morale, so integral to the British way of life was football perceived to be.

While the war interrupted a strong era for the champions, it did so no less for their opening-day visitors. Brentford were at the high point of their history thanks largely to the skills, industry and contacts of the great Harry Curtis. The Bees had been muddling along in Division Three South until Curtis was appointed secretary-manager in 1926. A former Football League referee, his first impact on the Bees came in that capacity, on 11 February 1922, when he expedited a snippet of club history. Officiating in the west London club's 2-1 defeat at Newport County, he sent off defender Alf Capper, the first Brentford player to be dismissed in a league match. The travelling Bees fans who offered Curtis some ribald thoughts from the Somerton Park terraces that breezy afternoon in south Wales had no idea that, four years later, he would take charge of their team and set about transforming it from Division Three also-rans to Division One thoroughbreds.

Having quit refereeing, Curtis went into management and, after warming up with a three-year stint at Gillingham, he took over at Brentford in May 1926. They had just finished 18th in Division Three South. Nine years later they were in Division One and, in their first season there, finished fifth – the top London club. Supporters swarmed to watch the Bees, home crowds averaging over 25,000, as less than 20 years after entering the league, they mixed it with, and matched, the likes of Chelsea and Arsenal.

Brentford's momentum continued into the war: in 1942 they beat Portsmouth 2-0 in front of 69,000 at Wembley to lift the War Cup. They would be no pushover, although *Daily Post* correspondent John Peel (in this era the vast majority of sports reporters wrote under pseudonyms) predicted, 'In spite of the counter-attraction of Liverpool races, I expect a big crowd will be present to cheer their favourites on. Although the London side will offer stout resistance, the Goodison side should start off the season with a victory.'

Brentford arrived in the north-west without their captain, the former Manchester United half-back Tom Manley, whose absence bore a backdrop which showed just how far from normality the country remained.

'Brentford's skipper, now resting because of a pulled muscle, is one of many players worried over housing,' reported the *Liverpool Echo*. 'His wife and family live at Great Budworth, near Northwich. For the past six years they've hardly seen him because of his army service. Now he's demobbed, the position is no better, for Tom is in digs down south and can't get a house.'

Brentford made light of their skipper's absence to prove John Peel wrong: they were rock solid in a 2-0 win with goals from Gerry McAloon and George Wilkins. The *Echo*'s verdict on the champions was blunt, 'Brentford played the better football at Goodison and fully deserved the points. There was method and precision in all they did. They passed to their own men and not, as Everton so frequently did, to the opposition. The Blues suggested the end, more than the beginning of the season, so often were they licked for speed. Brentford, with their liberal sprinkling of bald heads, were as lively as a bunch of spring lambs.'

Brentford's balding buccaneers licked the Toffees despite the wily Curtis having to react quickly with an enforced late team change, reported the *London Evening News*, 'London not only claimed the biggest attendance, it also produced the biggest surprise result of the day, for Brentford, in beating Everton on the latter's ground by 2-0. This, too, in spite of Brentford having to play in an emergency a young outside-left named Roberts who signed professional forms only last Thursday. He was one of the successes of the match and, before the game had run its course, Welsh FA representatives were inquiring whether Roberts was born in Wales. He was not. He is a Bristol man.'

For Maurice Roberts and the Brentford team as a whole, it was a flying start but for neither was it to be sustained. Roberts's professional career was to consist of just ten games, starting and ending in Liverpool. Having made his debut at Goodison, he lined up against Liverpool on 26 October and when the final whistle blew at Anfield, it terminated both Brentford's 1-0 defeat and Roberts's career.

Brentford's other players also failed to live up to their eye-catching start. With an ageing and much-changed squad at his disposal, Curtis, now 56, could not replicate his managerial masterclass of the prewar era. The Bees won four of their first five games but, at the other end of the season, just one victory from their last 17 sucked them down. Eight months after winning away to the champions, Brentford were relegated to Division Two, not to return to English football's top flight for another 74 years.

Curtis left the club in February 1949 with eternal gratitude, and a cheque for £1,370 from the board. Never mind Dean Smith and Thomas Frank – Harry Curtis is 'The Guvnor' of Brentford FC.

Everton also took time to shrug off the disruption and transition of the war years. They ended the season in tenth place and were never in contention to retain their title. Their crown was relinquished, though it didn't stray far – just a ten-minute walk across Stanley Park.

2

Football League Division One
Wolverhampton Wanderers 6 Arsenal 1 (HT: 0-0)
Scorers – Wolves: Pye (3), Westcott (2), Mullen; Arsenal: Lewis
Attendance: 50,845

'The Food Ministry is carrying out a nationwide inquiry to discover how many bread units a housewife uses each month.'

EVERTON KICKED off on 31 August 1946 on a mission to defend their title. Among those expected to challenge them hard for it were Wolves and Arsenal, two clubs which oozed history, charisma and, in the years leading up to the war, momentum. Their opening-day meeting at Molineux was a mouthwatering prospect.

Arsenal had become a great force in English football during the 1930s. In 1931 they became the first team from south of Birmingham to win the league; under Herbert Chapman and then George Allison they went on to be champions in five of the next eight years. Chapman built the golden era, although some suggested he bought it – Arsenal were known as the 'Bank of England club' due to their lavish spending. After Chapman died in 1934, from pneumonia which developed from a heavy cold with which he attended an Arsenal third-team match against Guildford City, former journalist Allison took over and seamlessly sustained the success.

Wolves were growing towards greatness. Founder members of the Football League 58 years earlier, they were hungry to lift their first title having finished second in each of the two years immediately before the war under the leadership of Frank Buckley. In 1938, Arsenal pipped them by a single point. A year later they were runners-up again, to Everton, with Arsenal close behind in fifth. This was truly an opening-day clash of the giants. One, it transpired, was much readier for the resumption than the other.

Buckley had signed a new ten-year contract as Wolves manager in 1938 but quit in February 1944 to join Notts County. The club entered the new era, under the control of former Bolton Wanderers and Wales winger Ted Vizard, full of hope that the elusive first title would soon be theirs. At five o'clock on 31 August, that hope appeared extremely well founded.

Despite a week of unrelenting rain – 'HARVESTERS AT WORK IN GUMBOOTS' announced the *Wolverhampton Express & Star* as Staffordshire's farmers battled to bring in the crops – Molineux was prepared for a huge crowd. Spectator safety was high in mind in light of the tragedy at Burnden Park four months earlier when 33 spectators died during a crush at an FA Cup quarter-final between Bolton Wanderers and Stoke City. The latest technology was deployed. On the eve of the match, under the headline 'WOLVES PLAN TO CONTROL 50,000 CROWD AGAINST THE ARSENAL', the *Express & Star* reported, 'A central control by telephones will be in operation at Molineux tomorrow for the Wolves-Arsenal clash so that the police and Wolves' staff will know exactly how many people are on the ground,' writes The Pilgrim. '"We will know to a hundred or two just what the attendance is," Superintendent G. Pendered told me today. Special arrangements have been made for the parking of cars and the police are anxious for as many motorists as possible to put their cars around the West Park where there is accommodation for 1,000 cars.'

The Pilgrim had also sniffed out a snippet of happy team news for Wolves fans, 'Late this afternoon Ted Vizard received the good news that Billy Wright, the club's international half-back, would be available after all and he will play at left-half in place of Crook. It was stated yesterday that Wright would be playing cricket for his army unit in the Aldershot district.'

While it was all coming together nicely for Wolves, Arsenal were sorely lacking in positive news. Many players instrumental to their prewar success, including greats Cliff Bastin and Ted Drake, had retired or relocated while star inside-left Bryn Jones was still on demobilisation leave and not back in training until the following Wednesday.

The *Evening News (London)* was upbeat about the Football League's return but wary about Arsenal's prospects, 'In the new football season which starts tomorrow there is every ingredient to make it the most enthralling season of all time. Considerable attention will be given to The Arsenal, who start the campaign with a difficult match at Wolverhampton, where Bryn Jones will watch his old club and his present club perform. Though the Arsenal have lost some of their stars, and their side looks strange in one or two places, I think they will nearly fill their Highbury home when they play there.'

Arsenal's difficulties during the war years had been exacerbated by the loss of their home. Early in the conflict, Highbury became a First Aid Post and Air Raid Patrol Centre with the main stand housing a wardens' reporting post. The dressing rooms became a casualty clearing station and a blast wall was built inside the main entrance to the iconic marble hall. The Gunners were forced to share the White Hart Lane home of rivals Tottenham Hotspur. They were thrilled to be back at their beloved Highbury but how they would fare there, certainly in the short term, was very much an unknown quantity.

In contrast to Arsenal's uncertainty, Wolves fans were full of optimism and to further lighten the mood on the eve of the big kick-off, the *Express & Star* shared a joke. The paper's Tonight's Smile feature delivered the following rib-tickler:

'How does your wife like that new washing machine you gave her for Christmas?'

'She hates the thing. Every time she tries to get in it, the paddles knock her black and blue.'

While the chaps chortled away at that cracker and considered manly issues like parking, where to put crosses on their coupon and who would play at right-half against Arsenal, the women got on with addressing minor matters like putting food on the table. The business of feeding their families was still heavily affected by shortages. Many foods, including sugar, meat, fats, bacon and cheese, were rationed during the war and in July 1946, to widespread dismay, bread was added to the list. 'But I thought we won the war?' was a common reaction to this additional hardship which brought twin extra pressures; another restriction on providing food, accompanied by the threat of prosecution for breaking the rules.

'BREAD SNOOPERS MAY CALL AT YOUR DOOR SOON' reported the *Express & Star*.

The paper continued, 'The Food Ministry is carrying out a nationwide inquiry to discover how many bread units a housewife uses each month. Trained investigators from a research firm which has carried out food surveys for the ministry all through the war have started to call on housewives with a questionnaire. This asks, how many bread units were spent by the family in one week? How many were changed into points? What cakes, biscuits and cereals were bought weekly? How many potatoes were consumed by the family in a week?'

It is not known how many of the 50,845 spectators at Molineux passed through the turnstiles with sandwiches lovingly prepared by wife or mum. Probably not many, due to fear of those trained investigators, but what is certain is that the vast majority left the stadium very happy. The duel of potential champions transpired to be a landslide.

Wolves were the better side in the first half without scoring. After the interval, the Gunners were blown away. Jesse Pye, making his debut following a £10,000 move from Notts County, opened the scoring two minutes after half-time and completed his hat-trick 11 minutes later. Longer servers Dennis Westcott and Jimmy Mullen, whose Wolves careers spanned the war, added three more goals in the last 25 minutes. Westcott scored twice and outside-left Mullen added the last having provided crosses for three of the previous five. The Bank of England had been well and truly breached. Reg Lewis's 87th-minute goal for Arsenal was no consolation. They had been routed in the rain.

'Ted Vizard's rampant, goal-mad young Wolves team rattled in four in the first 28 minutes following the interval,' reported *The People* the following day. 'Young Jesse Pye, wartime discovery, England inside-right and ex-desert veteran, smashed the ball into Arsenal's net three times in the second half for the first hat-trick of the season.

'Poor Arsenal! While the Midlands and north rejoice, this ageing, one-time "Bank of England" team faces, on paper, a tough, testing season. But it was only the first game. There are plenty more opportunities to climb back to their prewar peak and wipe off that £150,000 debt ... but the Highbury bosses will have to get cracking!'

Wolves' dazzling performance was driven by their wingers. While Mullen, a Geordie who Buckley had tempted away from under the nose of Newcastle United before the war, tormented Arsenal on the left, 5ft 4in Shropshire dynamo Johnny Hancocks sparkled on the right. That threat from both flanks was to become a huge component of Wolves' success, including that long-awaited first league title, during the next decade.

'Pye, who got three goals, can feel very satisfied and so can Hancocks, the new right-winger,' reported the *Birmingham Daily Gazette*. 'Success, in combination or as individuals, was a feature of the game. The spacing of the Wolves goals indicated the extent to which Arsenal were subdued. Few Arsenal sides visiting [the] Molineux ground have been made to look more inept than the one which crumbled up during the devastating second half. Before the interval the Wolves, though unable to score, had given proof that they were Arsenal's masters. The Wolves used the first half to wear down their opponents and then hit them for six.'

The brilliant display was a strong candidate for the front page of Monday's *Express & Star*, but Jesse and Co. had to be content with a place inside. The editor decided to focus instead on international politics – 'TITO TO MAKE NEW PROTEST AGAINST US PLANES ... ITALY TO BE ALLOWED TORPEDOES' – and the big domestic issue of: 'NO END YET TO BREAD RATIONING.'

On page seven, however, Vizard's side received due praise, 'Wolves' dazzling form in the second half was far too much for Arsenal who conceded six goals in 39 minutes to delight a bumper crowd of 50,845 on a wet and dismal afternoon. Arsenal were lucky to be on level terms at half-time, for their front line never showed much prowess. There was not one weak spot in the home side. It is hard to pick out individuals for special praise but Pye (3) and Westcott (2) must be applauded for their goals.'

The sensational start triggered a strong season for Wolves which saw them finish third, just a point behind champions Liverpool. They had to wait a little longer for that first title but it arrived in 1954 under the management of Stan Cullis, and they added further successes in 1958 and 1959.

Arsenal were soon to recover their powers but first endured an anxious few months. Their competitive return to Highbury, four days after the trouncing at Molineux, brought a 3-1 defeat to Blackburn Rovers and they collected just one point from their first four games. The Gunners entered December facing the unthinkable prospect of relegation but rallied to finish 13th before Allison retired and the appointment of former player and physio Tom Whittaker galvanised the team.

In Whittaker's first season, Arsenal were champions, finishing seven points clear of Manchester United, before the following year brought a truly momentous day in the club's history – though nobody knew it at the time. On 22 October 1949 they beat Blackpool 1-0 in front of 66,391 at Highbury. Lewis scored the only goal in an abrasive contest in which Leslie Compton received seven stitches in a gashed temple and Stanley Matthews suffered a bloody nose. That wasn't too momentous, but 497 miles away in Strasbourg, close to France's border with Germany, a baby entered the world. He was to be called Arsène Wenger.

3

Football League Division Three South
Mansfield Town 3 Crystal Palace 1 (HT: 2-1)
Scorers – Mansfield: Harper, Copestake, Hogg; Crystal Palace: Girling
Attendance: 8,000

'Although the water was nearly three feet deep in the shop, business continued and customers were served with chips while they waded knee-deep in water.'

ALMOST ONE million people, around one in 40 citizens of the United Kingdom, attended a match on 31 August 1946 to welcome back the Football League. Irene Lovelock was not one of them.

Almost a year on from the end of the war, life remained very difficult for much of the population. To address some of those difficulties, while fans flocked to 43 grounds around England and Wales to embrace the return of the competition, Irene was engaged in other business: that of the British Housewives' League.

In light of continuing and, in some aspects, increasing hardship and shortages, Irene sought to protect those without a collective voice. In June 1945, she created the British Housewives' League, of which she was now president.

'"I altogether disbelieve this food shortage ramp which is being used just as a political card," said Irene Lovelock, of Selhurst, founder of the British Housewives' League,' reported the *Croydon Times*. '"We are not just a protest league but we will fight against all injustices, whatever the government. We are out to make life very much easier than it is at present for the ordinary British housewife.'"

It was a noble cause and one which Irene and her many thousands of followers pursued to strong effect. When Clement Attlee's Labour government fell on 25 October 1951, the election was reportedly 'lost mainly in the queue at the butcher's or the grocer's'. Five years prior, however, a cause of greater immediate concern to many of Irene's neighbours in the south London ward of Selhurst was Crystal Palace's prospects for the new season. And first up, how they would fare in their opening Division Three South fixture, away to Mansfield Town.

Football supporters tend to view their team's prospects through a prism of negativity, but many Palace fans approached 1946/47 in a positive mood. Awaiting them was a rapid reality check. Every season, some clubs go in with high hopes which start to disintegrate by the third throw-in. Crystal Palace's, at the start of 1946/47, suffered perhaps the swiftest disintegration in the history of high hopes. They lost at Mansfield – 3-1. Four days later they lost at Reading – 10-2. The envisaged promotion bid unravelled very early, starting as the team trundled north to Nottinghamshire on the opening day in unlikely fashion, with a piece of fish on a train.

Media coverage of football in 1946 was not quite as advanced as it is today. Ahead of the big kick-off at 3pm or, as at Mansfield, 3.15pm, the latest information at supporters' disposal was what they had read in that morning's newspapers. Breaking news was reserved for spectators at the games when the teams were announced. Had the instant media of 2026 existed 80 years earlier, however, the season's very first hot news would have emanated from Mansfield. Across the bottom of TV screens would have rolled the revelation, 'Breaking news: Crystal Palace inside-forward Ernie Waldron taken to hospital after injury by fish.' Palace's season took a dive even before it began – the moment that Waldron ordered his pre-match meal.

'He was rushed to hospital from the station at Mansfield,' reported the *Croydon Times*, whose correspondent then dug deep, desperately deep, some would say, to find a football pun. 'By the time a surgeon came to examine him, the bone had disappeared but it had scored the gullet and Waldron was in no condition for football.'

Waldron was 'well looked after' at the hospital and recovered sufficiently to return to the ground later in the afternoon and travel back to London with his team-mates. By then, however, they were a dejected bunch, having been well beaten by a Stags side which, it was to transpire, produced its best performance of the season on its opening day.

Waldron's positive experience at Mansfield Hospital, two years before the creation of the National Health Service, owed something to the generosity of Mansfield Town's supporters. Seven days earlier, a 2,000 crowd gathered at Field Mill for a practice match – Probables v Possibles – and raised £85 10s for the hospital. Community spirit and resilience coursed through the residents of the colliery town, as illustrated by the fortitude they had shown in the face of that week's heavy rain and flooding.

'The torrent invaded the fish and chip shop owned by Mr Gelsthorpe in Bridge Street,' reported the *Mansfield Chronicle*. 'All the lower rooms were under two feet of water and although the water was nearly three feet deep in the shop, business continued and customers were served with chips while they waded knee-deep in water.'

Also rising to the occasion, the paper reported, was the town's constabulary, 'Two German prisoners of war who escaped on Friday from a working party at Kirby Muxloe, Leicestershire were recaptured in Mansfield by a police constable on Monday.'

That assiduous constable may well have been on duty at Field Mill five days later when the Stags supporters packed into the ground. A crowd of 9,580, paying gate receipts of £676, squeezed in, hoping for similar entertainment levels, but a different result, to the opening day of the aborted 1939/40 season. Palace, 3-1 down at one point, returned south that day celebrating a 5-4 win.

Palace manager George Irwin had compiled one of the strongest-looking squads in the division. Alongside prewar favourites including stalwart skipper and right-back Fred Dawes and muscular right-half Jack Lewis, Irwin had added some astute signings. Billy Bassett, a bald colossus of a centre-half, had joined from Cardiff City just before the war and would make his belated debut. Off the field there was friction – the board was in bitter conflict with the supporters' club which it wanted to either follow the club's agenda or disband – but the on-field prospects looked promising. On a damp, grey afternoon and a slippery, muddy pitch, that promise was swiftly harpooned by the Stags.

A goal fest similar to the 1939 game appeared to beckon when two goals arrived in the first nine minutes. Palace at first shrugged off the loss of Waldron to open the scoring after five minutes when Dickie Girling headed home a cross by Eric Coates, an amateur who had just applied for a trial with the Eagles having recently left the army. That silenced the home crowd, but Mansfield equalised four minutes later through Don Harper and then seized control. Bassett's debut took a downward turn on 30 minutes when he slipped on the greasy surface to gift the ball to Oliver Copestake who wellied the Stags in front from 30 yards. Mansfield led 2-1 at half-time and extended their lead four minutes after the break when Alf Calverley's perfectly weighted pass sent Freddie Hogg racing beyond a square back line to make it 3-1.

Mansfield held on comfortably against punchless Palace as the game petered out in energy-sapping conditions. Both sides tired, due partly, the *Chronicle* suggested, to the sustained limitations on their diet.

'Mansfield Town made a promising opening in the first postwar season and at the same time delighted a crowd of nearly 10,000,' the paper reported. 'Playing fast, open football, Stags were clearly superior in the first half and better marksmanship might have given them a bigger lead. In the last half-hour, however, the pace slackened – the cause may have been lack of training, an opening-match "feeling" or a restricted diet – but they clung to their two-goal lead. Bryant showed promise in his Third Division debut, although after his early liveliness, during which he opened Mansfield's account, he was somewhat subdued through the vigilance of the experienced Bassett.'

While Mansfield's performance was lauded, further south the inquest began. Glyn Lewis, called up late into Palace's team due to the fishbone crisis, proved to be a square peg in a round hole, the *Croydon Times* suggested, 'Lewis, an outside-left, stepped into the breach at inside-right. He is short of weight for an inside-forward and, on a day of drizzling rain and boisterous wind, he was not an effective substitute.'

The paper also flagged up the inevitable lack of cohesion from a team of players many of whom had only just been introduced to each other, 'Palace played only one public trial, at Selhurst Park. The

Possibles beat the Probables 3-1, Jones (2), Waldron and Jack Lewis scored the goals and it scarcely seemed that anybody but Hudgell and Lewis had ever played together before.'

If the defeat at Field Mill tempered the optimism of Palace's supporters, four days later came a result which completely squashed it. Irwin's side visited Reading and quickly went 2-0 down, then fought back commendably to trail 3-2 at half-time. The second half didn't go well. Final score: Reading 10 Crystal Palace 2.

'Forward,' the *Croydon Times* correspondent wrote. 'Palace look like needing all the tried and true supporters they can muster. The humiliating defeat at Elm Park disposed of any hopes they might have held out of being in the promotion running this season, short of a reversal of policy which would mean spending a lot of money on new players.'

Spending was not on the board's agenda. Instead, they were looking into a scheme to install a track around the pitch and bring speedway to Selhurst Park. Those plans went nowhere, as did Palace's season as they meandered to 18th in the final table.

They still finished nine points above Mansfield, though. After a solid start, the Stags floundered as the season lengthened. They lost only one of the first eight games, from which they collected ten points, but then added only another 18 points from the remaining 34 fixtures to finish bottom of the table, below Norwich City on goal average. The Stags and the Canaries had to seek re-election but their fellow clubs around the league were empathetic. As this was the first postwar season, with grounds and squads needing much reconstruction and many players still in the armed services, all four clubs seeking re-election – Mansfield and Norwich from the south and Southport and Halifax from the north – were re-elected without a vote. Logic also prevailed as Mansfield, just 30 miles from Sheffield, were switched from Division Three South to North.

Ernie Waldron made a full recovery from the troublesome fishbone but soon left Palace. In November, he signed for Aberdeen for whom he had scored 29 goals in 20 games as a guest during the 1944/45 season. He scored on his first game back for the Dons, against Hearts, but played only eight times before retiring due to ill health.

Irene Lovelock, meanwhile, carried on the fight, with increasing support from the local press. The *Croydon Times*'s front page carried a prominent picture headlined 'HOUSEWIVES AGAIN THE VICTIMS' with the caption, 'Croydon housewives were again the victims when the process workers and bottlers went on strike at the Leslie Park-road Co-operative Milk Depot. At the top of the picture the queue waits patiently for the little milk available while below is the idle machinery and empty bottles inside the depot.'

Food for thought for the *Times* readers. As was the intriguing headline beside it on the front page – 'WINDOW CLEANER WALKED INTO TOWN HALL AND TOOK TYPEWRITER.'

4

Football League Division Two
Millwall 1 Newcastle United 4 (HT: 1-2)
Scorers – Millwall: Johnson; Newcastle United: Milburn, Stubbins, Bentley (2)
Attendance: 39,187

'How will I spend that £750 a week?'

'NEARLY A million people, tired of the ersatz wartime soccer, welcomed back the bitter promotion and relegation struggle,' reported the *Sunday Dispatch (London)*. Nowhere was the welcome back more passionate, and promotion more craved, than at Newcastle United. With a team adorned by expensive signings, the Magpies were hot favourites to win promotion from Division Two and 39,187 people assembled at The Den to see their first assignment – a tricky visit to an ambitious Millwall side managed by colourful Cornishman Jack Cock.

Newcastle's history has often fluctuated between glorious and gruelling, and those fluctuations were encapsulated by their passage through the 1930s. Early in the decade, as a proud First Division club and four-time former league champions, they beat Arsenal 2-1 at Wembley to lift the FA Cup for the third time. Later in the decade, having already dropped into Division Two, they avoided relegation to Division Three North thanks only to a sliver of goal average and some gargantuan luck. They visited Stockport on a murky afternoon in the north-west desperately needing a win but were being held 2-2 with 13 minutes left when the light closed in completely and the match was abandoned. They won the rearranged game 3-1 and that additional point was to keep them up and send Barnsley down.

At least the unpalatable life in Division Two did not turn into the unthinkable, the mighty Newcastle United in Division Three North. But when the Football League resumed after the Second World War, the club was under intense pressure to return to Division One where their supporter base felt they belonged. Older fans recalled the club's domination of English football at the start of the century when they were champions three times in four years. Middle-aged fans recalled the FA Cup triumphs of 1924 and 1932; the thrilling, rain-lashed 2-0 win over Aston Villa in the second final played at Wembley; and the controversial 2-1 victory over Arsenal in the 'over-the-line' final eight years later.

In the 1924 triumph, legendary striker Stan Seymour scored the second goal to kill off Villa. Twenty-two years later he had switched from penalty box to manager's office and was supervising the Magpies' promotion bid. The *Newcastle Journal* was enthused, 'What seems certain to be a boom season for football starts today when players kick off in the first full-scale English soccer campaign since 1939. The play itself promises to be faster and better for, apart from there being the incentive of promotion, players have had greater opportunities for training than at any time since 1939. Leading teams of [the] 1938/39 season may well take the limelight once more but the north-east is looking to its clubs making something of a stir in the football world with Newcastle United's promotion bid the event of the season. It is a long, hard road to next May but the good wishes of all Tyneside sportsmen will be with the United team in their endeavours.'

Newcastle chairman George Rutherford, a coal mine owner, told the paper, 'The outlook at St James' Park is very happy indeed. We are especially well-situated regarding the quality of reserves. The Second Division promotion path will be a thorny one. We open with two away matches but hope there will be some points already in the bag when we play Swansea.'

Awaiting the Magpies on 31 August 1946 was not a banana skin, for bananas were still rationed, but certainly an awkward start with a 580-mile round trip to a resurgent Millwall under the flamboyant Cock. A former Lions striker, Cock returned to the club as manager in November 1944. He had scored 234 goals for Brentford, Huddersfield Town, Chelsea, Everton, Plymouth Argyle and Millwall and been decorated by his country for his endeavours in two arenas. During the First World War, he served in the 17th Service Battalion of the Middlesex Regiment (also known as the 1st Footballers' Battalion because it consisted mainly of professional footballers) and was awarded the Military Medal. In May 1919 he made his debut for England, against Ireland at Windsor Park, and scored after 30 seconds. Around that time, he also frequently performed as a music hall singer at the Granville Theatre in Fulham (in 1920 he played himself in a silent movie, *The Winning Goal*) before bringing the curtain down on his thespian career to concentrate on football. Dapper and dynamic, Cock was charged with continuing the mission, which was gathering momentum nicely until the war, to make Millwall one of London's top clubs. Promoted to Division Two in 1938, they were spoken of as a potential major force in football in the capital. Could Cock continue that rise?

The Den was ready to host football again thanks to the efforts of that most powerful and enduring force in British society – volunteers. On 19 April 1943, the ground had been extensively damaged following an air raid. 'Fire destroyed Millwall Football Club's main stand at The Den, New Cross, on Easter Monday, about an hour after the last game of the season – between Dulwich Hamlet and Tooting – had ended,' reported the *South London Observer*. 'A member of staff, after the crowd had gone, noticed smoke coming from the bottom of the stand. He at once reported it but within a short time the stand, which was erected in 1910 and seated about 2,000 people, was on fire from end to end.'

Millwall were forced to pay elsewhere, mainly at Charlton Athletic's The Valley, for the rest of the war, but the volunteers rebuilt enough of The Den for the Lions to return there for the big kick-off. They faced a Newcastle side hugely strengthened by spending power supplied by supporters who flooded to wartime games at St James' Park. During the last year of the war, crowds there averaged over 40,000 and that gave Seymour serious muscle in the transfer market. He lavished £8,500 on powerful striker Roy Bentley from Bristol City, £7,500 on Scotland centre-half Frank Brennan from Airdrieonians and £4,250 on midfield general Joe Harvey from Bradford City. They were big signings, though not the biggest around. Glasgow-born actress Deborah Kerr had just signed a five-year Hollywood film contract. 'How will I spend that £750 a week?' she quipped, before pointing out, 'When American taxation has been paid I will be left with £300 a week.'

The spending spree sent Newcastle into the season amid high expectations. Two days before the season dawned, Seymour gathered the players together for a pep talk. After training on Thursday, they assembled in the gym at St James' Park and heard the great man outline what he believed to be the ingredients of success: 50 per cent luck, 25 per cent ability and 25 per cent guts. The first, he told them, you hope for. The second you have. The third you must show. On a dark, dirty, rainswept day at The Den, they showed it.

The resilience showed early on when left-back Doug Graham took a kick in the ribs. With substitutes not introduced into the Football League until 1965, injured players had to simply soldier on or leave their team a man short. Graham carried on, hobbling doggedly up and down the left flank until the game was safe for the Magpies at 4-1.

Inspired by Graham's pluck, Newcastle's new signings dominated. After six minutes, Harvey dug out possession and launched a sweet five-man move which ended with Bentley teeing up Jackie Milburn to send a right-footed shot past goalkeeper Jock Purdie. Millwall equalised ten minutes later when Johnny Johnson scored from a tight angle, but the Magpies soon led again when Purdie punched Tommy Pearson's cross straight to Albert Stubbins who volleyed the ball directly into the net.

Leading 2-1 at half-time, Newcastle quickly sealed victory with two goals in three minutes soon after the break. Denied a blatant penalty when Purdie mugged Stubbins in the box, they increased their lead when Pearson skinned his full-back and crossed for Bentley to tuck home a debut goal. Then Harvey again won the ball and fed Bentley who netted a glorious 20-yarder.

At 4-1, with Brennan a towering presence at the back, Graham could safely leave the field. Cock's team never threatened and the Magpies headed for the train home happy. *Newcastle Evening Chronicle* reporter John Graydon (they didn't do pseudonyms up north) was most impressed.

'Never has football interest been greater on Tyneside than it is today,' wrote Graydon, 'and at this stage I should like to say that whoever goes to St James' Park this season can be assured of really first-class football. I write as an impartial observer, having no ties, but the Newcastle team I watched on Saturday ranks among the most promising sides I have seen for eight years. There is a wonderful team spirit among the young men who wear the famous black and white stripes. Team comes before self.'

Graydon lauded the debutants, 'Skipper Harvey, at right-half, led his men well and set them a good example by some determined tackling and goal-making passes. Brennan is a player who does the right thing without show and is among the most reliable defenders in the game today. Bentley is, I feel sure, a potential international. The new boy from Bristol City is the most promising inside-right I have seen since Willie Hall hit the headlines.'

Graydon was clearly convinced, though further south the *Sunday Dispatch (London)* was more cautious about the Magpies' prospects, 'Although Newcastle started off with a well-merited win over Millwall at New Cross, the north-eastern club will have to be less hurried in defence if they are to win back First Division status. Millwall's forwards were handicapped by the fact that Anderson, their centre-forward, was never able to master Brennan.'

The *Dispatch* writer was shrewd. Despite all the spending – a month later, Seymour signed Len Shackleton from Bradford Park Avenue for a record £13,000 – as the season progressed, Newcastle's defence could not match the efficiency of their attack. Shackleton netted six on his debut, in a 13-0 win over Newport County on 5 October, and the Magpies scored 95 goals, comfortably the most in Division Two, but they conceded 62. They suffered a wretched Christmas, losing home and away to West Bromwich Albion on Christmas Day and Boxing Day and at home to Millwall on 28 December, and won just eight of the last 22 games to finish fifth, ten points behind the top two. Seymour called for patience, which was soon rewarded: the following season brought promotion, and plenty of further glory was just around the corner. In the early 1950s, Newcastle won the FA Cup three times in five years.

Millwall's aspirations to join London's elite never materialised. They finished 1946/47 in 18th place and the following season were relegated to Division Three South where they spent ten years before becoming founder members of the new Division Four. Thirty years later, under John Docherty, they finally made it to the top flight where they spent three seasons.

Jack Cock left in 1948, his team having lost 44 of 86 games under his control. That concluded his football career and he later ran a pub with some exceptional tales to share with his regulars. Cock lived a full and exciting life, though if one regret existed it was perhaps his failure to exploit the potential solution to the Lions' lacklustre form early in 1946/47 as offered in the local paper.

'Unless two pints of bile juice flow from your liver into your bowels every day, your movements get hard and constipated and your food decays unnaturally in your 28 feet of bowel,' revealed the *South London Press*. 'The decay sends poison all over your body every six minutes. It makes you gloomy, grouchy and no good for anything. Carter's Little Liver Pills get those two pints of bile flowing freely.'

Could Carter's Little Liver Pills have turned Millwall into a footballing superpower? We will never know.

5

Football League Division Three South
Bristol Rovers 2 Reading 2 (HT: 1-2)
Scorers – Bristol Rovers: Curran, Lambden; Reading: MacPhee, Glidden
Attendance: 11,710

'Three pumps and some 50 workers with buckets partially cleared Eastville Stadium of thousands of tons of water.'

TWO WEEKS before the start of the new season, the directors of Reading Football Club, headed by chairman Bill Lee, arranged a pre-season treat for the players and staff. On a sunny Monday morning in mid-August, the workforce gathered at the club's Elm Park stadium and boarded a bus, ready for a trip to the seaside.

'The Reading Football Club players and their wives were taken at the invitation of the board of directors to Bournemouth,' reported the *Berkshire Chronicle*. 'Reading captain Tony MacPhee expressed thanks on behalf of the club personnel for the outing and Mr Lee, in response, referred to the happy family feeling there was in the club. Songs by the players and community singing enlivened the homeward journey.'

For a few hours, the pressures and worries of postwar life were parked and a thoroughly mellow day was enjoyed by all. MacPhee and his team were soon to deliver another very different sort of mellow day. Just around the corner lay the club's record league victory.

Those pressures and worries remained considerable, exacerbated by the recent development on the bread front. 'WILL LEAD TO CHAOS – BERKS BAKERS ON BREAD RATIONING' warned the *Reading Mercury*, whose headline writer then strayed into hyperbole with this revelation – 'SQUATTERS TAKE OVER IN READING.' A group of old army huts, rather than the entire town, had been occupied.

As their bus trundled back from Bournemouth to Berkshire on a warm late-summer evening, the thoughts of Reading's players were turning towards the big kick-off in 12 days' time. Their opening fixture was a relatively short trip to Bristol Rovers and how lovely it would be if the Football League was to resume in such weather. A sun-soaked Saturday afternoon with spectators in shirt sleeves and sun hats – that's what the Football Gods decreed. The Weather Gods had other ideas. The league's return was accompanied by a week of weather more suited to November, and a wetter than average November, than August. As Rovers and Reading prepared for their Division Three South fixture at Eastville Stadium, the entire nation took shelter.

The deluge was greatest of all over the west country and Wales. In the midst of harvest season, it was rotten news for farmers. 'Gales and heavy rainstorms which swept the whole of Britain yesterday caused ships to run for shelter and caused havoc to crops,' reported the *Western Mail*. 'Harvesting has come to a standstill and farmers state that a large percentage of the corn will be wasted. The bad weather is likely to continue. A gale warning is in operation for all coastal waters of the British Isles.'

Sport was badly affected. On the evening before the opening match at Eastville Stadium, across Bristol at the Knowle Stadium, Friday-night speedway was abandoned midway through the meeting. The hosts were trailing The Rest 36-24 after ten heats when the 6,200 crowd was told that conditions had become too dangerous. Twenty-five miles away, Somerset County Cricket Club's final championship match of the season, against Derbyshire at Frome, was abandoned as a draw, having failed to reach its third innings. There was just time for Bill Copson to take 5-37, one of 66 five-wicket hauls in the Derbyshire seamer's mighty career. Copson remains the only cricketer in history to take his 900th first-class wicket on a damp Friday in Frome.

The filthy weather only added to the fractiousness of commuters in Reading. In an angry letter to the *Reading Mercury*, John Maxwell lambasted the 'scandalous conditions which prevail each evening' in the bus terminus at the railway station. 'There appears to be no competent authority directing the forming of queues,' raged Mr Maxwell.

His diatribe drew a staunch defence of the transport staff from Mr H.G. Peacock of High Street, Slough. 'It is, in my opinion, up to the public travelling to use a little decency and take their turn and to help the official on duty,' wrote Mr Peacock. 'I admire the officials for their patience, civility and cheerful help. I have seen them lose their temper and so would you, Mr Maxwell, if you had to stand a few of the insults that I have heard hurled at them.'

Discord at the bus terminus notwithstanding, Reading's football fraternity approached the new season in a positive mood. Rovers, conversely, had endured a very difficult time on and off the field. Their final season before the war was a joyless grind which left them bottom of Division Three South, requiring an application for re-election. They survived, polling a solid 45 votes to see off challengers including aspiring Essex pair Chelmsford City and Colchester United who collected just one vote each, but the outbreak of war added off-field crisis.

Loss of income caused by the Football League's suspension forced Rovers to sell Eastville to the Bristol Greyhound Racing Association for £12,000. The club was given a 21-year lease to continue playing there but the greyhounds took priority. The dogs raced on Saturday afternoons, so the footballers had to play at the Ashton Gate home of rivals Bristol City, or at Kingswood. With such inconvenience alongside the financial strain, after competing in the regional competition in 1939/40, Rovers opted out of football until 1945/46.

They emerged from the war years needing new impetus as much as any club in the country and the team against Reading sowed the seeds of the required fresh start. Six of the 11 – Jackie Pitt, Vic Lambden, Harry Bamford, Randell Burnell, Barry Watkins and Arthur Weare – made their debuts and would go on to play more than 100 games for the club. One of those seeds germinated in a giant way. Pitt, a half-back who had joined from West Bromwich Albion, went on to play 512 games for Rovers, including 122 consecutive appearances in the early 1950s, a significant feat in an era when players wore boots like iron and thought nothing of depositing opponents into Row Z.

Pitt retired as a player in 1960, then joined the club's ground staff, where he worked at Eastville, and then Twerton Park when the club moved there in 1986. Seventy-five years after his damp debut against Reading, Pitt was inducted into Bristol Rovers' Hall of Fame to mark a truly mighty career. The *Western Daily Press* correspondent knew his onions when he sagely described the newcomer's debut as 'promising'.

Whether or not Pitt, Lambden, Bamford, Burnell, Watkins and Weare would actually make their debuts on the afternoon of Saturday, 31 August 1946 was still far from certain at lunchtime that day as rain continued to fall. Only half an hour before kick-off did the referee confirm the match would go ahead, following heroic work by the ground staff and volunteers.

'Three pumps and some 50 workers with buckets partially cleared Eastville Stadium of thousands of tons of water following Bristol's worst storm for 30 years,' reported the *Reading Standard*. 'Large pools had to be covered with sawdust and the ball often stuck dead in the mud, whilst players performed strange acrobatics in flying showers of water.'

'The rain had been continuous since the previous evening,' added the *Berkshire Chronicle*, 'and only the use of NFS pumps, followed by a "chain" of buckets, drained the ground sufficiently for the game to be played. Those parts of the ground that were not underwater were churned up with mud.'

A last-gasp postponement would have been unwise with an 11,710 crowd packing the ground for a game for which they had waited seven years. The match went ahead – and the comical conditions produced a cracker.

'Many parts of the field were waterlogged and the ball was frequently brought to an abrupt and disconcerting halt,' reported the *Western Morning Press*. 'Reading were perhaps fortunate to take the lead in the 15th minute when Weare, coming out of goal, misfielded the ball in a pool of water and MacPhee hooked the ball out of the goalkeeper's possession and rolled it into the empty net.' Seven minutes later, Rovers equalised after 'a series of misunderstandings by Reading's backs, worsened by the quagmire, enabled Curran to level'.

Reading regained the lead straight from the kick-off when Gil Glidden glided on to Doug Sears's pass and added a sweet finish, but

Rovers equalised again seven minutes after half-time. In an era when goalkeepers were not mollycoddled, if Reading's first goal involved a bit of roughing him up, Rovers' second did even more so. 'Lambden threaded his way through the backs and Groves, dashing out in a valiant effort to save, was kicked in the chest and was rolling in pain as the ball entered the net,' reported the *Morning Press*.

Reading attacked with as much pace and verve as the quagmire would allow. They pressed hard throughout the second half, but could not find a winner. Rovers keeper Jack Weare, a former sergeant and PT instructor in the Royal Air Force, made two fine saves in the dying minutes and the game ended 2-2, just as it did on the opening day of the aborted 1939/40 season. At the final whistle, the mud-covered players were applauded from the field by the rain-soaked crowd. The Football League, in all its down-and-dirty glory, was back. Both teams collected a point and the home side harvested a very welcome £907 in gate receipts.

After his side's promising start, Reading manager Joe Edelston had another nifty card up his sleeve ahead of their first home game of the season, against Crystal Palace, four days later. Vic Barney, an infantryman in the British Army, had played for Napoli the previous year after being sent to Naples to convalesce following a battlefield accident. The 24-year-old inside-forward had signed for the Biscuitmen and starred in the demolition of Palace. After a competitive first half, Reading led 3-2. The second half was not so competitive – the match ended 10-2 to the delight of Edelston, Barney, most of the 8,241 crowd and not least Harry Earl who had worked the turnstiles at Elm Park for 44 years.

Barney crowned his impressive debut with a goal and, according to the *Reading Mercury*, 'played an outstanding game in his first match as a professional, having been signed by Reading only a day or two before'. Captain MacPhee scored four goals and everyone in the team shone. Well, almost everyone. Right-winger Wilf Chitty, who had suffered shrapnel wounds when a bomb fell on Reading during the war, was cut no slack by the *Berkshire Chronicle* correspondent. 'The home attack pleased as a whole, with the possible exception of Chitty whose centres were not so telling as usual,' he observed, adding that, 'it was pleasing to see the absence of the exaggerated W formation which has been so often adopted in higher football circles.'

The Biscuitmen were on a roll: three days later, they beat Southend United 7-2 at Elm Park. These were happy days for Reading's supporters and most of all for those whose affection for football was accompanied by a passion for snails. The British Snail-Watching Society, incorporating the Yattendon Cochleological Society, which had been created locally to 'promote interest in and appreciation of the snail', was celebrating its first anniversary. Berkshire gave this noble institution to the world.

6

Scottish League A
Rangers 2 Queen's Park 0 (HT: 1-0)
Scorers – Rangers: Duncanson (2)
Attendance: 20,000

'Like all visitors to Ibrox, this party was astonished at the sumptuous equipment and gave vent to it when the Rangers' manager asked them to step into the cocktail bar to partake of hospitality.'

'TONIGHT, AT half past eight o'clock, a number of gentlemen met at No. 3 Eglinton Terrace for the purpose of forming a football club.' So read the minutes of a meeting held on Tuesday, 9 July 1867 in an apartment in a relatively new tenement building in the southern suburbs of Glasgow.

Meetings come in many forms. A good proportion of them are less than useful – tedious, tautologous, trivial or pointless. This one was momentous. From it sprang the formation of Queen's Park Football Club and, effectively, the start of organised Scottish football. 'The club set about laying down the foundation of the modern game, adopting a passing style of play which employed skilful ball control,' records queensparkfc.co.uk, with justifiable pride. 'The team worked as a unit, utilising team tactics, unlike that of their contemporaries of the day who played an "individualistic" style of game which used kick-and-rush tactics, "dribbling" with the ball, hacking and rough play.' The remarkable story of Queen's Park had begun.

The club eschewed the crudity of rough play and also that of players' pay. They set up on an amateur basis which they were to retain until 2019 when the relentless pressure of competing with professional opposition finally became too great. Until 2021, meanwhile, their home ground was Hampden Park, also home to the Scottish national team. Queen's Park FC's quirky and unique history is the most interesting and stylish in British football.

In 1872, although Glasgow-based, they participated in the inaugural English FA Cup, having become members of the Football Association in 1870. They generously contributed a guinea towards the cost of the first trophy, which they twice came close to lifting. They reached the finals of 1884 and 1885, both times losing narrowly to Blackburn Rovers at Kennington Oval. On 31 October 1903 they moved into the third Hampden Park. Nineteen years later they were relegated for the first time, but went straight back up the following year and remained in Division One until the war. On 31 August 1946 they crossed Glasgow for a derby clash with the giants of Rangers at Ibrox.

Almost 80 years after their formation, Queen's Park remained resolutely amateur which was causing a problem or two for Willie Gibson, a former Football League and FA Cup winner with Newcastle United, who had just been appointed as manager. Gibson's challenge was to deal with the loss of key players who, deprived of several years of full earnings by the war, decided to turn professional.

Queen's Park arrived at Ibrox viewed by many as cannon fodder for a Rangers side which was the dominant force in Scottish football. While Celtic were enduring the toughest period in their history (see Chapter 32), Rangers were flying. Under the mighty leadership of Bill Struth, manager since 1920, they won 25 of 34 first-team competitions they entered during the war. A November 1945 friendly with Dynamo Moscow drew 95,000 to Ibrox, a decent turnout, though not the biggest in the stadium's recent history. Their league match against Celtic on 2 January 1939 attracted 118,567. Struth's side ruled the Scottish football roost with the most recent arrival in their trophy cabinet being the Victory Cup, held in May and June 1946. They knocked out Stenhousemuir, Airdrieonians, Falkirk and Celtic before beating Hibernian 3-1 in the final at the home of Queen's Park.

While the final day of August brought football fans in England and Wales clamouring around the return of proper league football, those in Scotland were into their third week of it: north of the border, the season had got under way on 10 August. Rangers started well that day with a 4-2 win at Motherwell and approached the derby with Queen's Park on the back of a 5-0 win at Falkirk and a midweek 8-1 thrashing of Third Lanark.

It had been a good week all round for Rangers-supporting families: 13 goals in two games, accompanied by the welcome news that they would soon be able to sink into a tub at the Corporation Baths without getting up at 3am. 'NO MORE QUEUES AT THE "STEAMIE"' reported the *Sunday Post*, 'Glasgow housewives need no longer queue at the local "steamie" to book a stall or machine. The new system of advanced booking devised by the Corporation Baths Department comes into operation tomorrow. Seventy-five thousand applications were received from women anxious to book in advance at the 28 washhouses in Glasgow. This will end the spectacle of women, and sometimes school children, joining a queue at three or four o'clock on a winter morning for the opening of the baths at six o'clock.'

Alongside that happy news, *Glasgow Evening Times* correspondent Alan Breck previewed Rangers v Queen's Park in his All in the Game column. The league's return, with games every midweek, was already taking a toll on some squads but Rangers, reckoned Breck, had the depth to cope with the loss of star striker Willie Thornton who had powered the rout of Third Lanark.

Breck wrote, 'Now Rangers will reap the reward of that reserve array of theirs. They won't have a player so good as Thornton, who has a style all of his own and who was coming right into top form only to pull that muscle against Third Lanark. But Williamson is on call, and I suspect will be in that tack against Queen's Park at Ibrox. [Willie] Waddell may be absent too. You never can tell what will happen when Queen's go to Ibrox. They have had some sensational successes there, and if Whigham is not asked to carry too heavy a burden tomorrow, Rangers may be kept out long enough.'

Billy Williamson, it transpired, did not get the call. Struth gave the nod to South Africa-born Billy Arnison, having watched him score a hat-trick for the reserves against Hibernian the previous evening. Willie Waddell, a gifted winger who was to become one of the great off-field figures in Rangers' history, was fit to play.

Struth's side had won four of their five games while Queen's Park had won just one of five, but the professionals were made to work hard by the amateurs. 'Three minutes late, Rangers kicked off and were very soon fighting hard to stall a promising Queen's Park opening,' reported the *Evening Times.* There was certainly to be no repeat of the demolition of Third Lanark; Rangers were restricted to a pair of goals from Jimmy Duncanson. On 35 minutes, the Dennistoun-born striker ran on to a pass from Scot Symon, rounded a tackle, stumbled, regained his balance and buried a low shot past 15-year-old goalkeeper Ronnie Simpson. Eight minutes after half-time he headed home a cross by Waddell, but Simpson prevented further scoring, displaying the ability that would underpin a magnificent career during which he would win the FA Cup twice with Newcastle and the European Cup with Celtic.

Duncanson was the difference between the teams, opined the *Sunday Post* correspondent under the headline 'A RED-HOT RED-HEAD': 'But for this redhead, I fully believe the amateurs would have pulled off a draw. Not only did he toil to keep both Caskie and Waddell going, but his powerful thrusts always looked like finding the mark. Typical of this was the Ibrox opener. Falling after a Letham tackle, he regained his feet, crashed his way past two defenders to beat Simpson. For his second goal, Duncanson jumped high above the others to head through a Waddell cross.'

The match hit no great heights, perhaps, suggested the scribe, due to games coming thick and fast and the demands they placed on players, even professionals, still regaining full fitness after the disruptions of war, 'Maybe it was the general sultriness of the day or the after-effects of this two-games-per-week business. At any rate, this was all far removed from the joyous abandon these two teams infuse into things. In the air, out of play went the ball. Seldom along the carpet. And when we did see some glimpses of real football, ten backward forwards spoilt it by woeful finishing.'

Still, Struth had a solid win and two points to reflect upon as he settled into his office at Ibrox on Sunday morning. With a visit to Celtic looming the following Saturday, the industrious manager had plenty to do, only to find himself surprisingly required for a spot of hosting.

'One would think that managers would at least rest on Sunday, but not William Struth,' reported Waverley in the Spotlight column in the *Daily Record.* 'He was at work in his sanctum when a bus packed with English visitors arrived at the ground – on spec. The spokesman of the party, which came from Leeds, and the ladies and gentlemen with him, had heard so much about Rangers and their stadium that they felt they couldn't pass through Glasgow without a call – vaguely hoping there would be someone to open the gates. Like all visitors to Ibrox, this party was astonished at the sumptuous equipment and gave vent to it when the Rangers' manager asked them to step into the cocktail bar to partake of hospitality. No doubt about it, the Copland Road ground is a magnificent advertisement for Scottish football.'

In the *Sunday Post*, meanwhile, the Jack Harkness Here column explored the big talking point among Glasgow's football community ahead of the impending Old Firm clash: Celtic's controversial decision to charge 7s 6d for a stand seat for the game at Parkhead. Under the headline 'NEW PLANS FOR BIG GAME BOYCOTT', Harkness revealed, 'At one period last season we almost had a Rangers-Celtic match without players. On Saturday, we may have a Rangers-Celtic match without Rangers and Celtic supporters. Rangers Supporters' Association, a 6,000-strong body, have cancelled their total application for ground and stand tickets in protest at the charge of 7s 6d for a stand seat.

'Now here's the real cream of it. Celtic supporters are with Rangers in their protest! I've spoken with both George Littlejohn and Martin Carroll, respective supporters' clubs' secretaries. The Rangers boys made their decision on Friday evening. The Celtic boys have called an executive meeting for this afternoon. They will then decide whether to join in only the boycott of the stand or go the whole hog as far as the match is concerned. Then, on Tuesday evening, the two supporters' clubs are having a joint discussion. Whatever boycott action they may decide on remains to be seen, but they are definitely to forward a joint protest to the Celtic club. A most intriguing situation.' The boycott did take place: Rangers' 3-2 win was watched by only 28,000.

Saturday, 31 August turned out to be a highly significant day in the title race. Rangers took two points against Queen's Park while Hibernian took none from a defeat at Motherwell (see Chapter 46). Come the end of the season, Rangers won the league by two points – ahead of Hibernian. Struth's men also lifted the inaugural Scottish League Cup that season, and when the manager finally left Ibrox in 1954, after 34 years in charge, he had steered Rangers to 18 league championships, ten Scottish Cups and two League Cups, as well as seven wartime championships.

Queen's Park continued to proudly fly the amateur flag well into the 21st century. In 1996, for the first time, they accepted former professionals in the team, as long as they were not paid. Then, at a meeting (this time not at 3 Eglinton Place, which is now 404 Victoria Road) on Thursday, 14 November 2019, it was agreed to amend the articles of association to allow the club to turn professional. 'The two necessary amendments were voted through by more than 90 per cent,' recalls queensparkfc.co.uk. The quirkiest era in the history of British football had come to an end.

7

Football League Division Two
Plymouth Argyle 3 West Ham United 1 (HT: 2-1)
Scorers – Plymouth Argyle: Strauss (2), Rawlings; West Ham United: Wood
Attendance: 25,000

'No bananas fit for human consumption have been fed to pigs.'

THE DAY after the big kick-off, *The People* journalist Tom Morgan, in his Searchlight on Sport column, focused upon the colossal outpouring of affection for football. Morgan referenced his *People* colleague, astrologer Edward Lyndoe, as he waxed lyrical about the resurgence of the great game and celebrated the glorious uncertainty implicit in teams resuming after seven messy years.

Under the headline 'GREYHOUNDS WILL FEEL THE DRAUGHT', he also speculated that football's rebirth augured ill for one of its great rivals for British sporting affections, 'It doesn't even call for a Lyndoe to prophesy that the return to league football will coincide with the greatest boom the game has ever known. Yesterday's gates proved that the fan has cultivated a thirst for thrills since they were cut off in 1939 and most clubs must be wishing they had grounds the size of Wembley Stadium or Hampden Park. Britain at the moment is almost football mad and I should not be at all surprised if, for the first few weeks, even greyhound racing does not feel the draught. At one time the dogs were a definite threat to football but with Sunderland coming to Arsenal and Portsmouth going to Bolton and places beyond for the first time since 1939, football resumes its national interest and takes pride of place among sports fans.

'Quietest of all are the football clubs themselves. The usual bilge has been written about how each and all are going to win the cup and league, whereas actually every club is starting off without any idea of what is going to happen. Clubs who have hung on to old players will pull up with a jerk when they find that prewar stars are a yard slower while clubs who have signed on young, untried men will put everything into the lap of the Gods and cross their fingers for luck. The glorious adventure has started. Good luck to everybody.'

The nation embraced the Football League like a long-lost loved one and nowhere was that more heartfelt and appreciated than at Plymouth. Every club and every supporter had known danger or hardship in recent years, and the hardship continued, but few endured more than those of Plymouth Argyle and West Ham United who met at Home Park on the opening day.

The fall of France in the spring of 1940 left Plymouth, on the Devon coast, vulnerable to German attackers. During the next four years it was, other than London, the most heavily bombed city in the United Kingdom. The first bombs landed on Plymouth just before midday on Saturday, 6 July 1940. Three people – a 33-year-old woman, a 58-year-old man and a 13-year-old boy – were killed. Between then and April 1944, Plymouth was hit by 59 bombing raids, peaking with a seven-night blitz in March and April 1941. In that sustained onslaught, 1,174 people were killed and 3,209 were injured. More than 4,000 properties were destroyed and a further 18,000 were damaged.

At a time when the resilience of the British people was tested to destruction, nowhere was that more adamantine than in Plymouth. The city's strength and spirit was encapsulated in the hours after the blitz by one word painted over the west door of the bombed-out shell of St Andrew's Church on Royal Parade. *Resurgam.* I shall rise again.

Amid the devastation, Plymouth Argyle was forced into limbo. The Pilgrims played in the first season of wartime competition but in August 1941, travelling restrictions and the loss of their requisitioned ground convinced chairman Sir Clifford Tozer to withdraw the team from competitive football. Home Park was used for various purposes including the storage of furniture salvaged from wrecked buildings. The ground became home to more than 50 pianos but was then itself bombed. The 11-year-old grandstand was destroyed by fire from incendiary devices. The flames, fanned by a stiff breeze, were fuelled by the pianos and other furniture.

Argyle returned to competitive football, still under prewar manager Jack Tresadern, for the 1945/46 season in the Football League South. An old military hut was renovated to become the dressing rooms. Railway sleepers were used for footing on the terraces. League rules required the provision of some amenities for visiting directors, officials and the press, so the club borrowed a Plymouth Corporation double-decker bus. On matchdays the bus was deployed as a mini-grandstand. Between matches, it resumed its regular purpose, chugging around the city's streets as a training vehicle for new drivers.

Back on the field at last, the Pilgrims didn't fare well. Michael Foot, a passionate Argyle supporter freshly elected as the city's MP, had to wait until February for the first win of the season, 3-2 at home to Wolves. The ever-changing team (Tresadern used 72 players during the season) finished emphatically bottom of the table having collected just 16 points and conceded 120 goals. Ahead of 1946/47, expectations were not high.

More than 200 miles away, in east London, West Ham had also suffered heavily. The Hammers had entered the 1939/40 season on a high. Ted Fenton, wing-half and linchpin of the team, recalled, 'In 1939, we really and sincerely thought we were going to do it [win promotion]. We had the balance, the power and the experience necessary. We saw it as our season of fulfilment.' The season of fulfilment lasted only three games.

The suspension of the Football League brought serious financial implications for clubs and individuals, in the face of which West Ham's board took a heartwarming lead. Citing that footballers should not be punished for their patriotism, they decided that their players would be paid 30 shillings per week, even if absent on military service. At a time when clubs were battling to survive, it was a magnificent gesture.

West Ham's players responded by delivering the club's first Wembley victory. In 1940 they lifted the Football League War Cup having beaten Chelsea, Leicester City, Huddersfield Town, Birmingham City and Fulham to reach the final against Blackburn Rovers on 8 June. 'In front of 42,399 brave supporters, who braved the threat of a Nazi air raid,' recounts the club's website, whufc.com, 'Sam Small scored the only goal of the game to secure a welcome piece of silverware and boost the morale of east Londoners who had already been targeted by the Luftwaffe.'

While east London was hit many times, the Hammers' Boleyn Ground home avoided serious damage until August 1944 when a V1 flying bomb landed on the south-west corner of the pitch. Much of the South Bank terrace was destroyed, that end of the stand was damaged and the club offices were hit. They were forced to play all games away until December when, back at the Boleyn, they beat Aldershot 8-1 and Luton Town 9-1. Charlie Paynter's team finished the final wartime season placed seventh out of 22 in the South League. Solid, but could they recapture the spirit and confidence of the lost 'season of fulfilment'?

It was a question excitedly debated by West Ham fans from Plaistow to Mile End and Hornchurch to Sasolburg, but elicited little interest from the editor of the *East End News and London Shipping Chronicle*. In the run-up to the big day, the publication made no mention whatsoever of football, though it did bring good news for any ardent female Hammers fans seeking employment which would not impinge on their Saturday afternoon footy-watching. Bovril Limited advertised for 'women and girls for general factory work under best conditions' with those aged over 18 to be paid 64s 2d for a 44-hour week (no Saturdays). Those appointed would also enjoy access to 'excellent canteen and social facilities' at the factory at 148/166 Old Street, Shoreditch.

The *Evening News (London)* did offer a snippet of preview, 'West Ham United, lacking the services of their last season discovery, Travis, play Ken Wright at centre-forward who Charles Paynter says has the Corinthian style. He will probably move inside when Travis comes back from the army.'

Tresadern, meanwhile, plumped for a shake-up following Argyle's final pre-season friendly, a 6-3 defeat to Bristol City, which did nothing to alleviate their supporters' concerns. The manager made five changes with Stepney-born brothers Dave and Bob Thomas leading the attack. Bob had guested for West Ham during the war. In too came 21-year-old local lad Marcus Murphy, born in Tavistock, and previously with St Austell and Plymouth & Stonehouse Gas Company. 'Murphy, formerly with Gas Company and RN Torpedo Depot in the Plymouth & District League, makes his Second Division debut,' revealed the *Western Morning News.*

Most significant, it transpired, was Tresadern's decision to pick debutants on either wing. On the right was Sid Rawlings, a 33-year-old signed from Exeter City. On the left, Bill Strauss, a South African, was recruited from Aberdeen. On a filthy afternoon in Devon, the wingers took centre stage as Argyle gave the 25,000 crowd a day to remember.

West Ham started confidently and took the lead through Jackie Wood after 18 minutes but Argyle were in front within ten minutes thanks to goals from each of the wide men. Eleven minutes after half-time came the sort of moment for which the green legions had waited years. Strauss cut inside and let fly from 30 yards, leaving goalkeeper Harry Medhurst rooted in the mud: 3-1.

The home side, tails up, poured forward, and only a succession of fine saves from Medhurst prevented a deluge of goals to match the tumbling rain. Plymouth, having produced the shock result of the day, left the field to a huge ovation. *Resurgam.*

'Many of the 25,000 supporters went home with wet shirts but their spirits were high for, in one game, Argyle had done much to erase the memory of last season's doleful record,' reported the *Weekly Dispatch (London).* 'Few, in fact, noticed the heavy shower of rain which drenched them for five minutes as during that period Argyle scored two goals which reversed West Ham's early lead and inspired them to continue with a dash and determination which kept West Ham at sixes and sevens.'

'VICTORY WELL WON. TRIUMPH BY TEAM WORK' was the headline in the *Western Morning News.*

'Plymouth Argyle's clear-cut victory over West Ham United by three goals to one at Home Park on Saturday provided the biggest surprise among the results,' reported Tamar. 'There was no fluke about the win, however, no easy goals obtained against the run of play, but a fully merited decision by far and away the better side.'

Plymouth's storming start proved to be something of a false dawn but, fuelled by 36 goals from the Thomas brothers, they avoided relegation by four points, an outcome for which most of their supporters would have settled pre-season. An interesting decade followed. The 1950s brought two relegations and two promotions.

It took West Ham, stripped of key players by the lost years of the war, a decade to start moving forward again. Medhurst joined Chelsea, for whom he was to play 157 games, and also went on to play cricket for Cambridgeshire. He remains the only sportsperson in history to keep a clean sheet on his Football League debut, for West Ham against Fulham at Upton Park, and score 16 on his Minor Counties Championship debut for Cambridgeshire against Lincolnshire at Sleaford.

The vexed subject of bread rationing, meanwhile, rumbled on and Chalfont St Peter resident Mary Were took it to the very top. She wrote to the king, reported the *Daily Herald*, and while the monarch did not reply directly, Mrs Were did hear from the Ministry of Food. The ministry's parliamentary secretary, Dr Edith Summerskill, assured Mrs Were, 'No white bread has been issued to prisoners of war; No liquid milk is used in the manufacture of plastic,' and, crucially, 'no bananas fit for human consumption have been fed to pigs.'

8

Football League Division Three South Aldershot 4 Bristol City 3 (HT: 1-0) Scorers – Aldershot: Griffiths (3), Brooks; Bristol City: Clark, Rowland (og), Thomas Attendance: 6,400

'The gorilla Alfred is apparently in perfect health.'

THE EVE of the new season brought unwelcome news for Aldershot supporters who liked to partake in the good old footballing tradition of having a fag while cheering on their team.

'The cigarette shortage became even more acute locally during the week,' reported the *Aldershot News*, 'and most shops displayed "no cigarettes" notices. One possible explanation of the short supplies is that larger quotas are sent to seaside resorts during the holiday season. A leading tobacconist described the position as being worse than at any time since 1940.'

With bread rationing also starting to bite, these were particularly testing times for Aldershot fans who enjoyed a smoke and a sarnie during a match. However, the opening fixture of the new era, against Bristol City at the Recreation Ground, was a treat in itself. It was an absolutely cracking game with, for the home fans, the right result.

Bristol City went into the match as firm favourites. Aldershot were relative new boys to the Football League, having joined in 1932 and existed unspectacularly in Division Three South ever since. City's history was longer and much more illustrious. After entering the Football League in 1901, they quickly became a powerful force, finishing runners-up in Division One (to Newcastle United in 1907) and the FA Cup (to Manchester United in 1909). They encountered harder times after the First World War when a decade of yo-yoing left them in Division Three South, but the Robins retained plenty of kudos and continued to attract a big following. Their FA Cup tie against Preston North End in 1935 drew a record crowd of 43,335 to Ashton Gate.

That huge audience, which witnessed a tense goalless draw, included several employees of Bristol Zoo who had no idea of the traumas that lurked around the corner for the residents of their workplace. In April 1941 the *Western Daily Press* reported that the zoo 'had lost in the past year the giraffe Alphonse and his son Henry, also some kangaroos, wallabies and other animals'. There was also some better news, however, 'The gorilla Alfred is apparently in perfect health, notwithstanding the scarcity of fruit that was regarded as necessary for his diet.' Celeste the elephant had been transferred to Dudley Zoo.

Alfred and his fellow City supporters had been encouraged by their team's strong run in the 1945/46 FA Cup. The tournament returned a year ahead of the Football League, with all ties played over two legs to generate maximum revenue for the participating clubs. City relished the format and overcame Yeovil (5-2 on aggregate), arch-rivals Bristol Rovers (6-2) and Swansea Town (7-3) to earn an attractive fourth-round tie against Division One side Brentford. They rose to the occasion to beat the Bees 2-1 at Ashton Gate but lost the second leg 5-0.

'Both the City and Rovers showed promise last season,' reflected the *Western Daily Press* ahead of the kick-off. 'The former proved themselves one of the most attractive sides in the League Three South and by their displays in the FA Cup competition revealed that they are capable of holding their own in better class company.'

The reporter pinpointed Aldershot winger Ron Hobbs, who had first blossomed while representing Aldershot Shop Assistants on Wednesday afternoons, as the main threat, 'Hobbs may prove to be the fastest winger in the league. It is more than likely that, before the season is very old, some of the big clubs will be making enquiries about him.'

As mentioned in Chapter 5, the *Western Daily Press*'s Bristol Rovers correspondent showed his sagacity by describing Rovers debutant Jackie Pitt as 'promising' – 75 years later, Pitt was inducted into the club's Hall of Fame. The *Aldershot News*, it transpired, also employed a wise man. After watching the Shots' final warm-up fixture, an internal Reds v Blues match at the Recreation Ground, the *News* reporter, under the byline Our Own Correspondent, gave his verdict, 'Main conclusions that can be reached from the two trial matches are that Aldershot's attack is going to be substantially stronger. There is skill and artistry in the prospective front line … but there is still a need for a class centre-half.'

Our Own Correspondent had every right to radiate smugness behind his steaming Bovril in the ramshackle, wooden press box as Aldershot and Bristol City christened the season with a seven-goal thriller. Attacking skill and artistry were displayed in abundance, from Hobbs but most of all from his team-mate, experienced striker Steve Griffiths. Like thousands of other players, Griffiths had been denied his peak years as a full-time professional by the war. The Yorkshireman, fresh from Royal Navy service on the submarines, quickly started making up for lost time with a hat-trick on his Shots debut.

Griffiths scored the only goal of a relatively quiet first half: in the 38th minute he was fouled in the box and netted the penalty to give the Shots a 1-0 half-time lead. After the break, the rain turned from steady to heavy and goals flooded in. It was wonderful entertainment for the 6,400 crowd as three times Aldershot went two goals up but, on each occasion, City fought back to keep the game wide open.

Great fun though it was for the fans, it was a pretty challenging afternoon for two goalkeepers at opposite ends of their careers. Between the posts for the visitors was 43-year-old Alec Ferguson, a veteran Scot making his City bow 21 years after his Football League debut, for Wigan Borough. In goal for the Shots was 18-year-old Ron Reynolds, still to be born when Ferguson made his first professional outing. A local lad, Reynolds had recently signed his first professional contract on six pounds, 14 shillings per week – significantly less than Deborah Kerr. As the afternoon darkened past four o'clock and the rain lashed down, Ferguson and Reynolds were busy chaps.

Ten minutes after half-time, Aldershot went 2-0 up when Griffiths's smart finish gave Ferguson no chance. At that point young

Reynolds was contemplating the perfect start – a victory and a clean sheet – but that notion disappeared six minutes later, courtesy of one of his team-mates as Alf Rowland put the ball into his own net. Aldershot restored their breathing space when Griffiths completed his hat-trick but four minutes later it was 3-2 after City striker Don Clark shot low and the greasy ball squeezed through Reynolds's grasp into the net. It was the first of Clark's club-record 36 goals in the season. 'The City were playing at their best at this point,' reported the *Western Daily Press,* 'and Clark and Hargreaves went very near.'

It was Aldershot who scored next, however, when Harry Brooks found space among City's exhausted defenders to shoot home. A minute later, Griffiths had a golden chance to seal victory once and for all with another penalty, but this time he sent it wide. Instead, City fought back yet again and Wilson Thomas thundered a long-range effort past the helpless Reynolds in the 90th minute to make it 4-3. The Robins poured forward but the Shots, roared on by their supporters, held on. At the final whistle, the crowd rose in acclaim for both teams while the goalkeepers, wearing mud from head to toe, met in the centre circle and shook hands before heading for a much-needed bath. What a game!

In his match report, Our Own Correspondent had far too much dignity to recall his Delphic words a couple of days earlier. 'Aldershot won largely because they played the right type of football on the greasy ground,' he reported. 'They played fast, open football and never once relaxed. The forwards combined well and the defence stood up strongly against hot pressure.'

His *Western Daily Press* counterpart's prediction about Hobbs was not quite as accurate. The big clubs did not come in for the winger, who was still with Aldershot in 1951 when he shared a benefit game with Jack White against, somewhat strangely, Kilmarnock.

It was Reynolds who was to move up the Football League, through the unusual catalyst of a clandestine meeting at Waterloo railway station. In 1950, the club's directors sent Ron to Waterloo for a meeting with, he was led to understand, representatives of Arsenal. In fact, the gentlemen were from Tottenham for whom he went on to sign and play more than 100 games before closing an excellent career at Southampton.

The *Western Daily Press* attributed Bristol City's opening-day defeat to their failure to deal with the deluge, 'The City took a long time to settle down and, when they seemed to be getting into their stride, the rain and mud hampered them. One down at half-time, City came within a goal of equalising three times in the second half, yet could never do so. If Bristol could have got on terms at any time during the second half, it seemed likely that they would have won as Aldershot's defence, although playing soundly on the whole, was liable to make mistakes.'

The fortunes of the two clubs were to contrast vividly in the months ahead. While the Shots struggled and finished just one place and four points above the relegation line, City recovered to challenge hard at the top of the table. They finished third, six points below the promotion places. Aldershot's defence remained liable to mistakes, most spectacularly in the reverse fixture at Ashton Gate on 28 December. City's supporters in the 17,428 crowd gathered with growing concern, their team having won none of five games in December so far. Those concerns were emphatically put to rest. 'BRISTOL AVALANCHE' was the headline in the *Aldershot News*. City led 6-0 at half-time. Full time: 9-0.

'Bristol City gave a fine exhibition of football and overran a poor Aldershot team who were not a shadow of the side that took full points from City in the opening game of the season,' reported the *Western Daily Press*. Even from such a drubbing, however, the noble *Aldershot News* correspondent found a positive, 'Aldershot gave a clean and sporting display despite the fact that they were outplayed for three parts of the game.'

This was, of course, a time when, more than ever, sport could be viewed in perspective. Lives had been lost, given and shattered for the greater good. Millions had suffered, many in ways that would affect them for ever. A football result, even a 9-0, really didn't matter and no town in the country understood that more than Aldershot, home of the British Army since 1854. Aldershot's hospitals were the first to receive wounded troops from the Western Front during the First World War. The town's Cambridge Hospital treated thousands of wounded soldiers from the Second World War and some were still being treated there at Christmas 1946. Any Aldershot fan tempted to feel grumpy about the result at Ashton Gate needed only to glance down the same page of the *Aldershot News* for a portrait of defiance of adversity – and some perspective.

Under the headline A 'GENEROUS DINNER', the *News* reported, 'A Christmas dinner of turkey, chicken, pork, vegetables, plum pudding fruit, nuts and beer must have been just a dream to some people, but it was a reality to the patients at Cambridge Military Hospital, Aldershot. The wards were decorated by the patients and staff, and the keen competitive spirit between each one brought forth some magnificent displays. After some difficult judging, the prize for the best effort was awarded to wards five and six (surgical) with a special prize to the patients' dining room. On Christmas night the patients and staff made their own entertainment, and the sound of many happy "sing-songs" echoed through the building.'

On such inspiring resilience did the nation build its recovery from the wretchedness of war.

9

Football League Division One
Chelsea 4 Bolton Wanderers 3 (HT: 2-2)
Scorers – Chelsea: Spence (2), Lawton (2); Bolton Wanderers: Lofthouse (2), Forrest
Attendance: 61,464

'Admission by ticket only will have to come, for only by guaranteeing entry to the ground can anxiety be allayed, and it is anxiety on that score, rising to frenzy, that constitutes the greatest menace to safety.'

ON A day when fans flocked to games all over the country, the biggest crowd of all – 61,464 – gathered at Stamford Bridge to watch Chelsea play Bolton Wanderers. The match was of huge interest, not least for the presence of star strikers Tommy Lawton and Nat Lofthouse. It was also highly poignant: five months earlier, 33 Bolton supporters died in a tragic crush at an FA Cup tie at Burnden Park.

Stamford Bridge was no stranger to hosting huge crowds. A Division One fixture against Arsenal in 1935 attracted 82,905, and when Dynamo Moscow visited for a friendly in November 1945 74,496 people paid for admission – but the crowd probably exceeded 100,000 as fans squeezed through gaps in fences and gates. Such disorganisation was not uncommon and, while creating a tumultuous atmosphere, it was often uncomfortable and unsafe. Four months after Moscow's visit to England, it led to disaster when Bolton Wanderers hosted Stoke City in an FA Cup quarter-final second leg.

A crowd of 50,000 was expected but, as kick-off approached, there were already 65,000 inside Burnden Park with another 20,000 trying to get in. At five to three, when the players took the field, two barriers near a corner of the pitch gave way. In the chaos that followed, 33 people lost their lives and more than 400 were injured.

Home secretary James Ede appointed Mr R. Moelwyn Hughes KC to conduct an enquiry into the tragedy. The Welsh lawyer's report recommended that 'scientific calculation' should be applied to ascertain how many people could safely attend games. He also stressed the importance of crowd management outside grounds. Lessons, it transpired, were to be slowly learned.

It says much for the stoicism of the population of that era, accustomed to loss and, as much as possible, inured to it, that on the eve of the 1946/47 season, the tragedy was not even referenced in the *Bolton Evening News*'s pre-match coverage. Indeed, on the day the season opened, the paper's Town Topics column carried a lyrical tribute to the Wanderers groundsman and his 'green carpet' at Burnden Park without even mentioning the monstrous events which so recently unfolded there, 'There's a chap at Burnden Park who never seems to get into that limelight that means so much to a big, modern football organisation. He is the Master of the Turves and today as I watched the reserves battling against the North End Central League side, I paid him my respects, and in the same thought commiserated with him on the desecration that was spoiling weeks of fond care and hard work. It is a delight to see the green carpet at Burnden new as each September dawns, but it is gradually reduced to a black quagmire as the football days pass along. These hours of rain left the pitch today soft and yielding, and every tackle and every turn left a scar that will never be wholly repaired. Why, oh why, could we not have had a dry season's opening?'

A worthy salute to the Master of the Turves – though perhaps it would have been nice to name him!

Elsewhere in the paper, Olympian focused on the big match, 'Football form, notoriously fickle, will be more so than ever, for a beginning at any rate, but it is in the Wanderers' favour that they will field an 11 of tried and experienced players, with the success of last season to give them added confidence. There are good hopes of believing they will do well at Chelsea's headquarters.'

Bolton had happy recent memories of Stamford Bridge, having beaten Chelsea there to lift the War Cup 14 months earlier. The clubs met after winning their respective regional finals, Bolton beating Manchester United and Chelsea defeating Millwall at Wembley in the first club football match attended by Princess (later Queen) Elizabeth.

Bolton's return to the Bridge for the start of the 1946/47 season was a standout fixture, perhaps most of all for the match-up of Lawton and Lofthouse. Born in Farnworth and Bolton, just three miles apart, respectively, the two great strikers' careers had taken vividly contrasting routes. Lawton was a big-money, big-city star, having joined Everton from Burnley for £5,400 as an 18-year-old in 1937, and then Chelsea from Everton for a whopping £11,500 after he was demobbed in 1945. Lofthouse, six years Lawton's junior, was a homegrown legend. He joined Wanderers as a 14-year-old apprentice in 1939 and emerged as a powerhouse striker during the war years, alongside working as a Bevin Boy in the coal mines. A typical wartime Saturday for young Nat involved catching a 4.30am tram to the pit to work an eight-hour shift before catching the team bus to a game. Players of the 21st century may have consulted their agents about such a schedule.

Lawton and Lofthouse were a massive opening-day draw – and they delivered. They christened the season with two goals apiece, though a less vaunted individual was picked out as pivotal to Chelsea's win by *Weekly Dispatch (London)* reporter John Robertson. 'Chief snapper-up of unconsidered trifles, Dicky Spence, won this game by scoring two goals which should never have happened,' wrote Robertson. Spence had joined Chelsea from Barnsley for £5,000 in 1934, and played in the Arsenal game which attracted 82,905. Now 38, the winger was out of the traps like a yearling and took just seven minutes to score Chelsea's first goal of the new era.

Spence's early strike ('a sad sort of goal from the Bolton standpoint' commented the *Bolton Evening News*) was followed by heavy pressure from the visitors in which Scottish winger Willie Moir hit the bar. Ten minutes before half-time it was still 1-0 – then the main men got involved. Lofthouse sent a breathtaking 40-yard shot beyond goalkeeper Bill Robertson. Two minutes later, Lawton, 'springing a foot higher than anyone else', headed Chelsea back in front. In the final minute of a captivating half, Ernie Forrest, one of 17 players to have served with the 53rd (Bolton) Field Regiment in the preceding years, volleyed the visitors level again.

Bolton were denied by the bar again early in the second half when Ray Westwood's 20-yarder bounced to safety. Instead, it was Chelsea who took the lead on 70 minutes when Spence, yards offside, galloped clear to beat Bootle-born keeper Stan Hanson. Johnny Galloway, a £3,500 acquisition from Rangers, teed up Lawton to score from a tight angle to make it 4-2 but Bolton hit back yet again when Westwood's 'grand pass' sent Lofthouse through to score. In the dying seconds, the crossbar foiled Bolton a third time when Lol Hamlett rattled it direct from a free kick. On a day when the nation's heart was with Bolton, Lady Luck was not.

'If ever a team deserved to win and saw the points disappear in a thick fog of bad luck, it was Bolton,' wrote Paul Irwin in the *Sunday Express*. 'Bolton are going places,' added Robertson in the *Dispatch*. 'I like Moir, the inside right with the authentic Scottish touches, and Roy Westwood, darting about like a trout, showed that he is still far from a spent force. The trained-to-the-minute, electric Bolton attack, backed up by two go-ahead, aggressive wing-half-backs in Howe and Forrest, ought to have made victory certain before the interval.'

The *Dispatch* correspondent was less enthused by Chelsea's performance and also gave ref George Blackhall a kicking, 'A weird decision by referee G.S. Blackhall of Wednesbury midway through the second half proved the turning point in a pulsating, dramatic match of approved, prewar vintage. The Bolton defenders – old story of not playing to the whistle – stood with upstretched arms, appealing for offside, while Goulden pushed the ball forward to Spence, who was left with only the goalkeeper to beat. Some players would have stopped dead in their tracks and looked round for the referee. Not so Spence who ran on and banged the ball past Hanson. Bolton made a hullabaloo and the referee consulted a linesman who confirmed the goal, in my opinion, a bad decision which cost Bolton the match.'

The reporter then went to town on the Blues, 'Chelsea will have to tighten up their defence and their attack is altogether too sluggish. Robertson was shaky in goal and left-back Lewis was often left standing by Woodward. Williams kicked wildly. Galloway needs to put three yards on his speed, and Goulden unaccountably missed twice from easy positions. Though he scored twice, Lawton was too often caught in possession and Bain, who began well, faded away in the second half.'

Stanley Nelson, writing in *The People*, also put the boot in, 'Bain, I thought irritatingly slow. Galloway, the former Glasgow Ranger, certainly made Lawton's second goal but he will have to think much more quickly in English football.'

The national papers' scribes were unimpressed and not shy of letting their readers know it. Alongside them in the Stamford Bridge press box was greatly respected local reporter Haydn Berry of the *Bolton Evening News*; his writing was measured, warm and rounded. He touched upon the recent tragedy, 'In all bar the loss of the points the Wanderers made a successful start to the first, real postwar season. Of course, the points are important in their cut-and-thrust, survival-of-the-fittest season, but there are degrees of defeat. This, at Stamford Bridge, with its 60-odd thousand onlookers, was really a moral victory. Tactically, the side functioned well, except for a tendency to lift the ball (half-backs please note!) which is bad for a forward line lacking height. Financially, the club got off to a great start with a "cut" of the biggest "gate" of the day. It was Chelsea's lucky day all right, and on the display of the two teams, the "Pensioners" are the ones most in need of reinforcement for the stern campaign ahead.'

Below his match report, Berry reflected more broadly upon the Football League's return and considered the pertinent question of crowd control. It had not been brilliant at the Bridge – and the reporter's astute conclusions, under the headline 'CROWD CHAOS', were decades ahead of their time, 'Crowds generally confirmed forecasts that this will be the greatest boom season soccer has known. After Stamford Bridge I should like to see more tangible evidence that the great crowds are going to be more scientifically controlled. Police were nowhere in evidence when thousands of spectators outside the ground were crushing before the turnstiles before the match. "I would have given anything to get out of that jam," said a Boltonian who survived it. Burnden Park, before the tragic cup tie of 9 March, provided nothing as frightening as this, and yet nothing whatever was done about it except that the gatemen perspired at their turnstiles to pass spectators in one by one.

'One wondered if these willing Londoners, many in a frenzy of excitement, had read the story of the disaster. More than ever I am satisfied that admission by ticket only will have to come, for only by guaranteeing entry to the ground can anxiety be allayed, and it is anxiety on that score, rising to frenzy, that constitutes the greatest menace to safety.' Mr Berry's wisdom was to take half a century to permeate the thinking of those clubs who preferred to keep packing in spectators to maximise income.

In the immediate term, Bolton turned their attention to a Monday-night visit to face Stoke. They were to defeat a Potters side struggling to suit the skills of Stanley Matthews to the rest of their team (see Chapter 17). The town's womenfolk, meanwhile, could look forward to the honour of a visit from Arthur Mugford. Never mind feeding, clothing and organising their families in the face of shortages galore day in and day out, apparently the ladies still needed to pull their socks up, 'Another urgent appeal is being made to Bolton housewives for salvage of all descriptions, and especially books and paper. A special fortnight's campaign is to be held in the town between 7 September and 21 and Mr A.L. Mugford, senior campaign officer of the Board of Trade, is visiting Bolton with the object of trying to make the town more salvage-conscious.'

10

Football League Division Three North
Hartlepools United 1 Barrow 1 (HT: 0-0)
Scorers – Hartlepools United: Harden; Barrow: Mullen
Attendance: 7,229

'Tonight, millions of soccer fans throughout the British Isles will arrange their tomorrows with anticipation and satisfaction, and in the Hartlepools, the stream of men and women through Clarence Road will flow again towards the Victoria Ground.'

IT HAD been a turbulent couple of weeks for Mr and Mrs Cowperthwaite. They were chilling out one Saturday lunchtime, strolling along a quiet back street in Barrow, when they encountered that most audacious of road users, a boy racer. Around the corner he hurtled and Mrs Cowperthwaite bore the brunt as the boy and his horse and cart ran out of road.

Fortunately for the couple, justice was to be served. The town's chief constable, Sid Balance, took up the case and, 25 days later, the lad was up in court. 'BARROW BOY'S CARELESS DRIVING' was the headline in the *Barrow News*. '"This case has been brought to show to this boy and others that care has to be taken when driving a pony and cart," said Mr S. Balance at Barrow Juvenile Court. Before the magistrates was a 14-year-old boy summoned for driving a horse and cart to the common danger.

'At 12.30pm on 3 August, Mr and Mrs Cowperthwaite were in Back-Greengate Street, a very narrow street, when this youth, driving a pony and cart, turned into the street. Mr Cowperthwaite shouted at the youth to take care, but he did not stop, and Mrs Cowperthwaite was crushed against the wall by the cart, turned round several times, and received injuries which necessitated medical treatment.'

The boy was fined ten shillings and ordered to pay a further ten in costs. Mr and Mrs Cowperthwaite hoped he had learned his lesson. Sid Balance, chief constable of Barrow since September 1944, had done his job well.

It is not known whether the boy was an ardent supporter of Barrow AFC, though at a time when football utterly consumed the interests of many young men, it is very likely he was. In which case, four weeks on from the regrettable incident, Mr and Mrs Cowperthwaite could enjoy their Saturday lunchtime perambulation along Back-Greengate Street without fear. The boy would be 127 miles away for the big kick-off: Hartlepools United v Barrow at the Victoria Ground.

The town of Hartlepool, on England's windswept north-east coast, suffered damage in both World Wars, and so did the Victoria Ground, within a drop kick of the North Sea. In 1909, Hartlepools United, still to become a Football League club, undertook a tour of Germany, an ambitious and exciting venture for a team outside the powerful Football League and Southern League. Seven years later, their next brush with the Germans was less pleasant. On 27 November 1916 a Zeppelin on a bombing mission to the industrial centres of Teesside came under attack and jettisoned its load over Hartlepool. Some of it landed on the Victoria Ground, destroying the main stand, and the stadium was later further damaged by naval bombardment. After the war, the club somewhat optimistically contacted the German government to ask for compensation. Those in charge in Deutschland were a bit stretched at the time, so did not respond. They still haven't. The football club's case remains as valid as ever, so it may be worth them revisiting the subject.

Despite the lack of compensation, the dogged folk of Hartlepool soon had another grandstand in place. Designed as a temporary replacement, it was still standing strong when supporters packed into it for the big kick-off. The stand remained in use as late as the 1980s.

Excitement ahead of the 1946/47 season was as high in Hartlepool as anywhere but, as the big day drew near, their supporters faced a dilemma. At 3pm on Saturday, 31 August, the Football League would return with an intriguing fixture against Barrow. However, at 2.30pm that day, Hartlepool and the District Kennel Association was to host a dog show in the grounds of Oval Grange, Wooler Road (by kind permission of Mrs F.C. Pyman). Admission was just one shilling with all funds raised 'in aid of the local blind'.

On Friday evening and Saturday morning, debate raged in households across Hartlepool: Pools v Barrow or the dog show? About their evening entertainment, there was no doubt – greyhound racing at Hartlepools Stadium, starting at 6.45pm, admission two shillings. But what to do before then?

Some may have been swayed by Friday's *Hartlepool Northern Daily Mail,* which, capturing the mood of the town and the nation, salivated over the League's return. 'Tonight, millions of soccer fans throughout the British Isles will arrange their tomorrows with anticipation and satisfaction, and in the Hartlepools, the stream of men and women through Clarence Road will flow again towards the Victoria Ground.'

Stirring words and, sure enough, Clarence Road was streaming with blue-and-white-clad fans from two o'clock as more than 7,000 people plumped for the football. Those who chose the dog show, it was to transpire, were the wise ones. In this far-flung northern outpost of the Football League, the competition returned with, to deploy a technical term used by generations of supporters down the years, a crap game.

The *Hartlepool Northern Daily Mail* correspondent saw it coming. Under the headline 'BARROW ARE A POOLS BOGY', he added, 'While 20 football experts tip Pools to win tomorrow, it has been noted from the records that Barrow have rarely failed to get at least a point at the Victoria Ground in past seasons.' The reporter also passed on some welcome news on the transfer front, 'George Moses, the former Newcastle United inside-forward, who played for the Possibles in last Saturday's Pools trial game and scored for the Probables after changing sides towards the end of the match, has now signed professional forms with the Pools.'

Barrow were not the most glamorous opposition. They had joined Division Three North in 1921 and started with six successive defeats.

That set the tone for an austere Football League existence as they languished low at that level pretty much ever since. In the five years immediately preceding the war, they finished in the bottom half every season, yet, despite this mundane on-field existence, the club was, reported the *Barrow News*, a beacon of happiness.

'Following the practice game at Holker Street on Saturday, the chairman and directors of the Barrow AFC entertained the players to a reception at the Town Hall. The mayor (Coun A. Jones), welcoming them to the Town Hall, wished them great success in the coming season and spoke of the necessity of friendliness and co-operation between the players and management. Mr E.J. Davies, chairman of the club, said, "Eight years ago we had a similar gathering and it was the forerunner of a very happy family. For the two years before war broke out there was no happier team in the Third Division."'

On 31 August 1946, Barrow's team was happy enough to return west with a deserved opening-day point. Hartlepools' players were left to reflect on the enduring Barrow bogey. The spectators, never mind all that anticipation and expectation, were reminded of a timeless football truism – in terms of entertainment, a goodly proportion of matches come in somewhere between ordinary and poor.

Hartlepools gave a debut to Moses and took the field resplendent in brand-new, blue-and-white-striped shirts and black shorts. Those shirts were soon mud-brown and, as the rain tumbled down, a feast of football it wasn't. After a dreary, goalless first half, one or two in the crowd may have considered a quick switch to Oval Grange, half a mile away, to take in a bit of canine action. Those who stayed were at least rewarded with two goals.

Hartlepool-born Leo Harden, on his debut, put the home side ahead before they squandered a chance to bury Barrow when Fred Gregory missed a penalty. Instead, James Mullen's equaliser maintained the bogey and it could have got even better for the visitors but for a couple of athletic saves from United goalkeeper Napper Heywood. It was all a bit flat, though, and when referee Eddie Smith from Whitehaven, slumming it a bit after officiating in the FA Cup Final between Derby County and Charlton Athletic at Wembley four months earlier, delivered the final whistle, no one complained.

'POOLS DEFENCE LOOKS GOOD BUT FORWARD PROBLEM IS LOOMING' announced the *Hartlepool Northern Daily Mail* on the Monday. 'The game was a moderate affair, keen, vigorous, but not particularly clever and, on the whole, a draw was a fair result. Pools might well have won had they accepted half the chances that came their way in the second half. The attack was the weaker part of the team and there was hardly an individual who impressed. The need for at least one good inside-forward is evident. All the credit marks go to a defence which did not impress in the practice matches and yet rose to the occasion in magnificent style in this first league game.'

The *Barrow News* saluted a well-earned away point but, perhaps blasé at holding such a strong record against Hartlepools, was mildly insulting to the home side. Its report also maintained the long-standing tradition, which began with the dawn of newspapers and continues deep into the 21st century, of misprints of words that you really shouldn't get wrong. In this case, the name of one of the teams. 'Barrow well deserved a point in their opening game against Hartlepools on Saturday but they have got to meet much stiffer opposition in the Northern Section. Mullen, who scored Farrow's equalising goal, was outstanding in attack, and worked cleverly with Dunkley and Clark. Mullen will probably make – and himself score – many goals this season. Clark showed plenty of dash but he was shadowed everywhere by Lambert, the ex-Derby County centre-half.'

The Barrow boys arrived home late in the evening to discover that it had also rained heavily on the west coast. So much so that the enterprising cricketers of Lindale and Kendal fitted their North Lancashire League fixture around an impromptu visit to a rugby league game. 'With the ground unfit for play at 2.30, Lindale and Kendal's players piled into Kendal's bus and went to Craven Park to see Barrow beat Salford,' reported the *Barrow News*. 'Returning to Lindale, Kendal raced 57 on the board in an hour and then dismissed Lindale for 55 in a thrilling finish.'

Enterprising stuff, and while cricketers, footballers, dog show organisers and Mr and Mrs Cowperthwaite did their best to make the most of a wet Saturday, for the hardy trawlermen out in the North Sea it was just another working day. As reported by the *Hartlepool*

Northern Daily Mail, under a masterpiece of the headline writer's art – the whole story summed up in clear, concise and entertaining fashion: 'HARTLEPOOL FISH'. 'One English and two Danish seine netters landed a moderate supply. Two herring boats landed 50 crans. Prices: Herrings 91/- per cran, turbot 17/6-19/6, plaice 9/- to 12/10, witches 9/4, cod 5/6, codling 5/6, skate 5/5, crabs 7/- per stone, lobsters 2/6 per lb. The above prices include levy.'

11

Scottish League B
Dundee 5 Arbroath 0 (HT: 2-0)
Scorers – Dundee: Pattillo, Rattray (2), Ewen, Juliussen
Attendance: 14,000

'It takes some measure of restraint to refrain from indulging in a criticism which is wholly scathing of Arbroath's failure at Dens Park last Saturday.'

BETWEEN 12AM and 12pm on 31 August, it rained heavily in eastern Scotland. '2.5 MILLION TONS OF RAIN – DUNDEE'S BAREFOOT SHOPPERS' announced the *Sunday Post.* 'Dundee had its heaviest rainfall ever recorded yesterday. Between midnight and noon, 2.49in fell. About 9am, the weight of water in the sewers forced off manhole covers all along Dens Road. A raging torrent fed by tributaries from sloping side streets swept downhill to the city centre. Men and women went to work or shopping with their stockings in their pockets and their shoes in their hands or tied round their necks.'

Between 3pm and 4.42pm in that neighbourhood, it rained goals. The redoubtable ground staff at Dens Park ensured that the pitch was playable and Dundee's Scottish League B fixture with Arbroath could go ahead. Dundee's supporters were delighted that it did after their team resoundingly bounced back from a midweek implosion at East Fife. The Dark Blues had led 2-0 early in the Supplementary B Cup tie at Bayview Park but lost 4-2 after Henry Morris scored twice in the closing minutes of each half. Morris was a familiar face to the Dark Blues: Dundee-born and previously with junior club Dundee

Violet. His four goals triggered grumbles of 'we should have signed him' from Dundee's travelling fans and gave plenty for the chap on Bayview Park's first tannoy system, unveiled earlier in the year at the New Year's Day derby with Raith Rovers, to celebrate.

Bearing in mind the continuing demands of travel and players' workloads, the defeat at East Fife was not entirely unwelcome, suggested the *Dundee Evening Telegraph*, 'To be knocked out of the Supplementary B Division Cup is not all gloom. These midweek games put a tremendous strain on the players, and travelling difficulties are increased by night travel. For instance, a few of Dunfermline's players had to stay overnight in Dundee. Jimmy Ellis, the left-half of the East End Parkers, had to be up this morning at 5am for his work in the pit.'

The *Dundee Courier* reporter shared his *Telegraph* counterpart's lack of remorse at the cup exit, 'The late goal rush of East Fife which put Dundee out of the Supplementary Cup is causing no panic at Dens Park. In this game, as in others, there were times when they served up football of a high standard. The luck of the game swung against them. What Dundee now have to realise is that the big mission of the season is promotion. Every game will take on the aspect of a cup tie and the Dark Blues will have to play and fight for every point.'

Next came the visit of Arbroath, advertised in Thursday's edition of the *Dundee Evening Telegraph* as a 'Grand Football Match – B Division – Dundee v Arbroath at Dens Park. Gates Open 2.15pm. Tickets for the Reserved Stand are still on sale at the office of the Secretary, 20 Reform Street, between the hours of 9am and 12 noon and 2pm and 5pm.' For Arbroath fans, it was a short, scenic journey, 17 miles down the coast, through Carnoustie and Monifieth. A Football Special train, organised by Arbroath Supporters' Club, departed at 1.50pm. At Carnoustie, the Red Lichties fans could admire the historic station, opened by the Dundee & Arbroath Railway in 1838. At Monifieth they shared the excitement at the town's new street lighting. Sixty-two 250-watt vapour lamps, mounted on 25ft concrete columns, had been installed in the main street and another 130 in side streets. That evening, 14 of the lamps were to be lit as a trial – perhaps as the Arbroath supporters' train passed through on the return journey, if they were really lucky.

That thrilling possibility lay ahead but, as the visiting fans alighted at Dundee station, only one question was on their minds: could their boys evoke the spirit of Saturday, 12 September 1885? On that rainy autumn afternoon, Arbroath created a record that will never be beaten in senior British football. In the Scottish Cup, they beat Aberdeen-based opponents Bon Accord 36-0. The *Aberdeen Press and Journal*'s report did not dwell on the occasion: 'ARBROATH v BON ACCORD (ABERDEEN)'. These clubs played their cup tie match at Gayfield, Arbroath. The Aberdeen men received a merciless beating, the register at the end showing the unprecedented tale of 36 goals to *nil* against them.' End of report!

Sixty-one years later, while the cleaners at Arbroath High School threatened to go on strike for better pay, the players at Arbroath Football Club were trying to cope with the congested early season fixture list. 'Arbroath have a heavy cup-tie programme ahead of them in the next few weeks,' reported the *Dundee Courier*. 'On Monday, they travel to Brockville to play Falkirk in the first round of the Second XI Cup. On Wednesday, they face Dundee at Gayfield in the semi-final of the Forfarshire Cup, carried forward from last season. The second leg of this tie will be played at Dens Park on the following Wednesday, 11 September.' First up came the Division B visit to Dens Park, and after a bright start, they were taken to the cleaners.

For a quarter of an hour, Arbroath matched their hosts. Then, on 17 minutes, Johnny Pattillo put Dundee ahead, Peter Rattray made it 2-0 six minutes later and the visitors wilted. Ernie Ewen and Albert Juliussen added further goals in the space of two minutes shortly after half-time and Rattray rounded off the rout with his second, 19 minutes from time.

The verdict of the *Arbroath Guide* was blunt: 'MAROONS ON THEIR HEELS': 'It takes some measure of restraint to refrain from indulging in a criticism which is wholly scathing of Arbroath's failure at Dens Park last Saturday. To declare there were no fireworks from the Gayfield side would be an understatement. In contrast to the home team, the Maroons were sluggard. Slow to meet the valley, tardy in the tackle, the Arbroath players seemed to be rocking back on their heels and watching for the ball to come to them. They were never on their toes. When they did have a chance of carrying out some constructive movement, the positioning and action were so indecisive and haphazard it appeared as if there were no plan or purpose.'

What 'slow to meet the valley' means, who knows, but it was unlikely to be complimentary, and a similar theme was taken up by the *Sunday Post*, 'A one-horse race. Few expected the Maroons to display any fireworks – and they didn't. If "Juli" had had a right leg equal to his left, the score might have been greater. Murray played a strong half-back game at inside-right. Gregal, and occasionally Archie Coats, showed flashes of skill, but for the most part Arbroath had little forward power. The mid-line was good but overworked. The defence very ragged. Dark Blues, in white, were all right, but not top-class. Maybe the poor opposition dulled the fire of fellows like Smith and "Juli". These two were certainly "off". Best department was full-back, where Bobby Ancell and McIntosh played with coolness and ability. What they couldn't deal with, Gray and Bennett disposed of with ease. Reserves Andrews and Rattray earned bouquets, while the right-wing pair strolled through the game.'

The only vestige of praise for the visitors came from the *Glasgow Evening Times*, which opined, 'Arbroath swung it about to better purpose than Dundee in the early stages, but Bennett was much the better keeper. He was tested to the utmost with two spectacular shots from Smith, and then he foiled Coats by a daring rush out to the penalty spot. It was all against the run of play when Pattillo headed the opening goal in 15 minutes following an Andrews flag-kick.'

Arbroath's followers may have reflected that they would have been better off attending the 114th Dundee Annual Flower Show at the Caird Hall, opened by Major-General D.N. Wimberley CB DSO MC Officer. At least they could cling to the tantalising prospect of travelling home through Monifieth just as the new street lamps were being tested.

Arbroath continued to struggle. They finished 12th in Division B with only Dumbarton and Cowdenbeath below them, but Dundee flourished. The dismantling of the Red Lichties had left manager George Anderson with some pleasant selection issues. 'WEE ANDREWS SETS DENS A PROBLEM' announced the *Dundee*

Courier. 'A Juliussen fan kept count of the big centre's shots on Saturday. Ten with the right foot, seven with the left. Good thing for Arbroath Albert wasn't in his usual shooting form! Polished display of little Jimmie Andrews has set Dundee a problem – but the kind of problem no team objects to. Hill, Jones and Andrews are all first-class outside-lefts. Who gets the job?'

Anderson's plethora of attacking options proved highly effective in the months ahead. The Dark Blues scored 113 goals in their 26-game Division B programme to finish top of the table and won promotion as champions, three points ahead of Airdrieonians. A further 11 points back in third came East Fife for whom Henry Morris continued his hot form. Morris ended the season with 36 goals and ahead of him lay a truly niche achievement – to score a hat-trick on his international debut and never be picked by his country again.

Morris scored 59 goals in 48 competitive appearances in 1947/48 as East Fife won the Division B title. The following season, his first at the higher level, he impressed enough to earn his full Scotland debut, against Ireland in Belfast, on 1 October 1949. The match was a British Home Championship clash but also counted as a qualifier for the 1950 World Cup in Brazil. In front of 55,000 at Windsor Park, Morris scored two minutes into his debut. A minute from the end of it, he completed his hat-trick with Scotland's eighth goal in their 8-2 victory.

By all accounts, Morris was a modest, grounded individual – later in life he worked in a Leven foundry and a Markinch distillery – but if any trace of giddiness surfaced after his brilliant debut, it would have rapidly dissipated had he picked up the next day's *Sunday Post*. His hat-trick did not make the headline. Ireland's Johannesburg-born goalkeeper Pat Kelly, also on his debut, had that honour – 'IRELAND'S KEEPER WAS CREAKY SCOTS' BEST FRIEND'. Morris did not even get a name-check in the match report by Jack Harkness, 'A certain thing called Irish hospitality is known the world over. But never, surely, has it reached such heights as at Windsor Park. At least half a dozen times, the Irish goalkeeper said, "Have this one on me!" This amazing benevolence, rather than any Scottish brilliance, made the actual result of this game something very much haywire.'

Even when Harkness turned his attention to individuals, Morris did not get a mention. To Rangers winger Willie Waddell went the praise – or rather rampant adulation, 'Now the forwards. One player stands out a proverbial mile. Here we had Willie Waddell at his devastating best, the man who took the crowd's breath away – and also took the breath away from the whole left flank of the Irish team. Stanley Matthews at his greatest has never bettered the devastating period Waddell had during the first 20 minutes. It was Waddell's match. It was Waddell at his best, and that is wing play at its greatest. Other forward successes were Steel and Riley.'

The name of Morris surfaced only in a list of goal descriptions – and even those were not particularly complimentary. His hat-trick was completed when he 'half-hit a shot which trickled into the net – surely the softest goal ever'.

Scotland's next match was against Wales at Hampden six weeks later. Where Morris sat in the selectors' thoughts is unknown but anyway he picked up an injury in a preceding league match against Motherwell. By the time he regained fitness and form, other players had seized their opportunity. Morris's international career began and ended on that single day in 1949, as did that of Pat Kelly. The two chaps took forward different memories of the occasion.

12

Football League Division Three North
Stockport County 4 Halifax Town 1 (HT: 2-0)
Scorers – Stockport County: Chapman, Earl (2), Stock; Halifax Town: Quinn
Attendance: 7,987

'It was as if an electric shock had been administered – or a wholesale issue of monkey gland!'

IF READING commuter John Maxwell was full of wrath at the 'scandalous conditions which prevail each evening' at the town's bus terminus (see Chapter 5), similar levels of stress affected users of public transport in and around Stockport. One of these disgruntled individuals resided four miles south-east of the town in Hazel Grove, a village known as Bullock Smithy until its name was changed following a unanimous vote at a public meeting in 1836. In August 1946, this disgruntled individual, sheltering beneath the signature 'Long-Sufferer', unloaded his or her angst into the letters column of the *Stockport County Express*, 'Stockport, with its funny little ways, grows on one, but there are some ways which are far from humorous, as for instance, the transport to Hazel Grove. We Hazelgrovers patiently stand in a queue, sometimes about one foot from the traffic, while numerous Edgeley and Dialstone-lane cars draw up and pass on. We have been allowed to share a queue with Dialstone-lane passengers, but the latter get their own back by treading on our feet and tearing buttons off our clothes when passing us to board their convoy of cars. Meanwhile the hopeful (or hopeless) Hazel Grove passengers get splashed by mud and choked by exhaust fumes from passing traffic – all this after risking our lives getting through the traffic to the island. Tonight, after four Edgeley and two Dialstone-lane cars had passed, a tramways man asked two inspectors if they could not change a third Dialstone-lane car to Hazel Grove. The only reply he received was a pitying grin.'

Did Long-Sufferer have a point? Were the residents of Hazel Grove disrespected by bus schedulers and Dialstone-lane passengers alike? Was this bold campaigner bringing a much-needed injustice to light? Or did he (or she) just need to get out more?

If the latter was true, then if he (or she) visited Edgeley Park to attend the Division Three North fixture between Stockport County and Halifax Town on 31 August, then he (or she) will have received just the tonic required. The Hatters and the Shaymen put on a great show. If spectators at Hartlepools v Barrow had seen the Football League return with a bit of a stinker, those at Stockport v Halifax were treated to an absolute stonker.

'Few cup ties were ever harder-fought than this exhilarating match in which there was scarcely a dull moment for the 7,987 spectators (receipts £571),' reported the *Halifax Daily Courier and Guardian.* The Football League was back in all its fluctuating, unpredictable, inglorious glory.

Ahead of the game, there was little to suggest that such a feast was in prospect. Excitement was high about the Football League's return, but Stockport and Halifax both resumed an existence rooted more in attrition than achievement. County had largely occupied its bottom tier since joining the Football League in 1901. In 1937, at last came the joy of promotion, a crowd of 27,304 packing Edgeley Park for a title decider against Lincoln City, but it was followed by immediate relegation back to Division Three North. There they rejoined the Shaymen who were founder members of that level in 1921 and had bobbed along in it, mostly in mid-table or lower, ever since. Ironically, Halifax had shown signs of promise immediately before the war. An FA Cup run in 1939 included a stirring 7-3 victory over Rochdale and a marathon against Mansfield Town which culminated in a surreal third-replay victory at Old Trafford, watched by 1,219 – slightly fewer than the 42,000 who saw Manchester United v Arsenal there 11 days earlier. That win earned Town a third-round visit to Birmingham City, where the run ended with a 2-0 defeat, but manager Jimmy Thomson appeared to be building a team at last capable of climbing out of the third level. The Shaymen also started the 1939/40 season well with two wins and a draw. They sat second in the table, behind Accrington Stanley, when war was declared.

On the eve of the big kick-off, the *Halifax Daily Courier and Guardian* looked ahead with optimism, albeit expressed in a 57-word sentence that would perhaps have benefited from its luscious fruits being divided into two portions, 'Fortified by their fine performance on the same ground in the final match last season when they were narrowly beaten by the odd goal of five after leading 2-0 at half-time, Halifax Town should visit Stockport County at Edgeley Park (kick-off 3pm) in their opening league match of the season confident of giving a good account of themselves.'

The paper also brought the latest on a player availability matter, the likes of which Sir Alex Ferguson and José Mourinho, much though they found to moan about, never had to deal with, 'David Mycock, left half-back, is being demobilised from the forces today and will probably be unable to leave York in time for the match, in which case E. Turner will play.'

The *Stockport County Express* was also cautiously positive about the prospects of its team, 'Criticism of any kind is premature and form cannot be judged on practice games. One fact stands out. County have plenty of the right kind of men, the problem is to form a team.'

On the opening day, they formed a very effective team. Former Sunderland amateur Mycock, spotted by Town while playing in the Halifax and District Wartime League, did arrive in time to make his debut, but County's 'right kind of men' blended nicely. They dominated the first half, after which they led 2-0 thanks to goals from Eddie Chapman and Sam Earl. Former Derby County winger Jack Brinton sparkled on his debut and only the athleticism of goalkeeper Reg Elvy, not long back from serving with the Royal Air Force in the Middle East and Egypt, kept Halifax in the game.

It appeared a question of 'how many?' for the Hatters but the visitors came out firing after half-time. They pulled a goal back through Pat

Quinn and pressed hard for 20 minutes, in which Eric Binns, Harold Jackson and Quinn missed chances to turn the game right round.

It was the archetypal game of four quarters and the Shaymen paid heavily for not capitalising on the quarter in which they were ascendant. In the closing stages, out of nowhere, County relocated their rhythm and added further goals through Earl and Harry Stock. Elvy was superb despite sustaining an injured wrist, and a terrific match ended with an emphatic, if slightly flattering, scoreline which left Stockport joint top of Division Three North.

In Monday's *Stockport County Express*, it was reported by a scribe who belonged very much in Division One. Among the newspaper's staff was a football reporter who wrote with no byline or even pseudonym, but with enormous panache.

Under the headline 'COUNTY'S STORMING FINISH – NEW MEN PROMISING', this was this anonymous maestro's dazzling account of Stockport v Halifax on a grey afternoon in Lancashire, 'The ancient gods of Nature took an unsympathetic interest in the season's first match at Edgeley Park on Saturday. They frolicked and capered gleefully over 22 struggling men and 8,000 onlookers. Thor shook the heavens with his applause – or was it his merriment – whilst someone in the Director of Rains Department pressed a heavy hand on the downpour valves.

'The 22 men who chased about in the mud were: STOCKPORT COUNTY – Bowles; Gleave, Buckley; McCulloch, Morris, Brown; Shaw, Stock, Chapman, Earl, Brinton. HALIFAX TOWN – Elvy; Allsop, Green; France, Ruecroft, Mycock; Jackson, Wrigglesworth, Binns, Quinn, Waters. One man cheered and jeered alternately, but one who did but smile at the fickleness of the crowd was Mr J. Williams of Bolton, referee and a worthy man.

'It was a match of bright intervals and dull moments but from the general run of play it was obvious that County were the better team. In the first half the Stockport lads raided the Halifax goal from all angles (except from behind) and but for the fine goalkeeping of Elvy would have netted more than the two of Chapman and Earl. The second half saw County on the defensive for long periods – stout work, however, from Gleave and Buckley, the full-backs, stopped the

Halifax forwards from looking really dangerous. The heavy playing conditions seemed to have tired County and 14 minutes before the end, Quinn, the Town's inside-left, netted whilst County's defenders were appealing in vain for offside.

'Then something happened. It was as if an electric shock had been administered – or a wholesale issue of monkey gland! Stockport had the crowd on its toes with storming attacks on the Halifax goal, and a very exciting last few minutes saw two picture goals from Stock and Earl which put the result beyond doubt. There was a general air of optimism amongst County's critics after the match. It is too early yet to say if County have at last arrived at a team of great enough stature to keep them in the prewar Third Division North high standing. After wartime play of mediocre character it was a tonic to see a revitalised team so full of promise. Will the critics' optimism be justified? Time alone, they say, will tell.'

Whatever lay ahead for the Hatters, their supporters could look forward to thoroughly entertaining accounts of it in their local paper.

The *Halifax Daily Courier and Guardian* correspondent, meanwhile, was generous to both the home team and the Shaymen, 'Town's youngsters were not disgraced by the margin against them on a day of trying playing conditions, and against a team whose exhibition was the best seen at Edgeley Park for years and unquestionably of First Division vintage.'

Another season of attrition awaited Halifax's young team. Mycock scored in each of their first two wins, at home to Barrow and Rochdale in late September, but the campaign evolved into another gruelling one for Thomson's side. They returned to Edgeley Park in the FA Cup and were beaten 2-1. Eight successive defeats during December and January, two of which came home and away to Bradford City on Christmas Day and Boxing Day, left them bottom of the table. That's where they finished, persuading Thomson to quit after 11 years at the club. 'It has been a hard struggle at The Shay for several years,' he said, 'in fact for most of the time I have been in charge. But I am parting with the club on the best of terms.'

County could not quite maintain their vibrant start. They remained formidable at Edgeley Park, winning 17 of 21 league games there, but less productive away form prevented them building a serious promotion challenge. They finished a creditable fourth, though harder times – a long spell in Division Four after its creation in 1957 – lay ahead.

A brighter future was in store for commuters in Hazel Grove. Perhaps stirred up by Long-Sufferer's plangent plea in the paper, improvements were made to services into Stockport. Commuters in 2026 have the luxury, leaves on the line permitting, of 47 trains per day from which to choose.

13

Football League Division Two
Swansea Town 2 West Bromwich Albion 3 (HT: 1-1)
Scorers – Swansea Town: Haines, Paul;
West Bromwich Albion: Walsh (2), Hodgetts
Attendance: 32,000

'Fickle luck and a lynx-eyed referee thus dashed the hopes of 32,000 fans.'

THE PLEASURE generated by the return of the Football League extended far beyond the 90 minutes during which blokes hoofed a bag of wind around a field. With it also came back other much-loved components of the lives of the nation's sports lovers. High on that list was that Saturday evening institution, the sports paper.

Before the advent of the internet and local radio commentaries, the only way for supporters who were not at games to become fully informed about them was through the Saturday night 'Green 'Un' or 'Pink 'Un'. These flourished all over the country and one of the most read was the *Sports Argus*, in Birmingham. A 'Pink 'Un', the *Argus* was a staple of the West Midlands sports fans' week (it was so densely packed with articles and stats it took most of a week to read) with a circulation, at its peak, of 850,000. The return of the *Argus* on the day of the resumption triggered almost as much clamour as some of the games.

Swansea Town and West Bromwich Albion launched their Division Two programme with an incident-packed match of five goals, including a highly controversial winner, and a sending off. Lots happened and Albion fans not at the Vetch Field were among those who flocked to newsagents and street sellers that evening to buy the

Argus with its 'runner' report, detailing every spit, cough, shot and corner of the game.

On the Monday following the match, the *Birmingham Daily Gazette* prominently reported the scenes that greeted its sister paper's return. 'THEY FOUGHT FOR FIRST COPIES OF THE ARGUS' was the headline, as the report revealed, 'A crowd who had waited outside Newspaper House, Birmingham, on Saturday for the triumphant return of the *Sports Argus* fought to get their hands on the first copies to come off the presses. So great was the onslaught that several street sellers were only able to move a few yards from the loading deck before their supplies were sold out. Several times the crowd made rushes towards the publishing department and several forced their way into the building. Van drivers who were trying to get away to take early editions of the *Argus* to outlying districts had great difficulty in finding a way through the crowd and police assistance had to be called. Soon, however, the crowd dispersed – happily waving their first copies for over six years of the Midlands' favourite Saturday sports paper. Once they got through to the streets, sellers found a ready market.

'The presses had been set in motion by Alderman W.T. Wiggins-Davies, deputy mayor of Birmingham, who was accompanied on the platform by Mrs Wiggins-Davies and their son-in-law and daughter, councillor J.H and Mrs Lewis. After the informal ceremony in the machine room, the deputy mayor remarked, "I should imagine the sportsmen and sportswomen of Birmingham will remember this night equally as much as I shall, because they can once again read their favourite sports paper."

'The deputy mayor congratulated Mr C. Hardaker, director and general manager, on the expeditious and efficient manner in which the *Sports Argus* had been produced, and added, "The thing which struck me most was the happy spirit prevailing amongst the whole of the staff engaged in the production of the popular paper."'

For the reporter at the ground, delivering a sports paper 'runner' report could be a less happy task in either of two contrasting ways. A rubbish game devoid of incident meant that improvisation (and sometimes desperation – a murmuration of starlings over Gresty Road during a goalless draw between Crewe Alexandra and Birmingham

City, for example) was required to fill the ocean of planned column inches. Conversely, a highly eventful match created the opposite pressure with a battle to fit in all the facts. The Swans v the Throstles fell into the latter category.

The *South Wales Daily Post* correspondent Rolande saw it coming. Under the headline 'SWANS ATTACK SHOULD DO WELL TOMORROW – PROSPECT OF THRILLS IN OPENING GAME', he wrote, 'This week's heavy rain is bound to make the going heavy at the Vetch Field tomorrow but, wet or fine, there will be a huge attendance for Swansea Town's first match of the season, with West Bromwich Albion. The forward line certainly looks good and indications are that, because of the solid defence possessed by West Bromwich, there will be a first-class struggle.'

A first-class struggle it proved to be for a full house at a packed Vetch. The people of Swansea had suffered much. During three successive nights of bombing in February 1941, there were 230 deaths and more than 11,000 buildings were damaged or destroyed. The Vetch survived but was commandeered for use as an anti-aircraft base from 1941, so the Swans played two seasons at the St Helen's rugby and cricket ground. After they returned to the Vetch, they had to find money to repair the North Bank and wrecked pitch. Despite the extremely challenging times, they did so. On 31 August 1946 the club's resilience was rewarded with a big crowd and an entertaining game.

Albion took an early lead when Dave Walsh, a £3,500 signing from Linfield, scored from Frank Hodgetts's seventh-minute corner. Swansea hit back strongly and Jack Haines brought them level with 'a picture goal'. After young Swans striker Trevor Ford (who, 22 years later, would do a surprise half-hour 12th-man stint for Glamorgan against Nottinghamshire at St Helen's on the day that Garry Sobers hit Malcolm Nash for six sixes in an over) missed a sitter, the teams went in level at half-time.

Early in the second half, Walsh showed Ford how it should be done. 'Walsh is an opportunist as his first goal proved,' reported the *Evening Despatch*. 'His second goal was a lightning move which carried him round the centre-half and had the ball in the net before Swansea were aware of what was happening.'

The home terraces were roaring again when Roy Paul made it 2-2, but 12 minutes from time came the decisive, and highly controversial, twist. A long-range drive from Hodgetts was fumbled by goalkeeper Jack Parry and referee A. Ford ruled that it had crossed the goal line. A rumpus followed, during which Swans left-half Frank Burns overcooked his suggestions that Ford had made an error and was sent off. Albion held on to their 3-2 lead and after Ford blew the final whistle, he left the field to a reception which could not reasonably be described in that evening's *Sports Argus* as friendly.

In the *South Wales Daily Post* on Monday, Rolande dug out the ref. 'Mr A.T. Ford, of Ilford, the referee, is a newcomer to the list. Not all on the ground were in a position to decide whether the ball had gone over when Parry brought down Hodgetts' shot – and the referee himself was well away from the incident.'

Ford also copped it from the *Western Mail* correspondent who, perhaps accustomed to more respectful treatment of officials in the world of rugby union, also lamented the lack of grace shown by Swansea's players, 'Swansea Town lost their first match of the season against West Bromwich Albion at the Vetch Field on Saturday by what must have been the smallest fraction of an inch. Fickle luck and a lynx-eyed referee thus dashed the hopes of 32,000 fans. The goal that did the trick came in the 78th minute when Hodgetts, the Throstles' left wing, centred the ball, Parry fumbled it and Mr Ford ruled that the ball had crossed the line.

'Then came a regrettable incident – the Swans players gathered around the referee, protesting vigorously, accompanied by the roar of the crowd, and Burns, the Swans left-half, earned the doubtful distinction of being the first league player to be given marching orders. It was tough luck for the Swans, especially as Mr Ford was at least 25 yards from the goalmouth when Parry fumbled the ball.'

If Swansea's first team ended the afternoon feeling aggrieved, it appeared their reserves, away to Haverfordwest in the Welsh League, had a right to feel even more so. According to the *South Wales Daily Post*, 'The Swans possessed as much craftsmanship and purpose as the home side and had a fair measure of the play.' They must have been jolly unlucky, then, judging by a final score of Haverfordwest 7 Swansea Town Reserves 1.

For any Swans fans residing in a cluster of villages just to the north of town, the *Daily Post* carried yet more unwelcome news, 'Swansea Valley Licensed Victuallers' Association decided at Gwaun-cae-Gurwen that, owing to the shortage of beer, public houses in Cwmgorse, Gwaun-cae-Gurwen, Amman Valley and Ammanford would open from Monday next daily from 2pm till 4pm and from 8pm till 10pm, except on Thursday when they would be closed all day.'

Back in the Second City, the *Birmingham Daily Gazette* had plenty to celebrate: Albion's conquest of Swansea, Birmingham City's win at White Hart Lane (see Chapter 24) and the elation at the return of the *Sports Argus*. What the *Gazette* staff did not know, however, as they gaily compiled the *Argus* on Saturday evening, is that their rivals at the *Evening Despatch* had a world exclusive up their sleeve.

On Monday, 2 September, the *Despatc*h front page led on the big issue – 'BREAD RATIONING UNLIKELY TO END SOON – MINISTRY DISSATISFIED WITH THE WHEAT OUTLOOK'. The back page, meanwhile, brought news of a development which could change the face of football for ever. 'SOCCER EXPERIMENT IN BIRMINGHAM ... KICK-IN FOR THROW-IN GAME IS "SECRET"'. The report claimed, 'Although intimating it will not be officially recognised by them, the FA have officially granted permission to Mr Norman Bassett, West Bromwich Albion director, to arrange a game in which the kick-in will be substituted for the throw-in. But from the point of view of interested soccer fans, there is a snag – it must be played behind closed doors. That, however, is not unduly disturbing Mr Bassett, who for some time has been sponsoring the move for the change-over, and it is something of a feather in his cap to have at last induced the powers that be to allow thc cxperiment to be undertaken. Is it a straw in the wind?

'The game, Mr Bassett told me today, has been fixed for Monday next on the ground of Moor Green FC, between Moor Green and a selected Albion team. Mr George Dutton, the well-known international referee who has controlled international matches, will be in charge. Mr Bassett, son of the late Mr "Billy" Bassett, one-time famous England outside-right and later a well-known football legislator, informed me that he communicated with the FA following the Albion v Brentford league game last season when he made a check on the time occupied by the throw-ins. Out of the 90 minutes, there were 35 minutes when the ball was actually not in play.

"'I have ascertained that there is an average of 75 throw-ins during the course of a match,' he said, "and I feel that the introduction of the kick-in will call for the exercise of greater care from goalkeeper to outside-right and will result in improved football. It is common knowledge how much a game deteriorates in the later stages when a team, leading by a single goal, persists in kicking the ball out of play to frustrate their attacking opponents. If the kick-in was adopted they would think twice before adopting such time-wasting tactics. I feel that the football public is interested in the idea. I have received letters from all over the country, and even one from South Africa, backing me up in my efforts to have the throw-in abolished.'"

Eight days later, the *Despatch* carried no details, or even a mention, of the trial game. It was, and remains, a proper secret.

14

Football League Division Three South
Southend United 3 Walsall 1 (HT: 1-1)
Scorers – Southend United: Lane (2), Dudley; Walsall: Talbot
Attendance: 11,500

'In the failing light, many people, including myself, attributed the dribble to Gardiner, but Mr Warren assured me it was Moorton who was responsible for this fine piece of work.'

AMONG THE fascination for fans when the Football League resumed was the great unknown surrounding the form of teams and individual players. The war robbed many players of their peak years in full-time professional football and delayed the entry into it of many others. Most sides entered the new era with a clutch of debutants alongside more familiar faces, some of whom were approaching veteran status. So how would the new men scrub up? And were the prewar favourites still any good?

In the latter category was Harry Lane. After playing two games for Birmingham City, the Staffordshire-born striker joined Southend United in 1933 and scored 50 goals in five seasons before moving up to Division Two with Plymouth Argyle. His Argyle career truncated by the war, he returned to Essex and rejoined the Shrimpers. Lane was named up front in the team to face Walsall on the opening day of the 1946/47 season, but the fans asked, at the age of 37, does he still have what it takes?

They needn't have worried. Lane immediately and emphatically showed that he did. And so did Alf Smirk.

The people of Southend had as much reason as anyone in the country to rejoice at the end of the war. For seven years, the town, on the estuary of the River Thames guarding the gateway to London, was effectively in the front line. Southend seafront was commandeered for military use as soon as war was declared. On 25 August 1939 the Royal Navy took over the pier, which became a first line of defence. Housing and hotels around town were also requisitioned.

In the years that followed, Southend was heavily bombed. In 1942 its children were evacuated, some not returning home until 1945. To all this adversity, the population responded with steadfast courage and defiance. Southend Home Guard had 4,000 members. The town was seized by the war and transformed by it and, while its spirit and strength stayed strong, nowhere was a return to normality more craved and the return of the Football League more warmly embraced.

Ahead of the opening-day fixture at the Southend Stadium, the *Southend Pictorial* reporter The Onlooker looked on with confidence. Under the headline 'UNITED SHOULD BEAT WALSALL – TRANSFERS HAVE TAKEN STING OUT OF SADDLERS', he wrote, 'Southend United open their first postwar league programme today with a home encounter against Walsall and my considered opinion – not just a loyal, local hope – is that the United will start the season with a convincing win. The majority of critics plump for an away victory, and a few concede a draw, but no doubt they are working on the fact that Walsall took seven out of eight points against United last season, and the fact that the Saddlers reached the final of the intersection competition. What they have overlooked are the changes that have taken place in both teams since. The visitors have the same defence but have lost the sting from their forward line with the transfer of Hancocks to Wolverhampton while the veteran Alsop, who engineered the draw last March, is an absentee.'

The Onlooker was well informed. Saddlers legend Gilbert Alsop, scorer of more than 100 goals for the club, including one in their sensational FA Cup conquest of Arsenal in 1933, was unavailable while Hancocks was preparing to make his Wolves debut against the Gunners (he did rather well – see Chapter 2). The sale of Hancocks in May 1946 left a sizeable hole in Walsall's team but filled a similar gap in their accounts.

With four much bigger clubs – Wolves, West Brom, Aston Villa and Birmingham – close by, the Saddlers faced a perpetual battle for support and financial stability. The £4,000 received for Hancocks from Wolves would keep the wolf from Walsall's door for the foreseeable future.

The *Wolverhampton Express & Star* deemed this excellent news worthy of precedence over a preview of the Southend game. 'WALSALL ARE SOLVENT' was the simple headline, 'Walsall Football Club are today solvent. That statement was made by the chairman of directors, Alderman H.J. Barlow, at last night's annual meeting. When the balance sheet was drawn up to the end of June, the figure of £15,379 and 4s and 6d cash advanced by directors and others was included. Speaking of that item and the question of the legacy of £2,000 under the will of the late H.L. Fellows, chairman of the club for many years, Alderman Barlow stated, "Since June we have reduced the item 'cash advanced by directors and others' by £13,500 so it has almost been wiped off." It was not healthy for any football club to be carried on by one or two men, Alderman Barlow commented. A club should belong to the town and its policy decided through a board of directors appointed by shareholders.'

To head into the new era with such a solid foundation was certainly encouraging for the Saddlers, though Alderman Barlow then perhaps became a little giddy, 'If we can keep to the present policy, I think the day is coming for Walsall when we can confidently look forward to joining our other four big brothers.'

That was to prove a long-term mission, though the Saddlers did mix it with three of those brothers in the Championship early in the 21st century. For now, the struggle continued. They had limped into the war with successive applications for re-election and emerged from it with three successive defeats, starting with an emphatic beating at the Southend Stadium.

On Friday, 30 August, the *Essex Chronicle* reported that 'hollyhocks 15ft high are growing in the garden of Mr Gowlett, of Chalk Street, Rettendon'. The following day, more than 11,000 people made their way to the Southend Stadium in Grainger Road and handed over 1s 3d for ground admission or 3s 6d to sit in the grandstand. The open, windswept venue, designed principally for greyhound racing, was unloved (the Shrimpers had played there for only 13 years since moving from the Kursaal) and was to be little mourned when the club moved into brand-new, purpose-built Roots Hall in 1955. On 31 August, however, even in the rain, it was full of noise and fervour and Southend's players rose to The Onlooker's high expectations.

The home side took immediate control. Several chances came and went before Lane got the party going in the 30th minute when he curled a corner beyond Saddlers goalkeeper Jack Lewis directly into the net. Walsall levelled five minutes later when outside-left Ken Davies raced clear and crossed for Leslie Talbot to score, but it was an isolated spark from the visitors. Southend soon regained the lead when the speedy Smirk sprinted clear and crossed, then inside-forward Frank Dudley's shot was saved and Lane netted the rebound. Shortly after half-time, the Shrimpers added a third through Dudley. With Dudley orchestrating from the middle and Smirk sparkling on the wing, only the brilliance of Lewis denied Lane a hat-trick and more. There was no doubt about it. Harry Lane was back. And so was Alf Smirk.

'There was only one team in it from start to finish,' reported the *Southend Standard*, 'and the one goal the visitors scored was in the nature of a gift, through appealing for offside. Walsall were saved from a deluge of goals only by the skills of their goalkeeper, Lewis. What surprised spectators most was the amazing form shown by Harry Lane. Because he joined the club in 1933, when they were still at the Kursaal, supporters have gained an impression that he is much older than he really is, but many players have gained international honours when they have been older than he is now.'

The *Standard* correspondent did add a cautionary note, 'Although the victory netted all the praise the large crowd unstintingly gave, it does not mean either that the United have a promotion side or that they will go through the season winning with the comparative ease that they did on Saturday. For the opening match of the season, it was a splendid display, but the defensive weakness apparent in the trial games was even more obvious against Walsall.'

It was a splendid display, though, and not the only one in the area that week. Under the headline 'GIANT MUSHROOM', the *Standard* also reported, 'Mr J. Riley, whilst picking mushrooms at his meadow at Woodfield Poultry Farm, Hyde Wood Lane, Rochford, discovered among several large mushrooms, a giant of the species, which measured 12in in diameter and weighed 1lb 6oz.'

The news team on the *Wolverhampton Express & Star* could not compete with that revelation on the fungus front but did report the welcome bringing to justice of a heinous criminal, 'Mrs Elizabeth Garner (45), 15 Ashbourne Road, Wolverhampton, was fined £5 at Wolverhampton today for stealing socks from a local store on Saturday.'

The paper's football correspondent, meanwhile, was kind to the Saddlers after their slow start, 'Walsall's defeat at Southend was disappointing but there is no cause for despondency,' writes Saddler. 'They will play worse and win. Lack of cohesion between half-backs and the forwards was perhaps the most noticeable failing and Crutchley, working hard all the time, will be well advised if he does not allow his enthusiasm to get the better of him. The attack, never too well together, was even less effective after Darby, in a clash with the Southend goalkeeper, had suffered a badly cut tongue. Star of the Walsall team was unquestionably Lewis, whose goalkeeping well earned the generous plaudits of the home and holiday-making crowd.'

The correspondent's assertion that there was 'no cause for despondency' was correct. Walsall recovered from their poor start to finish a very satisfactory fifth. The *Southend Standard* writer's observations were also shrewd. Shrimpers manager Harry Warren had built an attractive, free-scoring side but the defence was error-prone. Sixty goals conceded in the 42 league games prevented a promotion push, although most of the 11,500 present on the opening day would have settled for a respectable eighth place in the final table.

Harry Lane was to enjoy three more productive seasons at Southend before ending his career at neighbouring Chelmsford. Alf Smirk played 100 games for the Shrimpers, then briefly joined Gateshead before returning to Essex and swapping dressing room for press box. He wrote for the *Southend Standard* and edited the *Laindon Recorder*.

Warren, meanwhile, was on the lookout for yet more attacking options and an enigmatic one surfaced when Southend reserves faced Charlton Athletic in the Football Combination. The winning goal in the Shrimpers' 2-1 win was a bit tasty.

'NEW PLAYER'S REMARKABLE DRIBBLE' announced the *Southend Pictorial*, 'The winning goal came in the closing stages from Moorton, a 19-year-old player signed on from Luton making his first appearance for Southend. He gained possession near the corner flag and dribbled through practically the whole defence and then passed to Hamilton, who had only to tap the ball into the net. In the failing light, many people, including myself, attributed the dribble to Gardiner, but Mr Warren assured me it was Moorton who was responsible for this fine piece of work. At other times, Moorton showed signs of nervousness and requires a little more experience.'

As there is no evidence of Mr Moorton ever featuring in Southend's first team, it appears that experience never arrived. Was that dribble against Charlton reserves the zenith of this gentleman's football career?

15

Football League Division Two
Barnsley 3 Nottingham Forest 2 (HT: 2-0)
Scorers – Barnsley: Robledo (3);
Nottingham Forest: Brown, O'Donnell
Attendance: 18,000

'I refer to that "little bit of muck" on top of the "knob" reserved for the 1s 3d supporter.'

THE BARNSLEY CHRONICLE and the *Nottingham Evening Post* adopted slightly different attitudes towards the start of the 1946/47 football season. The sports team on the *Evening Post* was evidently led by a cricket enthusiast. On the day the Football League returned and the sport entered a new era, the paper's front page contained a picture of Yorkshire openers Wilf Barber and Maurice Leyland walking out to bat against Nottinghamshire.

Headlines on the back page included 'YORKSHIRE BAT FIRST AT TRENT BRIDGE' (in the County Championship) and 'ROUSING SEND OFF – VOCE AND HARDSTAFF IN MCC PARTY' (the MCC squad had set sail from Southampton to contest the Ashes in Australia). There was also 'HORSE FALLS IN DYKE – BRIDGFORD RESCUE AFTER SIX HOURS' but no mention of Nottingham Forest and their impending tussle with Yorkshiremen.

The team on the *Chronicle*, on the other hand, 'read the room' a little more and devoted copious column inches to the Football League's return. Most prominent was a heartfelt celebration of the sport itself and how much it meant to the town. The *Chronicle* reported, 'Barnsley

Football Club will open the season's programme tomorrow in an atmosphere of goodwill and high hopes, generated by many thousands of well-wishers in South Yorkshire, who, encouraged by the splendid form demonstrated in the closing stages of the 1945/46 season, cherish the desire to see their team enter the First Division next season. Of one thing they may be certain: that the men guiding the policy of the club will spare no effort or initiative toward achieving that end: and the measure of their enterprise and foresight can be gauged by the extent of the alterations and improvements which have been made at Oakwell during the summer months, and which must also indicate their determination to cater for followers on ever-improving lines. A match-winning football team is a priceless advertisement for a town like Barnsley, and the benefits which can accrue, sometimes in indirect and unexpected terms, can be of worthy substance.'

The positivity continued across the page in a match preview headlined 'REDS IN GOOD TRIM FOR OPENING AT OAKWELL', and the article continued, 'English football on a prewar basis with all the keen rivalry engendered by the hopes of championships and promotion, and the fears of relegation, starts tomorrow after seven years of makeshift wartime soccer. The curtain-raiser at Oakwell is being eagerly awaited in Barnsley and district, the Reds being at home to Nottingham Forest.

'Practice games are something of a nightmare to club managements and, as a rule, they are glad to see the back of them without a star player on the injured list. Yet, Barnsley's final trial of Probables v Possibles on Saturday was not without its lessons, supplying as it did evidence that men likely to be first choice were up to concert pitch and that most of the positions were satisfactorily duplicated in case of emergency. The Reds won 3-0, the scorers being Baxter, Gray and Robledo. Gate receipts of £194 were in aid of the Mayor's Hospitals Comforts Fund.'

Such optimism was thoroughly vindicated by the Reds' performance. They made a storming start with George Robledo, a 20-year-old Chilean with an exceptional back story, at its heart.

Robledo was born in 1926 in the Atacama Desert, northern Chile, to a local man and a mum from South Yorkshire. When he was six years old, his parents decided to start a new life in England, but there was a late twist. On the day they were due to sail from South America, Mr Robledo said he was nipping out for some fags and never came back.

Mum and her two sons – George and Edward – set sail nevertheless. They settled in Wath upon Dearne where the boys' football talent soon shone. During the war, George, in his mid-teens, worked as a Bevin Boy in the coal mines while scoring goals for fun in local football. By the most unusual route, a jewel had fallen into Barnsley's lap. Over the next 25 years defences all over the world were to be pierced by his pace and power. Forest's was the first. In the South Yorkshire drizzle, the son of the arid Chilean desert delivered perhaps the most heartwarming story of the opening day with a hat-trick on his Football League debut.

Despite an afternoon of steady rain, 18,000 people packed into Oakwell. They arrived with high hopes but could only guess what the 90 minutes would bring. Neither side had distinguished themselves during the years up to the Second World War. Barnsley meandered along, alternating between the second and third tiers, while Forest didn't pull up any trees either. In 1874 they were the first English side to wear shinguards (albeit outside their socks) and in 1898 they won the FA Cup, beating Derby County 3-1 in the final at Crystal Palace, but it all went a bit flat between the wars.

Ahead of the 1946/47 campaign, manager Billy Walker had made some interesting signings, however. Former Celtic striker Frank O'Donnell arrived from Aston Villa, inside-forward Bert 'Sailor' Brown signed from Charlton Athletic, and ex-Leeds United and Queen of the South goalkeeper Reg Savage committed to the City Ground having guested for Blackpool, where he was based with the Royal Air Force, during the war.

Savage was a busy man as soon as the match was launched by the whistle of referee Arthur Baker. Barnsley, in red, poured forward. Forest, in their change strip of white with red hoops, put in a first-half performance described by the *Nottingham Journal* as 'too poor to be true'.

Robledo took just 16 minutes to score his first Football League goal. Two minutes later, he added a second. Barnsley's barnstorming start kept Savage at full stretch while home keeper George Rymer barely touched the ball in the first half. Robledo had 72 minutes in which to complete his debut hat-trick and it arrived 17 minutes after half-time when Jimmy Baxter 'waltzed past five defenders before giving Robledo one on a plate'.

Leading 3-0, the Reds eased up. Brown soon pulled one back for Forest and seven minutes from time he created the opening from which O'Donnell's header made it 3-2. It was too little too late for the visitors, though, and the *Barnsley Chronicle* hailed a 'well-merited win' crafted by the creativity of Baxter and Johnny Kelly and the finishing of Robledo, 'The liveliness of the forwards, with Kelly of the twinkling feet in his best form and Baxter scheming shrewdly and parting with the ball advantageously, gave the opposing defenders a gruelling time. Robledo's first goal came when O'Donnell was penalised for a heavy charge on Cunningham. The full-back, taking the kick himself, transferred to the centre-forward, who, racing round Davies, who slipped on the greasy turf, sent an oblique drive past the advancing goalkeeper. The shot was a winner all the way. The second, two minutes later, was smartly headed through from Smith's centre. He completed his hat-trick after the interval. Baxter enabled him to do this by means of a short pass "handed on a plate" by the inside-left after he had dribbled past four men.

'At one point, Barnsley enjoyed a three-goal lead and, if a point of criticism could be offered at all, it was that on the sodden ground, and with the ball getting heavy, they appeared to get rather leg-weary. The Forest, a bigger side physically, appeared to stay the pace the better but, though they narrowed the arrears down to one goal, there never seemed much fear of the South Yorkshiremen having the lead wrested from them.'

The *Nottingham Journal* did not gloss over the gulf between the teams, 'There was a glaring discrepancy between the two sides at wing-half and in the forward lines. Barnsley owed their complete superiority, particularly in a first half which saw Forest's display too poor to be true, to a couple of first-class attacking wing-halves and a fast and clever attack. Forest's attack was a one-man-band affair, and, of course, that one man was Brown. Here, there and everywhere, perhaps a bit too much everywhere, he was the hardest worker on the field.'

Forest's situation was to get worse before it got better. They finished in mid-table in 1947, then two places above the relegation zone in 1948 before dropping into it in 1949 to join rivals Notts County in Division Three South. Mansfield Town, 14 miles away, were in Division Three North.

Barnsley's vibrant start raised high hopes among their supporters, accompanied by the eternal question, 'But can we keep our best players?' It was an issue which chairman George Tomlinson addressed in Monday's *Chronicle*. 'People have been saying that Barnsley don't want to get into the First Division and that they cannot afford it. I say we can afford it and we are going to have a good try to get there. Don't let us have a recurrence of rumours that Barnsley are selling this player or that player: we are not selling any of our players.'

Another urgent matter was also brought to Mr Tomlinson's attention. In the paper's letters section, a resident of Outwood, Wakefield, writing under the nom de plume Oakwell, raised the vexed question of the 'knob': 'Arriving at Oakwell in good time last Saturday, I had a walk round the ground and was delighted (as were thousands more) with the smart appearance of the playing area, and with the alterations and improvements which had been made. What a pity the sun didn't shine to add to the beauty of it all! But I also noticed one black spot, one which caused quite a lot of rude remarks from many spectators, and one which brings no credit to those responsible. I refer to that "little bit of muck" on top of the "knob" reserved for the 1s 3d supporter. If this is the answer Barnsley FC are giving the chancellor of the exchequer to his appeal for the reduced admission charge to be passed on to the supporters, then I'm afraid if that gentleman had to pay a visit to Oakwell he would have more to say about the matter. I think the least the directors should do would be to make the whole of the Spion Kop end (apart from the boys enclosure) available to the 1s 3d supporter.'

Barnsley's happy start to the season continued two days later with a 3-2 win at Sheffield Wednesday, Robledo scoring twice. Their supporters were to be treated to the Chilean maestro's skills for two and a half seasons but, for a striker of his calibre, a move upwards was inevitable. In January 1949 he joined Newcastle United for £23,000. Edward, a defender, also signed for the Magpies and the pair helped the club win successive FA Cups in 1951 and 1952. George played in both finals and both brothers played in the 1952 final against Arsenal in which George scored the winner. A sketch of the goal featured on John Lennon's *Walls and Bridges* album in 1974. George scored 82 goals in 146 league games for Newcastle before returning to Chile in May 1953.

George Robledo lit up a damp afternoon in South Yorkshire in August 1946 and his skills blessed English football, from junior games in Wath to cup finals at Wembley, for more than a decade. His remarkable story is told in Spencer Vigne's excellent book, *Postcards from Santiago*, but let the last word come from the *Nottingham Journal*, which, back in August 1946, had important herring news, 'Surplus herrings caught in the North Sea this autumn are being turned into soap. A subsidy scheme is being worked out between the Ministry of Food and the Board of Trade and will begin at the end of next month. After food needs have been met, surplus fish will be sent to factories in Hull and London and oil extracted for soap factories.'

16

Football League Division Three North
Bradford City 3 Accrington Stanley 1 (HT: 2-1)
Scorers – Bradford City: Hinsley, Wass, Woollett; Accrington Stanley: Kearney
Attendance: 10,398

'Repairs to the roof of the main stand, damaged by young "hooligans" of the district, will cost hundreds of pounds.'

BRITAIN'S DECLARATION of war evoked many deep emotions: fear, anxiety, courage, patriotism. For Accrington Stanley's supporters, within those feelings also lurked a tinge of remorse. After two shocking seasons, their team started the 1939/40 campaign like a train only for it to be abandoned after three games.

The Reds trailed in bottom of Division Three North in 1938 and 1939, finishing a miserable 11 points adrift in the latter year. Both times they had to apply for re-election, but they survived and stuck with Jack Hacking, former Blackpool, Oldham, Manchester United and England goalkeeper, who had been manager since 1935. He rewarded that vote of confidence by orchestrating a flying start to 1939/40. Stanley opened with a 2-0 win at Bradford City, to the delight of their two trainloads of travelling supporters, and followed up with a 2-1 win at Barrow before beating Oldham 2-0 at home. Hacking's side was one of only two in the country, along with Blackpool in Division One, to have a 100 per cent record when the season was terminated.

On Saturday, 2 September 1939, the *Accrington Observer* broke some big international news – 'SHOCK OF GERMANY'S INVASION

OF POLAND. PRIME MINISTER'S GRAVE WARNING. THE COUNTRY MOBILISES'. However, it did not neglect local affairs – 'UNPAID RAIL FARE. OSWALDTWISTLE WOMAN FINED' – and also saluted the football club's good form ahead of their game with Oldham at Peel Park that day. 'STANLEY v HITLER' was the headline over the Sports Searchlight column in which Ajax reflected, 'From the crisis tensions, Stanley have provided their followers with a ready means of seeking relief. Well might one be accosted on every hand not with the question, "What is Hitler going to do?" but with, "Who's going to lick us?" If anyone had dared to predict last week that Stanley would by this time have been in possession of four points he would have been laughed at. But here we are safely over two of the stiffest hurdles the team is likely to encounter. History has been made. It is the first time since Stanley became members of the Third Division that they have won their first two games on opponents' grounds.'

Stanley duly saw off Oldham to make it three wins out of three but three days later, Tuesday's paper was a sombre edition. War having been declared the previous day, Ajax had to juggle the joy of Stanley's third successive victory with the sense of impending national catastrophe. He did so with immense skill, 'Though one writes heavily under the stress of calamity, it was in no such mood that the crowd of 6,000 at Peel Park on Saturday bade "Hail and farewell" to Stanley. It is difficult, now that even our great national pastimes have been reduced to pin points of importance, to recapture the Francis Drake spirit of this match. Sadly, one recalls the obvious determination of both players and spectators to squeeze the last bitter-sweet drop of enjoyment from the last hours of peace. With such gusto did they do so that it was the imminence of war that seemed unreal, not football on the brink of immense tragedy. Even after the flush of excitement had died down, and the ground had emptied, there were those ready to joke about Stanley finishing a season at the top of the league table for the first time in their history.

'The jest rings hollowly now, but let us for a minute or two try to recreate Saturday's happy picture and Stanley's glory as one of the two clubs in the entire league with all six points to their name. Even Hitler cannot filch pleasant memories from us.'

Stanley's brilliant start to 1939/40 thus entered eternal limbo. Seven seismic years later, when they prepared to revisit Bradford, much in the world had changed, yet some things remained the same. Hacking was still manager and Ajax was still covering the club for the *Observer*. On the opening day in August 1946 the paper's readers, having digested the story headlined 'THREE ENGLISH CHILDREN REFUSED AN OMELETTE', arrived at the sports page to find Ajax in a confident mood, 'Hacking, Eastwood, Webster; Conroy, Briggs, Lythgoe; Bond, Kearney, Morgan, Keely, Edwards. This is the Stanley selectors' answer to the problems they were set in deciding the Reds' line-up in the big league kick-off this afternoon as visitors of Bradford City. On paper at any rate, they look one of the strongest sides Stanley have fielded in the Third Division.'

Stanley's hosts boasted a proud history, though the glory days were becoming a distant memory. Home to two big clubs – City and Park Avenue – Bradford was an early powerhouse in English football. City won the FA Cup in 1911 and three years later the Bradford derby was a Division One fixture, but City's fortunes declined after the First World War. In 1922, they were in the top tier – 27 years later they finished bottom of Division Three North.

The war moved football into surreal territory, not least on Christmas Day in 1940 when the two Bradford clubs shared Len Shackleton. Quoted in Jack Rollin's *Soccer at War: the Complete Record of British Football*, Shackleton recalls, 'I played for Bradford (Park Avenue) against Leeds United on Christmas morning at Elland Road, had a cup of tea in Leeds, and at the invitation of Bradford City, Park Avenue's rivals, travelled to Huddersfield as a City guest player in the afternoon.' It must have been a remarkably empowering cup of tea.

By the resumption of the Football League, Shackleton was still a Park Avenue player, though just weeks away from a big-money move to Newcastle United. Both Bradford clubs, like most in the league, were under serious financial pressure, with City's exacerbated by the actions of local ne'er-do-wells, as the *Bradford Observer* reported, 'Bradford City are making an appeal for £2,000 for ground repairs, which will cost thousands of pounds. In addition, repairs to the roof of the main stand, damaged by young "hooligans" of the district, will cost hundreds of pounds.'

On the field, the club appeared equipped for a strong season under the management of former Derby County and England centre-half Jack Barker. They gave a debut to Charlie Woollett, who was – according to the match programme – 'secured at great expense from Newcastle'. The blond winger shone and scored on his debut.

Accrington began the game with some neat passing moves but didn't threaten the home goal and were punished when Bradford took the lead through George Hinsley's 20-yard free kick. Stanley equalised when Sid Kearney headed home a cross from Arnold Lythgoe and should have gone ahead when Ron Morgan, unmarked on the six-yard line, put his header straight at goalkeeper Matt Middleton. Instead, City went in front a minute before half-time when Woollett's cross was headed against the bar by Jimmy Isaac and Bill Wass was allowed time to collect the rebound, control the ball and score. Former miner Wass took the handshakes of his team-mates unaware that it was the only goal he would ever score in professional football.

Bradford took complete control after half-time. In the 54th minute, Woollett, 'in complete isolation' according to the *Accrington Observer*, headed a third goal and only wasteful finishing from the home side saved Stanley from a hiding.

The *Yorkshire Post and Leeds Intelligencer* expressed its approval in concise fashion, 'Bradford City produced two clever wing-forwards in Wass and Woollett and a sound goalkeeper in Middleton from Plymouth and deserved their win.' Monday's *Bradford Observer*, with much to celebrate, offered a little more. On the back page, City's victory was lauded in a measured and analytical fashion, 'If Bradford City can find a good left-back they have the makings of a strong team. Against Accrington Stanley, the forwards worked smoothly. Woollett, the young outside-left, and Whittingham, at centre-forward, often tricking the visitors with quick positional changes. Bond, Accrington right-winger, son of Anthony Bond and nephew of Dicky Bond, two former City wingers, and Kearney worked well in the visitors' forward line with Briggs a power in defence.'

The front page, meanwhile, reported a happy day for Mrs H. Barrett of Pontefract: 'YORKSHIRE WIVES LAND IN GERMANY – MOST THRILLED OF ALL A PONTEFRACT

WOMAN': 'After a pleasure trip in perfect weather, the *Empire Halladale*, converted German luxury liner, docked at Coxhaven this morning with more than 500 "Operation Main Union" passengers on board. Germans standing near the dock were sullenly silent as they saw the British wives and children standing on deck and taking their first look at Germany. Two hundred and 86 wives and 266 children were reunited with their husbands and fathers. Perhaps the most thrilled of all the travellers were Mrs H. Barrett and her two boys, Michael and Brian, for although she has been married for nine years, Mrs Barrett had spent only nine months of this time with her husband and has never been out of Yorkshire before.'

Back in Accrington, Ajax was in a reflective mood as he considered the first team's reverse at Bradford and the reserves' even more bracing start – a 5-1 home defeat to Marine, 'New memories of a Football League kick-off for old – and what a contrast for Stanley between 26 August 1939 and 31 August 1946! Seven years ago, the Reds went to Bradford with modest expectations and came away rejoicing in a 2-0 victory. On Saturday, City's ground, which they visited with bright hopes that really seemed to have substance, was their Gloom Valley (Parade). The castor oil taste of disappointment for the Stanley officials and fans was in the fact that the sound beating was at the hands of a side who, to quote one of City's unimpressed supporters, "are not going to get far on this form". It is too soon to panic, despite the additional shock of the reserves' rout at home. There will be plenty of upsetting of calculations other than Stanley's before clubs "bed down" in league football again. But Stanley cannot afford a repetition at Barrow on Thursday of forward play as feeble as Saturday's in conditions ideal for orderly football – grassy and yielding, yet not miry, turf, no rain and no wind to speak of.'

There was no repetition at Barrow. Far from feeble, Stanley recorded a rousing 3-1 at which the long-serving Ajax was not present. Was he injured? Was he suspended pending investigation into the word 'miry'? Did he cry off having heard about the reckless horse and cart drivers around the back streets of Barrow (see Chapter 10)? We will never know. But Jason, promoted to first-team duty having covered the reserves on the opening day, brought them the best of luck. 'Away with gloom, Stanleyites!' he wrote. 'You can forget the misery at Bradford on Saturday and revel with me in the glorious display which brought a smashing win at Barrow.'

It was the first of 14 league wins that season which ensured that Stanley did not have to apply for re-election this time round. For the town's sports fans, there was also further cause for celebration, 'Good news for local cueists. The Accrington and District Sunday School Billiards League, like the Observer Cup competition, is emerging from suspension.'

17

Football League Division One
Stoke City 2 Charlton Athletic 2 (HT: 1-1)
Scorers – Stoke City: Ormston, Steele; Charlton Athletic: Duffy, Welsh
Attendance: 32,335

'After much heated argument, many of the crowd were allowed, having paid 3s 6d, to transfer to the paddock – admission 2s 6d – without any refund, to be soaked during the afternoon.'

STOKE CITY v Charlton Athletic was a truly mouthwatering prospect, a meeting of two teams seen very much as potential title challengers and containing some of the top stars of the day. The home side included Stanley Matthews – the 'wizard of dribble'. Matthews's magical talents had adorned the right wing of the Stoke and England teams since before the war. He was one of the superstars of his era, although his extravagant skills did not always knit comfortably with those of the rest of the Potters' players.

Matthews's objective on the opening day of the 1946/47 season was to get the ball past one of the best goalkeepers in the country. Sam Bartram joined Charlton in 1933 and had barely missed a game since. A master of his craft, he was integral to the club's surge through from Division Three South to Division One in successive seasons in 1935 and 1936. With towering composure and consistency, Bartram remained a cornerstone of Charlton's subsequent serious challenge for the league title in their first season in the top flight, and their passage to three Wembley cup finals in four years.

A great goalkeeper and humble, likeable man, South Shields-born Sam was a hero to the Addicks' supporters. Just before the new season, he had a very special visitor. The *Kentish Independent* brought the story under the headline 'SERVICEMAN'S LAST WISH': 'A smartly dressed young man walked into The Valley last week and asked if he might be allowed to speak to Sammy Bartram. When Sammy came out from the electrical room, the young man presented the goalkeeper with a parcel which contained a new set of "gear", boots etc., saying, "Sam, my brother was a goalkeeper and he had to have a leg amputated. He asked me to bring his gear along to you, hoping that it would fit you. My brother has since passed away and here is his gear." Shaking hands hurriedly, the young man left the ground without leaving his name or address. He will be pleased to know that the boots do fit Sammy and they are being "broken in" for Charlton's international goalkeeper.'

Wonderful gestures all round: from the young hero who tragically passed away, from the visitor to The Valley who expedited his brother's dying wish with such dignity, and from the Charlton star for coming out to receive them. A very powerful story and its location in the paper was further proof of the lack of melodrama of the era. Rather than a front-page splash, the story was tucked away near the bottom of an inside page, its power all the greater for its discreet position.

Above it, on the same page, attention focused directly on football matters and Charlton's visit to Stoke, with a nod to Hugh Dalton. The chancellor of the exchequer had sanctioned a reduction in Entertainment Tax, 'Better football at cheaper prices should be provided for fans in the season starting tomorrow. Ersatz wartime fare will be replaced by cut-and-thrust league competitions with promotion and relegation issues. There will be no second chances for clubs in the FA Cup. And thanks to Mr Dalton, supporters will pay threepence less for admission – a remarkable state of affairs in a world of rising prices.'

More than 32,000 people took advantage of Dalton's largesse and packed into the Victoria Ground to see if Matthews and Co. could beat Bartram. The home fans were upbeat. After a difficult time in the 1920s, Stoke had built a promising team around Matthews. 'The feeling that they were about to dominate English football was manifest far beyond the boundaries of Stoke-on-Trent,' reports the club's website, stokecityfc.com. 'The war wiped out a six-year period which may indeed have proved to be a golden one.'

Charlton's website, charltonafc.com, reflects upon the war years with a similar lament of what might have been, 'Having finished second, third and fourth, Charlton were well placed to claim the Football League title and may well have done had it not been for the outbreak of the Second World War.' Under charismatic Yorkshireman Jimmy Seed, the Addicks had charged through the late 1930s. They reached Division One for the first time and in their first season there they almost crowned their sensational ascent with the title, finishing just three points behind champions Manchester City.

The Addicks' momentum continued during the war. In 1943 came their first appearance at Wembley, in the Football League (South) Cup final. They lost to Arsenal but were back next year when they beat Chelsea and collected the trophy from General Dwight Eisenhower. When the FA Cup returned in 1945/46, Seed's side reached Wembley again. They lost to Derby County but their momentum was high and Stoke and Charlton each entered the 1946/47 season realistically eyeing the top prize, their first league title. One of them was to come agonisingly close to clinching it.

Stoke had signed off from the Football League on 2 September 1939 with a trying day. Having lost 2-1 at Middlesbrough, they made the long journey home from the north-east in filthy weather and a blackout with only sidelights permitted on the bus. They got back to Stoke at 4am. Seven hours later, war was declared.

Seven years later, *Staffordshire Sentinel* correspondent Potter justifiably bigged up the opening-day clash, 'Stoke City are faced with a formidable task in their opening match of the season tomorrow, for Charlton Athletic, last season's cup finalists, are considered one of the most complete sides in the country. Stoke, however, will not let the reputation of the visitors worry them and are determined to carry into effective reality the impressive form they have displayed during training and in practice matches. As expected, Ormston and Baker form the left wing and Matthews, who is at the top of his form judging by last Saturday's display against Scotland, will be partnered by Antonio. Incidentally, Matthews received another presentation at

Manchester, in the form of a writing set. Owing to military duties, full-back McCue will be unable to play. Of interest to Stoke supporters will be the appearance of John Oakes, Charlton's veteran centre-half. At 43 years of age, he is still considered one of the best in the country.'

Roared on by the passionate home crowd, Stoke started strongly. 'Matthews was beating Shreeve with ease and delighted the crowd with his amazing ball control,' reported the *Sentinel.* In the 21st minute, the early pressure told when centre-half Neil Franklin charged 50 yards upfield and fed left-winger Alex Ormston who 'closed in to score with a grand drive'. Charlton had hardly shown as an attacking force but equalised nine minutes later when Chris Duffy beat goalkeeper Dennis Herod from close range. 'There were some who thought Herod should have saved Duffy's shot, but from the press box, it appeared as though he were unsighted,' continued the *Sentinel.*

A flash of Matthews magic led to Stoke regaining the lead through Freddie Steele five minutes after half-time. 'Matthews, over on the left wing, was surrounded by three players, but placed the ball to Ormston who had gone inside. The winger sent Steele away, and the centre-forward, shaking off Oakes's challenge, beat Bartram with a high-powered drive,' the *Sentinel* explained. Don Welsh levelled again for the Addicks, again against the run of play, after a slick one-two with Bill Robinson. Stoke poured forward in the later stages but were denied by flawed finishing and flawless goalkeeping.

'Star of the Charlton team was Bartram, the goalkeeper, who proved that he is still one of the best in the country,' reported Potter. 'He made innumerable saves and was fortunate on only two occasions – when Oakes's outstretched leg diverted a Steele shot and when Antonio hesitated less than a couple of yards from the goal-line.'

The *Daily Herald* correspondent, meanwhile, concurred regarding Stoke's superiority but also raised the intriguing question of whether Matthews's skills suited the team. 'Scoring opportunities fell to Stoke in the ratio of four to one but Charlton, having snatched two goals, came near to snapping up both points a few minutes from the end of a hearty rather than spectacular tussle. A late, ripe chance fell to Duffy, put through by the craft of Welsh. Fortunately for Stoke, he shot inches too high. It would have been less than justice had the Duffy near-miss struck home, but a salutary lesson to Stoke, who may one day solve their everlasting problem of how to fully exploit the genius of Matthews. Omissions by the inside-forwards became epidemic, and I am early inclined to the view that a bit more height might help a lot.'

The *Sunday Mirror* suggested mildly, on page 14, that 'it was definitely not one of Charlton's best days, and the team may require time to settle down'. The paper's front page headline was less mild: 'SHOULD THE NAZIS HANG IN PUBLIC?'

On Monday, as Stoke prepared for another big home game, against Bolton Wanderers, that evening, they were given some food for thought by Thos. E. Moore of Werrington. In a letter to the *Sentinel*, he wrote, 'I wonder if you would enlighten the public as to what has been done on the Stoke City football ground to put into practice the lessons learned from the Bolton disaster last season. I arrived at the ground at 2.40pm on Saturday, and made my way to the queue in front of the entrance to the Boothen Stand, Block D. After a few minutes, we were allowed to pay 3s 6d each, only to find the stairway leading to the stand entrance was absolutely full and every seat taken. All this time the turnstiles were still clicking merrily, and late comers merely added to the confusion within. After much heated argument, many of the crowd were allowed, having paid 3s 6d, to transfer to the paddock – admission 2s 6d – without any refund, to be soaked during the afternoon while some, including myself, stayed at the top of the steps leading to the stand to have a very poor view of the game. Ought not the men on the turnstiles to know exactly when they have admitted the correct number of spectators? If this cannot be done on the stands, where the number of seats is definite, what earthly chance is there of regulating the number on other parts of the ground?'

Mr Moore and his fellow Potters fans tasted Monday-night disappointment. The visitors won 2-1, after which the *Bolton Evening News* took up the *Herald*'s point about Matthews, 'The great Stanley amused his admirers quite a lot, but his trickery did not get his colleagues very far, and I'm sure they wonder at times if an average, straightforward winger wouldn't suit them better.'

Matthews's time at his hometown club was coming to a close. As the season deepened, speculation grew over his future, with Blackpool cited as his likely destination. His skills helped Stoke to build a title bid which sent them into Easter placed fifth in the table but, with three games left, the Tangerines got their man. Matthews moved for £11,500 after the Stoke board, having rejected the player's transfer request, relented when he threatened to retire.

Despite the saga, the Potters, under manager Bob McGrory, sustained their tilt at the title. Seven wins in eight games sent them into their last fixture, against Sheffield United at Bramall Lane, knowing that victory would make them champions. They were two points behind leaders Liverpool, who had finished their season, but had a better goal average. Any win would do, but a 2-1 defeat in South Yorkshire presented the title to the Reds of Merseyside.

The defeat dropped Stoke to fourth in the final table – a classic example of how, in sport, opportunities must be seized when they arise. The Potters were so close to being champions. Will they ever get that close again?

18

Scottish League A
Heart of Midlothian 1 Queen of the South 1
(HT: 1-1)
Scorers – Heart of Midlothian: Kelly; Queen of the South: Armstrong
Attendance: 22,000

'Ping-pong has been accelerated from a diversion suitable for the trembling invalid to the swift combativeness of table tennis, demanding agility and some stamina.'

AS SUPPORTERS of Heart of Midlothian and Queen of the South gathered in the pubs, clubs and cafés around Tynecastle Park ahead of their Scottish League A match on Saturday 31 August 1946, they found rich food for thought in that day's edition of the *Edinburgh Evening News*. In an eloquent, colourful and prophetic piece, the paper's editorial writer considered the evolution and future of not just football, but all sport, under the heading 'CRAZE FOR SPORT NOVELTY', 'Croquet, they say, is enjoying a boom in Hollywood. On the spacious lawns of filmland's select, the game which we so readily associate with leisurely summer afternoons, ladies with long, sweeping skirts and picture hats, and men in rather tight trousers and high, stiff collars, has found new life and vigour. Especially vigour. It has changed in the course of transportation to the farther coast of America, and the tap of mallet against ball has given way to a solid thump. Croquet, in short, has been "pepped up" and made more exciting, according to modern standards.

'The trend of all kinds of games and entertainment is in the same direction. Ping-pong has been accelerated from a diversion suitable for the trembling invalid to the swift combativeness of table tennis, demanding agility and some stamina; the older Scottish style of football has been losing popularity because it is not fast enough to satisfy the appetite of spectators; there are recurring agitation for the "brightening" of cricket.

'Years ago, the pundits asked, "Where will the craze for speed and excitement lead to?" (and some of them under their breath added, "Woe! Woe!") but, as the craze is still unsatisfied, the question, largely rhetorical, remains unanswered. We do know that it has led to the rise and popularisation of sport and entertainment like speedway, racing and ice hockey, but who can say what it will yet bring forth? Some new form of contest, with a novelty that tickles the crowd's fancy, may descend upon us overnight, either as a home product or as an importation from America, Australia, Tibet or Xanadu, and in no time there will be district leagues, national championships and international matches. The sport "kings" work quickly and they organise in an impressively ample way. Apparently, they find it pays. If they need the assistance of the bookmaker to draw the thousands within their doors, it is forthcoming readily enough but, as is pointed out elsewhere in our columns today, one of the sports which is enjoying remarkable patronage at the present time, speedway racing, has no betting attached to it.'

Lovely prose – and, in conclusion, the writer deployed an empathy and wisdom that had eluded the Churches Committee on Gambling (see Chapter 1), 'It can be left to the moralists and the Simon Pures to argue whether the dedication of so many man-hours of mass attendance at sport arenas is good or bad for the nation in general. Suffice it to say here that for many it means a touch of colour which otherwise would be absent from the weekly round. And the gladiators of the new sports certainly do their best to appear (at least in print) anything but drab. The riders of the speedway have names, assumed or real, which must be the envy of up-and-coming stage stars. As for the ice-skaters, they run riot with their Tigers and Panthers, their Vikings and Pirates. When it comes to sport, there's quite a lot in a colourful name. We may yet see thousands roaring their heads off at a needle (new style) croquet match between Edinburgh Atomicians and Glasgow Rocketeers.'

As names go, Heart of Midlothian and Queen of the South are two of the more evocative in British football, and both clubs have a pretty evocative provenance. The former has Terpsichorean roots. 'In December 1873, the best players of Queen's Park and Clydesdale played an exhibition match at Raimes Park, Bonnington (now Victoria Park) to introduce Football Association Rules to Edinburgh,' relates the club website, heartsfc.co.uk. 'Among the 200 spectators were a number of the dance hall footballers who then decided to adopt Association Rules during the early months of 1874. Their restructured side was called Heart of Mid-Lothian Football Club after their other favourite pastime.' heartsfc.co.uk also quotes a subsequent *Edinburgh Evening News* report which adds to the colourful story, 'The Hearts had a curious inauguration for, in 1875, they had their origin from the Heart of Mid-Lothian Quadrille Assembly Club. The members of this dancing party one evening adjourned to the Meadows, got the loan of a ball from a cricketer named Howie, and played until the ball burst. Their vigorous enthusiasm did not stay here, as Mr James Reid discovered that he had sufficient to buy a new ball.'

Queen of the South arrived on the Scottish football scene almost half a century later. The club was created following the First World War, forged from a desire to combine the various strands of football interest in Dumfries into one club. The idea advanced during a series of meetings in 1919, the first at Dumfries Town Hall and the second at the New Bazaar Hotel. During the latter, Mr A. McGeorge, presiding, proposed that no future meetings should be held in licensed premises. This was supported by 14 votes to seven and the next meeting was held at the YMCA.

Queen of the South joined the Scottish League in 1923 as founder members of the new Division Three. They won promotion (pipping Annan-based Solway Star on goal average) in their second season and were promoted again, to Division One, in 1932. There they remained until the Second World War by which point, up in Edinburgh, Hearts supporters were growing impatient. 'The public was weary, waiting for Hearts to mould fine players into a winning side,' the club website reports.

The Queens fans arrived in Edinburgh with traumatic recent memories of the city. Three weeks earlier, they opened the season with a visit to the Scottish capital to face a Hibernian side widely viewed as strong contenders for the title. In front of the biggest crowd of the day, 30,000, at Easter Road, Hibs won 9-1. 'The Dumfries lot did not provide them with the right trial tackle,' was the disparaging view of the *Edinburgh Evening News*. 'The home half-backs and forwards were masters from the start.' Three weeks later, the 'Dumfries lot' returned to Edinburgh having rallied impressively. Their early form was erratic – in two home games after the opening-day drubbing, they beat Third Lanark 4-1 and lost 6-1 to Motherwell – but they then won at St Mirren (2-1) and Falkirk (3-2). A home draw with Partick Thistle in midweek confirmed their place in the top half of the table. They would be no pushover.

Sure enough, after Archie Kelly gave Hearts a 17th-minute lead, Matt Armstrong, who scored 137 goals in 191 league games for Aberdeen before the war, equalised 11 minutes later. The defence that capitulated so totally at Easter Road stayed strong at Tynecastle, abetted by some over-elaboration from the off-colour home side, according to the *Sunday Post*, 'With a surplus of class inside-forwards available, Hearts encountered bad luck in fielding two who were definitely having an off day. Tommy Walker and Alex McCrae, both of whom have done valiant work for their club, ought to have had this game well won in the first half hour. Instead, they indulged in pattern-weaving and confusion with Kelly. And it was indicative of their general waywardness and their goal-shy state that each missed a sitter. All this without detracting from the merits of the Dumfries performance. The Palmerston Park side have improved beyond recognition since their tragic first call at Edinburgh. There was no nine-goal panic apparent in defence, where Henderson, Savage, Denmark and Holt towered about their courageous colleagues.'

The *Glasgow Evening Citizen*'s Inside Sport column, by Harry Young, saluted the Queens' admirable response to their traumatic start to the season, 'Queen of the South, who started by losing nine goals to Hibernian, have made a remarkable rally and are now in the top half of the table. In their last four matches they are undefeated, and in drawing with Partick Thistle at Dumfries, and Hearts at Tynecastle, they have shown other clubs that they cannot depend on Dumfries to hold one of the two bottom places in the league next spring. The Queens are fighting.'

'And what of Hearts?' added the *Daily Record*. 'Not setting the heather on fire yet. A draw at home doesn't win championships. We expected them to beat Queen of the South but perhaps we have not yet measured the strength of these rejuvenated southerners. Four games without defeat – and three of them away from home – looks as if we hadn't.'

Sunday Post scribe Jack Harkness, meanwhile, revealed that during his midweek visit to Dumfries, he had helped Partick Thistle manager Donald Turner to foil an English raid on Scottish football, 'I sat out the Queen of the South v Partick Thistle midweek game with Mr Jim Taylor, Preston North End's chief. "I've five Scotsmen in the Preston team just now," said J.T., "but I see one who could make it half a dozen." Then he asked me a Thistle player's age – and I added ten years just to put him off the scent. Anyway, my fears turned out groundless. Mr Donald Turner saw to that. His parting remark to Mr Taylor in the boardroom was like music in my ears, "I'm sorry, Mr Taylor, not even for all the money in England."'

Hearts' title challenge never fully materialised. They finished the season in fourth place, eight points behind champions Rangers and six behind Edinburgh arch-rivals Hibs. The title would return to Tynecastle (they had won it twice while Queen Victoria was on the throne) in 1960. Queen of the South finished 12th, a commendably solid effort after such an appalling start, with Queen's Park, St Mirren, Kilmarnock and tailed-off Hamilton Academicals below them in the final table.

Next up for both sides was another midweek assignment, Hearts away to Hamilton and Queen of the South at home to Morton. It was the fourth successive midweek round of fixtures since the season began, a hectic schedule that was engaging the fans but having an adverse impact upon employers and the national economy, reported the *Daily Record*, 'First-class football legislators in Britain are giving careful consideration to the question of midweek games in relation to their effect on absenteeism in industry. While soccer authorities contend that their sport does not interfere with production any more than racing and speedway, they are anxious not to cause any hold-up in the national effort. A number of midweek fixtures, including the Scotland v Ireland international on 27 November, have been arranged, and visits by continental clubs, also for midweek games, are in prospect. Nevertheless, it is only in areas of heavy industry, such as coal mining, that the problem is regarded as acute. It might be solved, as it was in some cases last season, by workers voluntarily putting in an extra shift in the evening when they went to see a football match in the afternoon.'

19

Football League Division Three North
Wrexham 3 New Brighton 2 (HT: 1-2)
Scorers – Wrexham: Gardner, Haycock, Pritchard; New Brighton: Buist, Prendergast
Attendance: 10,024

'Stockings may also be knitted for the reserve team, members of Vale of Conway Area League.'

THE PRESSURES and shortages of war caused many problems for sports clubs. Enterprise, decisiveness and selflessness were required to solve these problems and, as is the case in all walks of life, the solutions were often provided by women. For example, when Llandudno Junction's rugby team encountered a sock crisis, it was the ladies who stepped up.

'KNITTERS AT JUNCTION MATCH', reported the *North Wales Weekly News*, 'Another team attended the Llandudno Junction-Caernarvon match at Nant-y-Coed on Saturday – the "team" of 11 women supporters each of whom undertook to knit a pair of maroon and white (club colours) stockings for the senior team's Welsh League debut. Told that stockings ordered by the club had not arrived, the supporters' club promised to help and six women committee members and five others, including wives of players and committee men, volunteered to tackle the job. They had no difficulty in getting "coupon subscriptions" for about 68oz of wool. Supporters' club treasurer Mrs G. Whiteley, wife of club captain Jack Whiteley, said that the knitters worked hard against time. Ten pairs were finished on Thursday and the rest were completed on Friday. "We are very grateful to our women supporters," said club chairman E. Daley. Stockings may also be knitted for the reserve team, members of Vale of Conway Area League.'

It was a display of pressure knitting from the very top drawer and prevented the chaps taking to the rugby field sockless and vulnerable. The influence of women across society was rising – and ready to expand in new directions, revealed the *Liverpool Echo*. Under the headline 'SALLY, THE BRICKLAYER' (Sally was no doubt an amused relative of the headline writer), the paper mused, 'Women coming out of the services are asking employment exchanges for light jobs on housing sites and building trade unions are now discussing the request. Said a building expert, "The industry thinks it will not be long before we see women bricklayers, carpenters, plumbers, decorators and electricians."'

The voluntary skill and commitment that delivered those crucial socks was essential to the survival of many sports organisations during wartime. Professional clubs faced, beyond significant running costs, the additional burden of wages to find, and for many it was a massive struggle. Fifty miles east of Llandudno Junction, Wrexham approached the 1946/47 season, and their opening fixture against New Brighton, in relatively rude health, but it had been a battle. On Christmas Day 1940 the Reds played local rivals Chester home and away to generate desperately needed revenue. They met at the Racecourse Ground in the morning before the game at Chester kicked off at 3.15pm. With the war at its height, Wrexham's match programme that day included some notes which revealed the depth of the struggle: a plea for help mingled with a splash of sadly misguided optimism, 'Despite the strenuous times through which we are passing, there is no reason why we should not make the best of things and during the brief respite which the curtailed Xmas holiday brings, enjoy ourselves to the full. What is the use of doing otherwise? All being well, next Christmas we should be halfway through a postwar season under proper league conditions. Every effort has been made to provide the best possible football for our patrons, but the support accorded the club has been poor, so much so that, despite reduced running expenses, the receipts have not covered expenses on several occasions. Let one of your new year resolutions be, to support your club better.'

Sufficient support did materialise and Wrexham, the third-oldest professional football club in the world, went into the campaign aiming to add a first Football League promotion to their long history. After joining Division Three North in 1921, they spent much of their first decade low in the table but then improved to record three top-three finishes in five seasons. Were they capable of breaking new ground and climbing to Division Two?

On the eve of 1946/47, *Wrexham Leader* correspondent Spartan spoke to the club's main man, Rhyl-born Tom Williams, who had been in charge since April 1942, 'Fewer men today could be busier than Wrexham's indefatigable secretary-manager, Tom Williams, for upon his shoulders rests the unenviable task of placing Wrexham in its rightful position on the football map this coming season. In between numerous telephone calls from far and near, he managed at his Racecourse office to outline to me his club's prospects for season 1946/47 – the season in which normal peacetime football gets back into its stride. On Wrexham's prospects, Mr Williams struck an optimistic pose, but he tempers his optimism with the realisation of the difficulties involved. "The prospects are quite good. There are, however, one or two more star players we would have liked to have signed, but for various reasons we could not get them," he stated. He attributes some of the difficulties to the fact that experienced players are extremely difficult to get hold of at the moment and also the fact that full-time players refuse to sign unless housing accommodation is found for them.'

First up for Williams's team was a local derby against New Brighton from 40 miles away, beside the seaside on the Wirral Peninsula. Created in 1921 from a crisis which engulfed another club, New Brighton were destined to encounter plenty of their own. Formed from the ashes of the bankrupt South Liverpool, they joined Division Three North in 1923, playing home games at Sandheys Park in Rake Lane, hence the nickname the Rakers. 'New Brighton never really pulled up any trees,' recounts footballheritage.co.uk, 'and apart from the occasional top-ten finish, more often than not were a bottom-half of the table club that enjoyed the odd cup run.'

To their ongoing on-field mediocrity was added off-field trauma in 1942 when a bombing raid wrecked Sandheys Park. The club moved to the Tower Athletic Ground and had to pretty much start all over again. In June 1946, former Manchester United, Everton and Liverpool half-back Neil McBain, a resolute Scot, took on the mighty challenge of asserting the Rakers back in Division Three North.

The *Liverpool Evening Express* correspondent predicted that McBain's men might cause an opening-day upset, 'The newly constituted New Brighton are, of course, an unknown quantity, but from what I have seen of them in training, they certainly lack nothing in enthusiasm. Few teams return with anything tangible from the Racecourse, but the Tower men may provide a surprise.'

New Brighton did seize a surprise half-time lead. Wrexham scored first, in the ninth minute 'thanks to the skill and energy of [Tommy] Gardner', but the visitors levelled within seconds when Forsyth's shot was fumbled by goalkeeper Frank Williams and Buist tucked home the rebound. 'Uncertainty in defence led to Buist registering an equalising goal for the Rakers,' reported the *Wrexham Leader*, 'who, Dr Tom Mathew, the New Brighton chairman, told me on Saturday, will still be known by this name although they have been compelled to move their playing pitch from Rake Lane to New Brighton Tower grounds.'

New Brighton regained the lead after 30 minutes when Patterson's free kick rebounded from the bar and Bill Prendergast accepted a tap-in. McBain's hegemony appeared to be heading for a victorious start, but Wrexham's strength showed after the interval. Right-winger Gardner, who became the club's record signing when he joined from Burnley in December 1945, created their second goal, for Fred Haycock. Then 'a lovely open forward movement, in which Gardner shone on the right wing, was successfully finished off by [Vince] Pritchard, the new centre-forward from Dumbarton, and this third goal gave Wrexham both points'.

The Rakers fought hard and were denied an equaliser when Prendergast netted late on but, to the relief of most in the raucous 10,000 crowd, his effort was deemed offside by Warrington referee E. Plinston. Wrexham took both points, slightly fortuitously, as admitted in Monday's *Leader* by a reporter working under the enigmatic pseudonym of XYZ, 'Over ten thousand people saw Wrexham open the season at the Racecourse on Saturday with a victory over New Brighton, who are back in the Football League once more after an absence of six years, due entirely to the war. Wrexham won the match by three goals to two. It was a very close call, and there were moments when it looked as if Neil McBain's proteges from Merseyside might signalise their return to Third Division football by an away victory. From this necessarily brief outline of the game, it should be seen that Wrexham had to struggle to win. New Brighton, who have had to restart operations from scratch, fielded an 11 which, on this first day's display, may be expected to give their fellow members of the Northern Section a very good run this season. One thing which struck me on Saturday was that several of the Rakers had very useful extra inches in stature. The Wrexham inside men appeared to me to need these extra inches.'

The *Liverpool Daily Post* pinpointed Gardner as the difference between the two sides, 'New Brighton almost brought off a surprise win at Wrexham. They led 2-1 at half-time but Wrexham's stamina told. Spearhead of all Wrexham's raids was Gardner, outside-right, who scored their first goal and made the second for Haycock. Pritchard got the third. The Rakers' scorers were Buist and Prendergast. Cyril Jones especially was outstanding in Wrexham's defence, and for New Brighton, Hill was a splendid pivot. Attendance 10,000. Receipts £800.'

Wrexham went on to finish a respectable seventh in Division Three North. New Brighton finished 18th with McBain carving himself an enduring place in history along the way. For the visit to Hartlepools United on 15 March, the manager found himself without a goalkeeper so did the honours himself, aged 51 years and 120 days. 'Owing to four non-arrivals, even manager Neil McBain, who is over 50, had to turn out for New Brighton at Hartlepools,' reported the *Liverpool Daily Post*. 'He played in goal, this being his first game since his retirement as a centre-half in 1931.' Hartlepools scored after only three minutes and went on to win 3-0 but McBain acquitted himself well. He remains the oldest player to play in a Football League match, a record which will never be broken.

Further peril awaited; New Brighton finished bottom of the table the following season but survived the re-election vote, fending off competition from aspiring League clubs Shrewsbury Town, Scunthorpe & Lindsey United, South Liverpool, Nelson, North

Shields, Northwich Victoria, Wigan Athletic and Workington. Three years later they were bottom again and this time were voted out, replaced by Workington. The Rakers dropped into the Lancashire Combination, then the Cheshire County League, and the club was dissolved in 1983.

Tom Williams left Wrexham in 1949, his last match in charge, ironically a 2-1 home win over New Brighton, to be succeeded by Les McDowall. The Reds' pathway to Division Two was to prove long and winding. Two spells in Division Four were to precede their first ascent into the second tier in 1978.

Back on 31 August 1946, Wrexham's supporters filed out of the Racecourse in the rain with two hard-earned points to celebrate. The welcome and exciting win took their minds off the giant issue which was dominating conversations in the town at the time. As the *Western Mail* explained, 'Wrexham Town Council have decided to ask Wrexham Rural District Council to meet them and discuss the report recently published by Denbighshire County Council on the county's water supply scheme which involves an expenditure of more than £1,000. The council's view is that East Denbighshire should be treated as a distinct unit.'

20

Football League Division Three South
Clapton Orient 2 Ipswich Town 2 (HT: 2-0)
Scorers – Clapton Orient: Brown, Willshaw; Ipswich Town: Connor (2)
Attendance: 12,530

'Today heralds the big kick-off all over the country and football is back to the good old days before the war, when a steak was a steak and a bottle of whisky cost – well, you know.'

TWO CLUBS could not have approached the resumption of the Football League in more contrasting moods than Clapton Orient and Ipswich Town. Ipswich couldn't wait for the season to start. Having played as amateurs since 1878, the club turned professional in 1936 and immediately the professionals flew. They won the Southern League at the first attempt and gained entry to the Football League at the expense of Gillingham, polling 36 votes to the Kent club's 28. This astonishing progress had been financed by chairman John Murray Cobbold following a chance meeting with Arsenal chairman Sir Samuel Hill-Wood and a visit to Highbury. Under the stewardship of 'Captain' Cobbold, and manager Scott Duncan, Ipswich finished a solid seventh in their first season in Division Three South. They started the following campaign strongly and were fourth, and unbeaten, when it was aborted. Suffolk's first representative in the Football League had started in style.

Captain Cobbold served with distinction in the Scots Guards during the First World War and acted decisively at the start of the second. He immediately suspended all football at Portman Road. The club's supporters' association, representing nearly 10,000 fans, wrote to him urging him to reconsider, pointing out that football was continuing elsewhere. He declined, issuing a statement that it was 'in the interests of the club to close down all operations at the Portman Road ground as and from 30 September 1939'. Cobbold was a man of deep resolve. He was also a decent shot and remains the only chairman of a Football League club ever to have killed two woodcock with a single shot, a feat achieved only a couple of dozen times in British history. Aged just 47, he was killed by a flying bomb in Birdcage Walk, London, in June 1944, but his legacy at Ipswich, as the Cobbold dynasty went on to deliver decades of high achievement, is immense.

Ipswich again prospered when they reopened for the 1945/46 season. They finished fifth in Division Three South (North) and beat Norwich City home and away to lift the Norfolk Jubilee Cup. On 31 August 1946 they travelled from East Anglia to east London aiming to take up where they left off in the Football League proper.

It was rather different for Clapton Orient who had been fighting financial trouble for years. In 1933 they were suspended by the Football League and threatened with expulsion for failing to meet a £2,000 payment. They survived, helped by a donation from Edward, Prince of Wales, who had retained a soft spot for the club ever since watching them beat Notts County 3-0 in 1921. Life remained hard for London's smallest professional club. Orient stayed open during the war but limped along, rarely above the bottom two of the league table, as they struggled to attract players and fans. Wartime brought some hefty defeats – 10-3 at West Ham, 15-2 at Arsenal, 16-1 at Portsmouth. When the FA Cup returned in 1945, Orient were dumped out by the amateurs of Newport, Isle of Wight.

A week before the start of the 1946/47 season, an extraordinary general meeting of the club passed a resolution to change its name from Clapton Orient to Leyton Orient. The switch ended 48 years as Clapton and it was hoped the new name would trigger a new era. Manager Charlie Hewitt was a frustrated man, however. A Welshman, who began his managerial career at Mold, Hewitt was at loggerheads with the board about the lack of money for new players. To improve the atmosphere around the club, a trip to the theatre was arranged.

'Clapton Orient players, directors, relatives and friends attended the Adelphi Theatre, Strand, one night last week to see Mr C.B. Cochran's show *Big Ben*,' reported the *Walthamstow and Leyton Guardian*. 'This was the first of several social engagements arranged by the club to foster goodwill among the players and the directorate.' A generous gesture, though Hewitt would no doubt have preferred the board's generosity to have been directed towards his team-building budget.

Orient's lowly location in London football's pecking order was clear from their brief mention in Friday's *Evening News*, 'London's fifth match tomorrow is at Leyton where Ipswich visit Clapton Orient. The Orient side will be bedecked in their new colours and it is hoped that this will coincide with a new lease of life for the club.'

Come Saturday afternoon, 12,530 packed into Osborne Road (soon to be renamed Brisbane Road) willing that new lease of life to begin. Those who invested two pence in a match programme were warmly greeted on the front page by some earthy notes from writer Forester, 'Good afternoon, friends. So the show is on! Today heralds the big kick-off all over the country and football is back to the good old days before the war, when a steak was a steak and a bottle of whisky cost – well, you know. Anyway, competition will be keen among all clubs in all leagues, and many new stars will be born to hit the headlines and become the idols of thousands. We may look forward to tense excitement, thrills and disappointments. What the future may hold, no one can say. The Orient are resolved to take their place among the elite. Our aim is promotion.'

Forester also reminded the fans that a big difference awaited when the players came out, 'Today we present ourselves in new colours: white shirts with a blue chevron, black knickers with a three-inch black seam, and blue stockings. Gone is the red chevron which has been associated with the club's colour scheme for more than half a century. But Orient is still Orient.'

New colours. New names on the way for club (which became Leyton Orient on 2 October) and ground (which became Brisbane Road on 9 November). New era on the field? At the interval, it appeared so. Orient led 2-0 after scoring twice in the last seven minutes of the first half. Hackney-born left-winger George Willshaw was the architect of their advantage, creating the first goal with a perfect cross which was netted by Buster Brown, then scoring the second himself. A surprise result beckoned, but Ipswich stayed calm and reeled in the lead in the space of 100 seconds, eight minutes after the break. Former Albion Rovers striker Jack Connor capitalised on an error by big centre-half Ron Fenton to make it 2-1. Then, according to the *Walthamstow and Leyton Guardian*, 'Scarcely had the groans of the home supporters died away when, almost directly from the kick-off, Ipswich raced for the Orient goal. A shot by Mackay was smothered by Lewis, but he unaccountably allowed the ball to be snatched from his grasp and once more Connor accepted the gift.' Both sides had chances to win it, one of the best falling to Orient's Doug Hunt. 'One right-footed drive, which was heading for the Ipswich goal like a rocket, was intercepted by Parry, the right-back, who was rendered unconscious for two minutes or more by the force of the ball,' added *The Guardian*.

On Monday, the paper's Orient correspondent, JEB, laid it on the line about the team's defence – 'UNPARDONABLE ERRORS BY ORIENT. PLAYERS WERE OVER ANXIOUS' – having first spared no detail about its new costume, 'Wearing their new colours – white shirts with blue chevrons. Black nickers with three-inch white seams and white stockings – Clapton Orient began their opening campaign in the League Three South at Leyton on Saturday in none-too-enterprising style. They were held to a draw – two goals each – by Ipswich Town, who were able to equalise as a result of two defensive errors which were described by their severest critics as "unpardonable". Much may be said for the over-eagerness and the over-anxiousness of all players in making their debut in such an important occasion. The strain is prevalent and obvious, with every player keyed up to concert pitch and endeavouring to give only of his best. Is it not a fact, therefore, that slips occur, and will occur? On the whole, the football was very much of the first-of-the-season nature, although on occasion there were flashes of brilliance in which the ball was directed from man to man with almost perfect precision.

'Ipswich, it seems, have knotted together a very formidable side this year, and on their showing on Saturday there was not one outstanding weakness. Their approach work was excellent and they were capable of bringing off the unexpected. Fenton, Orient's "giant" centre-half, was given an exacting test for his first match of the season and though he did not, perhaps, come through the ordeal with full marks, he has the qualities and makings of a good centre-half. Unfortunately for him, he was the first member of the defence who erred when a goal resulted and Fenton, no doubt, will take a long time to forget the incident. Lewis, in Orient's goal, was below form and he was lucky to escape with three glaring mistakes which might have brought goals for Ipswich. As it was, the equalising point came when he dropped the ball at the centre-forward's feet. Lewis, too, might have been overawed by the occasion, although he is a player of considerable skill and experience and should not have suffered in any way from "stage fright".'

The *Ipswich Evening Star* correspondent was impressed with the Blues' display, 'Ipswich would not have been flattered had they claimed both points for they were far the better balanced team and much the more polished. With the somewhat unusual experience of having the support of a 12,000 crowd, Orient were fortunate not to be heavily in arrears in the first half-hour.' The *Eastern Daily Press* account of the game, meanwhile, was concise, 'At Leyton, Ipswich shared four goals with Clapton Orient, after being two goals in arrears at half-time. Connor (centre-forward) who was top scorer last season for Carlisle, scored both goals for Ipswich.' In light of the deepening housing crisis affecting the country, the paper devoted greater space to the latest squatting news, 'Squatters have been busy in the Yarmouth area during the weekend. The former RAF air-sea rescue hut at the foot of Baker-st at Gorleston has now been occupied, two more huts at Mautby Decoy have been claimed, and four families have staked their claims to army huts at West Caister.' Further details followed, including an interview with a Mrs Minns who revealed, 'I have been married four years and this is my first chance to do my own housekeeping.'

The *Weekly Dispatch (London)* divided praise among the two teams, 'Ipswich impressed as a solid, well-balanced team. In Mick Burns, they have a goalkeeper of class. Right-back Rumbold played well against his old club. Inside-forwards Harry Baird (Irish international from Huddersfield) and Angus Mackay (former Hamilton Academical) worked to good effect. Orient have sound backs in Clark and Ritson.

William Brown, former Romford centre-forward, and Fenton, centre-half from Gainsborough Trinity, should do well with more experience.'

The *Dispatch* also carried a potential career opportunity for young fans to consider. 'NATIONALISATION MAKES COAL-MINING A CAREER' announced an advertisement from the National Coal Board. 'WAGES. Colliers, 21 years old or older, earn £5 a week minimum, working underground. NATIONAL SERVICE. If you are 17 and due to register in September, you can choose coal mining as an alternative to the services. REORGANISATION. The government had advanced £150,000,000 to be spent in five years by the National Coal Board in reorganising the industry and on improved welfare facilities.'

It was a little late for Charlie Hewitt to go down the mines but he was seriously considering his career path. A few days after the Ipswich game, his disagreements with the board came to a head when he resigned. William Bulloch Wright, the trainer, took over but not for long. Nineteen days later, Hewitt returned and supervised Orient to 19th in the final Division Three South table before departing again, this time for keeps, the following season after a goalless draw at home to Port Vale.

21

Football League Division Three North
York City 4 Chester 4 (HT: 3-1)
Scorers – York City: Nettleton, Allen, Carr (2); Chester: Burden (2), Gledhill (og), Hamilton
Attendance: 6,000

'The director in charge, Mr Stan Bartley, and Mr F. Brown had the bright idea of holding up private cars, the drivers readily agreeing to come to the rescue.'

EXCITEMENT AT the return of the Football League was widespread across cities, towns, villages, hamlets, factories, schools, prisons and lighthouses across the country. Widespread, but not unanimous. The sense of anticipation had not spread to at least one community in the north of Yorkshire. The *Driffield Times* sports correspondent, Winger, revealed that residents of that parish still had other things on their mind, 'Once again there is very little to report on the football front. The harvest is in full swing and the country clubs have no time at present to bother with anything else.'

For those in that rural community who would be preparing football pitches when the time came, Winger added a note of warning: keep an eye on your posts, 'Apropos my remarks about the Cranswick goalposts last week, I find that, since writing the notes, the posts had been damaged by livestock. They have now been repaired and repainted.'

Driffield's indifference to the Football League coming back was not shared 30 miles away in York. Football fans there were avidly looking forward to 31 August 1946, and the first Football League fixture at

Bootham Crescent since 26 August 1939, when York City drew 2-2 with Chester. That was a decent game. 'Chester deserved a point at Bootham Crescent because they had the more enterprising half-back line' was the verdict of the *Yorkshire Post and Leeds Intelligencer* – and the fixture usually produced goals. In fact, it boasted some spectacular recent history when it came to high scoring. For York, painful history.

On Saturday, 1 February 1936, York visited Chester for a Division Three North fixture, eager to improve upon their previous outing – a 7-2 defeat at Accrington Stanley. Prolonged heavy rain raised serious doubts about whether the match would take place but, although 'ankle-deep in mud', the Sealand Road pitch was deemed playable. The home fans were glad that it was. Chester won 12-0.

'CHESTER DELUGE OF GOALS IN FOOTBALL TALE OF TWO CITIES' announced the headline in the *Chester Chronicle*, followed by sub-headings 'FORWARD REVELRY IN SEA OF MUD' and, intriguingly, 'TWELVE GOALS, BUT GAME WAS NOT ONE-SIDED'. From the stats, it would appear that the game was pretty one-sided. York goalkeeper George Wilson, or one of his colleagues, retrieved the ball from the back of his net in the third, fifth, seventh, 14th, 22nd, 36th, 38th, 43rd, 49th, 72nd, 85th and 87th minutes.

'Goals came so easily that the York players smiled at their own discomfiture, and the goalkeeper (he was not exactly brilliant) was the only perturbed player on the field,' reported Austin in the *Chronicle*. 'Chester were not only captivating, but irresistible, and might easily have scored 16. Were it not for the barren 20 minutes between the ninth and tenth goals, I shudder to think of what the score might have been!'

York were down, but far from out. Having conceded 19 goals in two games, they responded by winning their next two, at home to Lincoln (2-1) and away to Rochdale (3-2). It is perhaps the greatest display of 'bouncebackability' in the history of football.

Ten years later, the teams reconvened at Bootham Crescent for the big kick-off. Again, it was a wet day at the end of a wet week with the field more mud than grass. And again, goals flooded in, this time, to the relief of the Minstermen, much more evenly.

York and Chester were both relative newcomers to the Football League, having joined it in 1929 and 1931 respectively. Neither had risen from Division Three North but both delivered a highlight or two for their fans. In 1938, York beat First Division clubs West Bromwich Albion and Middlesbrough on the way to the FA Cup quarter-finals before losing to Huddersfield Town in front of 58,066 in a replay at Leeds Road. Chester's supporters were treated briefly to the sublime goalscoring skills of Arthur Gale. During the 1930/31 season, the Salford schoolteacher scored 73 goals in 39 Cheshire League games, and 107 goals in all. Chester replaced Nelson in the Football League for the following season (without Gale who joined West Bromwich Albion) and competed solidly in Division Three North, regularly finishing in the top ten, up to the war.

On the resumption, Chester's supporters faced a choice. For those who didn't fancy the 224-mile round trip to Bootham Crescent, the *Chronicle* offered an enticing, more local option. Under the headline 'RECORD ENTRIES FOR DOG SHOW', it reported, 'A record number of entries (560 to date) has been received for the Chester City and County Canine Society Dog Show, to be held in the Drill Hall tomorrow (Saturday). Alsatians, cocker spaniels and fox terriers are well-represented among the 234 dogs entered for the show.'

The paper also went big on the football. Newspapers of this era mostly used photographs small and sparingly due to limitations of technology and a desire to cram in as many articles as possible. On this momentous day, though, the *Chronicle* spread a team picture across four columns of page three with the headline 'CHESTER ALL SET FOR BIG KICK-OFF'.

Below it sat a preview that explored the captaincy issue which had split the fans: Trevor Walters or Eric Lee? The article continued, 'Chester supporters view with mixed feelings the deposing of last year's captain, Trevor Walters, in favour of Chester-born Eric Lee. I know that Mr Frank Brown [the team's manager] found it difficult to choose between them, but Lee's youth and ability decided him. For the time being at least, Walters skippers the Cheshire League side; but, as I hinted previously, it is indeed a wealthy club which can afford to exclude either he or Lee from the senior side. A great personality and an excellent clubman, Walters will accept the decision like the good sportsman he is.

'Meanwhile, Eric Lee still plays as an amateur and has steadfastly resisted all offers to turn professional. Recently demobilised from the RAF, he intends training as a schoolteacher. From what I know of him, there is little danger of him ever leaving Chester, because his love for the club is as great as his love for the game. It may well be that Lee, with all his attributes, will become one of the outstanding pivots of postwar football. He has size but, more important, natural football ability. Chester will open the 1946/47 season at York on Saturday with a side including six local players. It is doubtful whether any club competing in the Football League can emulate this.'

Frank Brown and his largely local lads boarded a train at Chester station on Saturday morning with two points in their sights. Never mind defeating York, however, their first challenge of the season turned out to be getting to the ground on time. After encountering train trouble, they were rescued by a bright idea and some generous-hearted random residents of York. 'The train arrived in York one hour late, and then it was impossible to secure taxis to convey the players to the ground,' reported the *Cheshire Observer*. 'The director in charge, Mr Stan Bartley, and Mr F. Brown had the bright idea of holding up private cars, the drivers readily agreeing to come to the rescue. Nevertheless, the kick-off was 15 minutes late and then the referee was stranded in Bridlington and the game taken by the senior linesmen who did very well.'

The Bootham Crescent audience was kept waiting for kick-off but was then treated to a thriller in the rain. The match burst into life in the 14th minute with three goals in as many minutes: Ernie Nettleton opened the scoring for York, Tommy Burden equalised with a slick finish from a pass by Jackie Arthur but then, back in the Chester goalmouth, Lee's defensive header fell straight to Billy Allen who restored the lead. The frenzy of scoring subsided for a while before 'a picture goal by Frank Carr' from a corner put York 3-1 up at the break.

Chester came out flying in the second half and reduced the deficit when Arthur again sent Burden in to score. Carr's second, in the 65th minute, restored York's two-goal lead and they were still 4-2 up as the last ten minutes arrived. With the light fading fast as the match ran late on a dirty, grey afternoon, Chester poured forward and ten minutes from time an own goal by Sammy Gledhill made it 4-3. The comeback was completed in dazzling style with three minutes left when a loose ball in the box fell to Bobby Hamilton and his shot on the turn flew into the roof of the net. It was 4-4 – and could have got even better for the visitors.

'There were three minutes left for play when the equaliser came,' reported the *Chronicle*, 'and York were so played out that in that time Burden had another goal disallowed. Another five minutes must have seen a victory for Chester, but in all fairness they did not deserve to win. They had only themselves to blame that they were two goals behind at the interval; it was just that the defence never settled down.'

It was an energy-sapping contest on a heavy pitch and, with the travelling complications, added up to a gruelling day for the away team. The *Chronicle* also considered the physical demands on footballers who were still serving in the armed forces. Two Chester players had travelled, as the headline shared, '1,300 MILES IN A WEEK': 'When they take the field against Tranmere on Saturday, two of Chester's service players, Tommy Burden and Bob Hamilton, estimate that they will have travelled the best part of 1,300 miles in the first week of the season. They arrived in York in the early hours of Saturday morning from their station in the south of England and returned there on Saturday night. Wednesday night they were on their way to Chester for the Doncaster game and will be coming up north again on Saturday. Burden is a sergeant-instructor in the army and not to be "demobbed" until November. A west countryman, he is a natural footballer and a great club man. He was one of Frank Buckley's "nursery" at Wolverhampton. Tommy saw the rigours of the early landings at Normandy and suffered a wound in the back which threatened to end his football career. Courage and a wonderful physique triumphed.'

Hopefully, Tommy got back down south on Saturday night in time to put his feet up with a pint and then chill out on Sunday and properly digest his side's eight-goal thriller at Bootham Crescent. While he did that, back in Chester, more than 400 people and 200 dogs were reflecting on a most pleasant occasion. 'A record number of dogs competed at Chester City and County Canine Society's limited unbenched show in Chester Drill Hall,' reported the *Cheshire Observer*. 'Almost 600 entries were made, with well over 200 dogs competing and the "gate" exceeded 400 people. Alsatian, cocker spaniels and terrier classes were outstandingly good. The mayoress of Chester, Mrs E.E. Ashton, interrupted her flag-day selling campaign to attend the show, and present two of the trophies. The gesture was much appreciated and her collecting box was well filled as a result. An interesting spectator was the GOC in chief, Western Command (Lt.-Gen Sir Brian Horrocks).'

22

Football League Division One
Sheffield United 0 Liverpool 1 (HT: 0-0)
Scorers – Liverpool: Carney
Attendance: 30,000

'Lightning kept flashing round the ground, but even the thunder which followed it failed to drown the groan of disappointment which went up when Jones put a first-time shot well outside the post.'

WHEN LIVERPOOL'S supporters crossed the Pennines to visit Sheffield on 31 August 1946, none of them gave a moment's thought to 14 June 1947.

Why would they? All attention was on Bramall Lane and the Reds' fascinating opener against Sheffield United, reigning League North champions and among the contenders to lift the first postwar Football League title. A cracking game was in prospect. But 14 June 1947? A distant day in a different year when cricket would be centre stage and the football season a fading memory.

What those Liverpool fans could not know was that a marathon season, caused by prolonged freezing weather, lay ahead. It would still be going on 14 June 1947 and on that day the Reds would clinch their fifth Football League title. In fact, it was to be the most glorious day in Liverpool's glory-filled history: the day they won two trophies in 15 minutes.

The 1946/47 First Division was to be Liverpool's – and it would not have been had George Kay's team not started with a victory in the Steel City 287 days earlier. Without those two points at Bramall Lane, the championship would have eluded Merseyside and instead gone to the Potteries (see Chapter 17).

Liverpool entered the season fresh from a groundbreaking tour to the USA and Canada. Organised by visionary chairman Bill McConnell, the trip built team spirit among Kay's squad while also enabling them to benefit from a diet freed from the constraints of rationing. The squad returned to England happy and strong, albeit not further strengthened through the transfer market. 'I am going to be candid,' Kay told the *Liverpool Echo* on the eve of the season. 'We are not satisfied – only Income Tax collectors can say that. But we have a good lot of lads and, as and when we can improve the team, we shall do so. We want you to see a successful team.'

The *Echo* correspondent was supportive, but cagey, 'The fact that there are no newcomers to the Reds' side is not the fault of the board who have made pretty strenuous efforts without being able to do the trick. If things so pan out that Liverpool work out their salvation without any new names so much the better. I have some fears about it, but meantime let all supporters give the side every possible encouragement.'

Awaiting Liverpool on the opening day was one of the country's leading teams at one of the world's most historic sporting venues. Bramall Lane opened as a cricket ground in 1855 and hosted its first football match – Sheffield FC v Hallam FC, in aid of the Lancashire Mills Distress Fund – seven years later. It lasted for three hours and ended 0-0.

It was at Bramall Lane, in 1883, that fixed crossbars were used for the first time in senior football, settling the many arguments, still heard on playgrounds today, of 'that was too high … no, it wasn't, it was a goal'. In 1902, the stadium hosted an Ashes cricket Test. In 1913, young Warwickshire all-rounder Percy Jeeves hit Yorkshire great Wilfred Rhodes for successive sixes there. Seven weeks later, P.G. Wodehouse saw Jeeves play at Cheltenham and was so struck by his dapper appearance, he named one of his most famous characters after him. A brilliant cricketer, Jeeves appeared destined to play for his country. Instead, he died for his country. On 22 July 1916, Jeeves disappeared without trace at High Wood. On 25 June 1913, Yorkshire's members, a tough jury, had applauded him into the Bramall Lane pavilion.

Sheffield United were firmly among English football's elite. Thirty-seven successive seasons in Division One had ended with a dip into Division Two for five years in the 1930s, but they regained top-flight status in the last season before the war. In 1936, their FA Cup tie against Leeds United was watched by a crowd recorded as 68,500, though it was probably closer to 80,000, thousands more having piled through a broken gate to watch from the cricket field side.

Bomb damage to Bramall Lane during the Sheffield Blitz in December 1940 caused the club to briefly play home games at the Hillsborough ground of neighbours Sheffield Wednesday. They returned to Bramall Lane in September 1941, still under Ted Davison, secretary-manager since 1932. In 1945/46, Davison steered them to the League North title in emphatic fashion. The Blades won 27 of 42 games, scoring 112 goals, to finish five points clear of second-placed Everton and encourage hopes that a second Football League title could be coming to Bramall Lane. It was overdue. Celebrations of the first had followed shortly after those of Queen Victoria's Diamond Jubilee.

A splendid match was in prospect, laced with pace, according to the *Liverpool Evening Express*, 'One of the fastest games of the day will be at Bramall-lane where Liverpool go in an effort to show that last season's champions, Sheffield United, will not find it such easy going this time. The United were the speediest team I saw last season, and when it comes to pace there are few better than Liverpool. I think the success of the Reds depends mainly on the defence, for the Blades are magnificent in attack. With Willie Fagan absent, Nieuwenhuys, the senior professional, will captain Liverpool.'

Cape Town-born Berry 'Nivvy' Nieuwenhuys was one half of a Reds pace threat forged in South Africa. He lined up on the right wing. On the left was Robert Priday, born in Kroonstad, 74 miles from Reitz, who had signed for Liverpool on the liner *Cape Town Castle* at Southampton docks.

The *Evening Express* also brought other international news, featuring the Morath brothers. Among the city's most prestigious jewellers, the German brothers, especially renowned for their cuckoo clocks, placed an ad to confirm their continued part-time opening, '1839-1946. 107 years of service and quality. Morath brothers,

Clockmakers and Jewellers, regret that they must still close Monday, Wednesday and Saturday, owing to staff shortage. 71 Dale Street, Liverpool 2.'

Whether the Morath brothers' staff took advantage of their free Saturday to head to Bramall Lane is undocumented. If they did, they read, in the match programme, 'Here we are back again with high-powered league football with its immense competitive drive.' Then they saw referee Harold Wright (Macclesfield) begin the match, which was, indeed, highly competitive, but faded rather after a lively start before yielding a late winner – a title-clinching late winner, it was to transpire.

The *Sheffield Star*'s 'Green 'Un', also returning after seven years, carried a blow-by-blow report of the match. 'NO-PLAY-RAIN – BUT IT'S SOCCER' was the front-page lead, 'The Green 'Un greets you again after seven years. We are as happy to be here as, we hope, you are to see us. We have known some queer starts to football seasons, such as when players have collapsed right and left through heat. But there was no heatwave today. Instead there was terrific rain. The rain did not help United to a goal rush but no doubt we shall have to wait until later on for Bramall Lane to get nice and muddy.'

On page six, Frank Stainton furnished readers with a detailed and colourful account of the game, starting with some big team news. Billy Liddell would become a true Liverpool legend, but his Football League debut was delayed, 'Liverpool had to make a last-minute change – and an important one too – for Liddell, the Scottish international, had pulled a thigh muscle and was unable to turn out. His place at outside-left was taken by the South African, Priday, so that Liverpool's outside men hailed from the Union, the other, of course, being Nieuwenhuys.'

The Blades started brightly, 'United kept on launching attacks on the Shoreham Street goal, with Collindridge putting in an enormous amount of work. In the first 20 minutes only a couple of attacks had come from Liverpool.' But on a dirty day in South Yorkshire, the game and its pacy stars became bogged down even before half-time.

'Lightning kept flashing round the ground, but even the thunder which followed it failed to drown the groan of disappointment which went up when Jones put a first-time shot well outside the post. A good deal of the earlier play had been promising, to say the least. Now it had become scrappy and rather pointless. It would, of course, be grossly unfair to criticise too harshly, with the season barely on its way, but so far this hardly looked like soccer of what we used to call First Division quality.'

As the second half deepened, however, and the game failed to improve, Mr Stainton did dabble in criticism, 'Liverpool were guilty of a good deal of pushing and elbowing, and this may have had some effect on the Sheffield United rhythm, but whatever it was the game was not of the standard which the First Division will provide us with this season.' The reporter's final paragraph then delivered an unwelcome late twist for his readers, 'After 87 minutes there came a goal – but to Liverpool. United's backs and centre-half had run well upfield in order to throw Liverpool offside but "Nivvy" was standing in a perfectly legitimate position. He snapped up the ball, more or less ambled down his right wing, measured his centre perfectly and Carney was able to head through from close to the post.'

By hewing out a narrow, hard-fought victory, Liverpool had shown the hallmarks of champions. Withstand an injury blow. Absorb pressure. Stay strong. Grab a late winner. The *Liverpool Echo*'s reporter was pleased, but not getting giddy, 'Liverpool's victory at Sheffield was a grand "send-off", yet that the side is not "set" in attack is evident and no one, least of all the board, will be satisfied until the front line show more punch. When only two directors accompany the team at the start of the season you may depend upon it that others have football missions elsewhere. I gather that director Ronnie Williams was in Scotland over the weekend. Chairman Bill McConnell's chest trouble prevented him going to Sheffield.'

The *Liverpool Evening Express* reporter, Radar, having travelled with the team, got in a nifty bit of name-dropping, 'It was a happy party on the return journey, during which Nieuwenhuys commented to me, "This is a fine start. Now if only we can just have that little bit of luck that is so vital if a team is to get among the honours, I think we shall have a great season."'

The blunted Blades had not lived up to expectations. Perhaps that's why Monday's *Yorkshire Evening Post and Leeds Intelligencer* made no mention at all of the match. Instead, the paper reassured their readers that a dangerous criminal of the parish was safely locked up. Under the headline 'ACCUSED OF BUN THEFT', they reported, 'Charged at Otley today with breaking into a lock-up shop in Shipley Glen, and stealing one bun, James Henry Hiles (48), woolcomber, of Fern Bank street, Baildon, was remanded in custody.'

A great season it proved to be for Nivvy and his colleagues. When the big freeze finally thawed out, Liverpool blew hot with five wins and a draw leading up to their huge final fixture, away to top-of-the-table Wolverhampton Wanderers. Kay's side dug out a 2-1 win to climb to the summit. But would they stay there? A tense fortnight followed before Stoke City visited Sheffield United on 14 June for their final game. If the Potters won, they would be champs.

On that momentous day, Liverpool faced Everton at home in the Liverpool Senior Cup Final. Kick-off at Anfield was 15 minutes later than at Bramall Lane and, despite thoughts understandably straying elsewhere, the Reds beat their neighbours 2-1. The closing minutes of the match, however, were surreal after news came over the loudspeakers. Stoke had lost 2-1. Let the celebrations begin. Liverpool's 1946/47 title triumph had been completed, just as it had started, at Bramall Lane.

23

Football League Division Three North
Hull City 0 Lincoln City 0 (HT: 0-0)
Attendance: 25,586

'If an opposing player does something with which you are not in entire agreement, do not beseech your own men to "kick him in the teeth".'

LIFE IN 1946 contained more than its share of traumas and they came in many forms. People had to endure all manner of hardships and deprivations, as illustrated by a gentleman of the East Riding who suffered that cruellest and most unforgiving of experiences, a long wait to be served in a pub.

'Queued-up' of Driffield poured his rage into a letter to the *Hull Daily Mail.* He was quite clear about the cause of the problem – women: 'I visited a public house in Bridlington this week and had to wait in a queue for at least 15 minutes for a glass of beer. I suggest it would be easier if public houses had one room for women, one for men and one for mixed, a waitress for each room, allow one drink only, and no serving to queues. That would be fair and more comfortable. While waiting for my turn, there were 19 people in front of me and 17 were women, while of those sitting down, 85 per cent were also women. Beer is refused to men because the landlord has already sold out to women who, because they did men's work in the war, now think they should drink, smoke and swear. They are supposed to be the weaker sex, but the quarrels I have seen in public houses have been started by women. If they want to go drinking, then they should be in a room of their own. Beer is a man's drink and there would not be a shortage of it if women would stick to what is imported for them, a cup of tea.'

The thoughts of Mrs Queued-up are not recorded. It is not inconceivable, of course, that there wasn't one.

At the start of the 1946/47 season, there were many Hull City supporters, male and female, who richly deserved a pint. The Tigers' opening game, against Lincoln City, would be the first played at their new ground, Boothferry Park. The ground's existence, and indeed the football club's continued existence after some deeply precarious years, was a tribute to the efforts of the fans and local community, much of them given voluntarily.

Hull almost folded in the summer of 1938 when several directors, including chairman Jim Baraclough, quit. They had been worn down by sustained financial pressure, exacerbated by uncertainty over both the future of the club's Anlaby Road home and plans for the proposed new ground. On 14 January 1939, City beat Carlisle 11-1 at Anlaby Road – 'It was the fourth time on record that their score has reached double figures and, curiously enough, all of these notable performances came in late December or early January,' reported the *Hull Daily Mail* – but it was an isolated respite from a deeply worrying time.

Anlaby Road's destiny was ultimately decided by the Luftwaffe which targeted Hull relentlessly due to the town's importance as a port. Severe damage to the football ground, added to the perpetual financial problems, forced the club into temporary closure. It reopened for the 1944/45 season but, with the new stadium requisitioned by the military, the team had to play at The Boulevard, home of the Hull FC rugby league club. City used 85 players in a difficult, messy season which convinced the board to bail out again for 1945/46. In *A Century of City – The Centenary History of Hull City AFC*, Mike Peterson wrote, 'Abstaining from that season was a signal to many that the sun was setting on Hull City, and that the end was in sight for the club. In hindsight, it was merely the dawning of a new era.'

A new board, led by local builder Harold Needler, bought the club in December 1945. They stabilised it off the field and pressed on with the construction of Boothferry Park. It was a serious challenge to get it ready for 31 August 1946, not least because its use as a storage depot had left the pitch in a shocking state. Thanks to an army of volunteers, painting, labouring and tea making, that challenge was met.

On the opening day, a *Hull Daily Mail* scribe, writing under the rather grand pseudonym of Three Crowns, reported, 'Long after eight o'clock last night the erection of turnstiles and barriers was still proceeding; even when darkness had set in, an army of phantom-like figures kept on working in a race against time. Official tests of the stability of the two stands have already been undertaken by officials of the Hull Corporation as a safeguard, and the provision of numerous crush barriers in the standing portion of the ground has been another safety measure. Club supporters have painted these barriers, fencing and barrier rails, in addition to helping with construction of terracing.'

The paper revealed that among the prestigious guests on the big day would be the lord mayor and lady mayoress of Hull, councillor and Mrs H. Harrison. 'The lord mayor will perform a ground-opening ceremony a quarter of an hour before the kick-off,' stated Three Crowns, 'but speechmaking will be cut to a minimum.'

That's always a good idea and the point was also taken up by the *Lincolnshire Echo*'s well-informed correspondent, NHB, as he briefed Lincoln's fans in a fulsome 61-word sentence, 'While the lord mayor, sheriff and members of Hull Corporation will attend the first match on the new ground, it is proposed to limit speechmaking to a minimum, for chairman Harold Needler and the other six Hull men who form the new board are workers rather than talkers and they have raised tremendous enthusiasm in the city already through their enterprise.'

Lincoln had also weathered plenty of interference at their Sincil Bank ground. Early in the war, the South Park Stand and rooms below it were requisitioned by the Air Raid Precautions service. The ARP also subsequently took over the St Andrew's Stand, in which Morrison Shelters were stored. The players' recreation room became a 'decontamination, clothing and reception room', which led to the removal of its table tennis and snooker tables. To the loss of the latter, another blow landed on the cuemeisters in the Imps squad when Lincoln Billiards and Snooker League followed the Football League into suspension.

The proximity of several air bases meant that Lincoln were able to call on several stars, including George Robledo, Neil Franklin and Peter Doherty, as occasional guest players, but their fortunes were mostly thin. The amorphous nature of football during the war is illustrated by Lincoln's finishing position in the various competitions (sometimes two per season). They finished seventh of 11, ninth of 36, second of 38, 19th of 51, 11th of 48, 36th of 54, 15th of 50, 53rd of 56th, 51st of 54 and 46th of 60. Some matches were abandoned when air raid sirens sent players and spectators racing for cover. When the sirens often turned out to be false alarms, Lincoln, like many clubs, posted spotters on lofty perches to signal 'play on' unless aircraft actually appeared on the horizon. Spotters were soon banned by the Ministry of Home Security.

In September 1945, a small quantity of South African oranges arrived in Lincoln's shops. In August 1946, the *Lincolnshire Chronicle*'s preview of the big kick-off included a snipe at manager Joe McClelland regarding Harry Parr, a creative inside-forward later to combine playing for the Imps with working in the city's General Post Office's telephone manager's department.

The *Chronicle* wrote, 'One of the outstanding features of Lincoln City's practice match at Sincil Bank on Saturday was the display at inside-right by Harry Parr, who has recently signed amateur forms for City. I felt, however, he would have had a fairer and sterner trial had he played for the Whites, composed mainly of newcomers, than for the Stripes, who consisted of last year's players with two exceptions. Parr showed enterprise and speed and was able to assist Cheetham in scoring seven goals. Parr had two himself.'

On Saturday morning, work continued at Boothferry Park and the volunteers' brilliance was rewarded. It was ready! The freshly installed turnstiles were soon clicking merrily as supporters flooded in to generate hugely welcome match receipts of £2,720.

Added to those receipts was dosh from the sale of programmes in which supporters who invested the requisite six pence in the publication were encouraged to be passionate, but peaceful. 'Be as vociferous and full partisan as you like in encouraging your own team,' fans were urged, 'but if an opposing player does something with which you are not in entire agreement, do not beseech your own men to "kick him in the teeth".'

Perhaps understandably for a match including 17 Football League debutants, it was a scrappy spectacle. Boothferry Park was christened by thunder and lightning, heavy rain and football high on effort and physicality but low on finesse. The game ended goalless, though interest was sustained after half-time by a spot of siege mentality among the home team and fans when Hull goalkeeper Billy Bly left the field injured after a collision with striker Tommy Cheetham. Down to ten men, and with full-back Arthur Watson, a former Imp, in goal, the Tigers resisted tigerishly to hold on for a draw. It almost got even better for Frank Buckley's side when Bert Knott, who scored four goals on his debut for Margate in 1934, found the net but the effort was disallowed. The match concluded as one of only two goalless draws on the opening day of the new era.

'Hull City provided a splendid example of an ordinary side, handicapped by injuries, being inspired by the encouraging roars of 26,000 supporters to hold Lincoln City to a goalless draw,' reported NHB in the *Lincolnshire Echo*. 'Major Frank Buckley's side did not impress on anything but its capacity to fight back when everything seemed against them.' NHB expressed his disappointment in the player he had bigged up. 'Parr was not as good as I expected,' he commented. Perhaps, the General Post Office's telephone manager's department worker-to-be would have been more impactful had he played for Whites the previous week.

The *Hull Daily Mail* saluted Watson, 'The game was rather patchy with Hull reserving their best work until the late stages. It was an uphill fight for the home side, labouring for the greater part short-handed, first through an injury to Bell, and then one to Bly. Watson kept goal splendidly while Bly was off.'

Despite the absence of goals, it was a momentous day as, fuelled by a phenomenal community effort, Boothferry Park came together just in time. However, the front page of Monday's edition featured a picture not of football but of a pillow fight. 'Pillow duel at the sports held by Thomas Holmes and Sons Ltd. recreation club. H. Wallis and C. Saxby weigh each other up and then start mixing it,' explained the caption.

Elsewhere on the front page came news of a furry hero as 'GOOLE DOG GAVE ALARM' to save its owners, 'A dog gave the alarm when a fire broke out at the house of Mr and Mrs T. Dickens, 76 Swinefleet-rd, Goole. The occupants had gone to bed, and were aroused by the barking of their dog. On going downstairs, they found that a clothes horse in front of the fire had overbalanced, and the clothes were ablaze. Goole NFS were called, but by the time they arrived, neighbours had assisted in putting out the fire.'

Few alarms lay ahead in the coming months for Hull and Lincoln as they ended the season solidly side by side, 11th and 12th in the Division Three North table. The Tigers stayed strong in defence but a lack of goals cost them a promotion bid – only bottom-of-the-table Halifax Town scored fewer than Hull's 49 in 42 games. As suggested by the opening fixture, Lincoln, too, needed to strengthen up front. In October, McClelland addressed the situation when he signed Jimmy Hutchinson from Bournemouth for £750, the deal completed on Grantham railway station at midnight.

24

Football League Division Two
Tottenham Hotspur 1 Birmingham City 2 (HT: 1-2)
Scorers – Tottenham Hotspur: Foreman; Birmingham City: Jones, Mulraney
Attendance: 57,256

'Optimistic Spurs in their official programme published a 1946/47 league table with their own club leading the field, but they found Birmingham City also in promotion mood.'

'FOOTBALL ENDED for the time being with last Saturday's games. Here is a scene at St Andrew's, the Burnley goal having an escape when Duckhouse, the Birmingham centre-forward, narrowly missed a scoring chance.' So ran the caption under a picture on page seven of the *Birmingham Mail* of Monday, 4 September 1939. Above it sat the ominous headline 'LAST OF FOOTBALL'. No details of the match, not even the scoreline, were given. The newspaper's eight broadsheet pages were crammed entirely with information and speculation about the impending war.

Amid the torrent of towering international matters, sport surfaced in only one other small corner of the paper and that was to confirm its marginalisation for the foreseeable future, 'All sports events, whether to be held indoors or outdoors, which would attract crowds of spectators, have been banned by the government. There is no ban on sport, as such, the point being the discouragement of gatherings of people.' Birmingham City's 2-0 win over Burnley was immediately interred in history. The season was abandoned, the result annulled and the goals of Don Dearson and Ted Duckhouse counted for nothing.

Duckhouse, a local player – born in Shelfield, near Walsall – had not long turned professional with the Blues after first signing as an amateur. His career had just begun to take flight, but the 31-year-old had starred in the last match of the club's prewar era. Seven years later, the Football League returned and Birmingham re-entered it with a visit to north London to face Tottenham Hotspur. Duckhouse had played for the Blues sporadically during the war years and made 26 appearances in 1945/46 as they won the Football League South title. At White Hart Lane, he lined up, as ageing centre-forwards do, at centre-half and was an 'unqualified success' as Birmingham won 2-1. The 38-year-old starred in the first match of City's postwar era.

Irrespective of it being a second-tier fixture, Tottenham v Birmingham was one of the standout games of the day. Both were big clubs only their fans believed, on loan to Division Two. When Spurs joined the Football League in 1908, they arrived already cloaked in charisma. Seven years earlier they had become the first non-league side to win the FA Cup, an achievement for ever to remain unique. They won immediate promotion to Division One and another FA Cup followed in 1921, but it wasn't all glory as they fluctuated between the top two divisions. They had been in Division Two since 1935 but retained a colossal fanbase, as shown by the 75,038 who packed White Hart Lane for an FA Cup tie with Sunderland in 1938.

Birmingham spent 18 successive seasons in Division One before relegation in 1939. In the first of those campaigns, 1921/22, top-flight football was some compensation for the fans for whom there was no FA Cup involvement because the club forgot to enter the competition. They remembered to enter it in 1931/32, however, and reached the final for the first time, losing 2-1 to West Bromwich Albion. Their long stretch in the First Division ended in the last season before the war when they finished 21st, just one point below 20th-placed Chelsea, but in 1945/46 they were strong again. They won the League South title, edging out neighbours Aston Villa on goal average, and reached the FA Cup semi-final. Such a powerful season put them among the favourites to return to Division One in 1946/47.

Supporters of both clubs awoke on 31 August 1946 with much in common. They expected their team to challenge hard for promotion.

They knew the taste of glory and craved to recapture it. And they headed for White Hart Lane on a damp, grey morning cheered by an uplifting tale about a kitten.

The cockles of Spurs fans' hearts were warmed by the *North London Press* account of 'RESCUED KITTEN FROM TREE IN SNOW STORM': 'When PC James Greer, of Stoke Newington, attached to Highbury Vale Police Station, was called into the back garden of a house in Adolphus Road, Finsbury Park, and saw a small kitten piteously clinging to a tree branch 50ft above the ground, he ignored the darkness and the snow storm, stripped off his greatcoat and tunic and climbed to the rescue. Pussy had been stranded for two days! This week he received a framed testimonial from the RSPCA for his "courage and humanity" in rescuing the kitten at a personal risk.'

Blues supporters, meanwhile, enjoyed a happy ending to 'KITTEN'S 34-MILE RIDE ON CAR AXLE' in the *Birmingham Daily Gazette*, 'After a fruitless search for a kitten which a child said ran under his car while it was standing at Great Bridge, Birmingham, Mr R. Massey, of Woodville, Burton-on-Trent, drove home a distance of 34 miles, and was then astonished to see the kitten jump off the back axle. After lapping some milk, the kitten, covered with oil and dust, played about skittishly. A search revealed the place on the back axle where Pussy had ridden securely.'

The *Gazette* also reflected favourably on the Blues' prospects, 'The stage is set. Dress rehearsals are over, and this afternoon – zero hour is 3pm – players and spectators will welcome the raising of the curtain on the first full-scale football season since 1939. No other part of the country can surpass the Birmingham area in its enthusiasm for the great game, but indications are that this season will exceed anything we have known before. High things are expected of Birmingham City in the Second Division promotion fight. On paper, they look like a team of world-beaters. In Harris and Mitchell they have a pair of half-backs who know all there is to know about setting the attack moving, and if the forwards get moving as they did so often last season then opposing goalkeepers will be kept busy.'

Evening News (London) writer J.G. Orange concurred with the *Gazette*'s view, 'Another side of meteoric possibilities playing in town is Birmingham, of whom we saw quite a lot last season in the League South. They play the Spurs at Tottenham, and I consider Birmingham a very nicely balanced side, a fair prospect for promotion.'

For such a big game, some measure of crowd control was required and, with more than 50,000 people inside White Hart Lane well before three o'clock, the police ordered the turnstiles to be closed. Thousands of fans were left to monitor the match from outside where, even from that distance, it was soon clear that football was back with a bang. Roars from the crowd greeted two goals in the first three minutes.

The opener was the first anywhere in the country in the new era and it came from Birmingham striker Wilson Jones. 'Duckhouse sent a long, diagonal pass to Mulraney, whose prompt centre to Jones, centre-forward, was met with the perfect header,' wrote the *Birmingham Daily Gazette*. Spurs soon levelled thanks to another header, from former West Ham striker George Foreman, before the 18th minute brought what transpired to be the winning goal. It was a long-range effort from Ambrose Aloysius 'Jock' Mulraney on which press box opinions differed. It was 'the tragedy of the match' according to a London-based observer, or 'a grand 30-yard drive' according to a gentleman of the Second City.

Either way, it was 2-1 to Birmingham and their lead would have been greater but for the excellence of Spurs goalkeeper Ted Ditchburn. The visitors faded after half-time, though, and it was their keeper Gil Merrick's turn to shine as he kept his side in front, assisted by a home attack which did not impress the watching scribes.

'Birmingham's win came about mainly because the Tottenham forwards were below standard,' reported the *Daily Herald*. 'Tottenham were sadly short of a controlling forward. And they did not shoot like the Birmingham forwards who had the makings of goals all along the line.' The report in *The People*, meanwhile, did nothing to reduce the belief among many in the Midlands that the London-based press lacks a little neutrality when clubs from the capital meet those from elsewhere. A clue to the tone of the piece came with the headline 'SPURS TRAGEDY OF A LONG SHOT'. After Birmingham took their instant lead, *The People* reported, 'Spurs supporters did not have time to feel sad, for within a minute Foreman took a leap at the ball, centred high and the scores were level. Ten minutes later, Hotspur experienced the tragedy of the match. Mulraney, with the wind assisting, tried a shot of something like 28 yards. There might have been a swerve unseeable form the stand, but it seemed as if Ditchburn misjudged the ball and that was the end of the scoring.

'The league champions (South) forgot that they have enough clever players to be a good team. After showing us that they could play the swift-moving, get-goals football which is now the fashion, when it can be done, they degenerated and were nothing like as good as when they were scoring two goals in the first quarter of an hour. During the last ten minutes the Spurs made a magnificent effort to get level. They forced even Merrick to get flustered, although he made several fine saves. Neither side could have been sure how it was that the home team did not manage to equalise.'

A more balanced account was offered by *Daily News (London)* reporter Gerard Walter, 'If Birmingham play as they did in the first 30 minutes at White Hart Lane they would rocket back into the First Division. In that period, their football was intelligent, incisive, fast, every move a threat. Tottenham then threw off their role of anxious defenders. With Willis performing prodigies at the back and Burgess finding time to send Medley and Skinner away on the left, they began to have as much of the play as their opponents. The fact is that the Spurs imposed their inferior style upon the run of the game. The football deteriorated as the excitement increased, for the home forwards were frequently getting through the other defence, and Merrick was often called upon to prove his quality, which he did by more than once denying the equalising goal.'

The *Birmingham Daily Gazette* also lauded Merrick, a future England goalkeeper and also a talented cricketer. Merrick would make 36 for Birmingham against Aston Villa at the Wolseley Motors Athletic Ground in July 1952 before being dismissed by Tom Cartwright (the future England Test player was a bit of a ringer in the Villa team!). The *Gazette* wrote, 'In the closing minutes Spurs geared themselves up to a series of cumbersome raids in which Merrick achieved considerable distinction in keeping his charge clear. Optimistic Spurs in their official programme published a 1946/47 league table with their own club leading the field, but they found Birmingham City also in promotion mood. The unqualified success of Duckhouse at centre-half was the best feature of Blues' game, and Wilson Jones was always a great trier.'

For one member of the press, the angle of his report was already known before kick-off, whatever the score turned out to be. *Sunday Mirror* correspondent Stanley Russell got wind of the fact that world snooker champion Joe Davis was in the crowd. Davis had won the first world title in 1927, claiming prize money of £6 10s, and scooped all 15 since, most recently beating Australia's Horace Lindrum 78-67 in the 1946 final at the Royal Horticultural Hall, London.

Stanley made hay with his scoop, and the headline writer joined in with the not particularly football-relevant 'THIS WAS GOOD POTTING', 'Joe Davis, King of Snooker, was at White Hart Lane yesterday watching the Spurs and Birmingham City play out another game of angles and potting and snookering on an outsize green cloth', writes Stanley Russell. There were 22 men instead of balls and they moved perhaps even faster than he does. 'There was some Davis-speed potting – two goals in the first three minutes – yet they lacked one thing Joe has always had, finesse.'

Davis had won his last world title, but another notable achievement remained in his locker – the game's first officially ratified 147 break. His historic maximum was recorded in an exhibition match against Willie Smith at Leicester Square Hall, London, in January 1955, by which time Ted Duckhouse was lining up for Rushden & Diamonds as his playing days drew to a close. The end of Duckhouse's long career as a professional footballer would mean the start of another working life. In those days, and here is a phrase rarely used in 2026, footballers were poorly paid.

'After his football career finished, Ted could be seen catching a bus to Darlaston each morning, as one of the hundreds of factory workers employed in the town,' reveals David Oakley, a contributor to the excellent brownhillsbob.com. 'I wonder how many of his fellow passengers realised how close they were sitting to a man who some years earlier had 40,000 spectators following his every move, and whose face had appeared on cigarette cards, they may have collected as youngsters?'

25

Scottish League A
Clyde 0 Aberdeen 2 (HT: 0-1)
Scorers – Aberdeen: Harris (2)
Attendance: 30,000

'The outstanding feature is her range of action. The Christian *can proceed to Great Yarmouth, fish for six weeks, and return to Aberdeen without having to refuel.'*

CLYDE AND Aberdeen met at Shawfield armed with plenty of positivity from their midweek matches. Three days earlier, Aberdeen had beaten league leaders Hibernian 1-0 at Pittodrie to terminate the visitors' unbeaten record and move to just a point behind them at the top of Division A. The Dons' fans were delighted by their team's strong performance, excited by a potential title challenge ahead and intrigued by a cryptic message which was taken on a half-time lap of the ground. 'Pittodrie's 20,000 spectators at last night's Aberdeen v Hibs match were puzzled by an SOS issued at half-time,' reported the *Aberdeen Press and Journal*. 'Chalked on a board carried round the enclosure was a message asking one of the spectators "to come home tonight".'

While Aberdeen were overcoming Hibs, 150 miles to the south Clyde showed formidable fighting spirit in their home match with Kilmarnock. The game ended 3-3 after Clyde dug deep despite centre-forward Davie Mathie sustaining a first-half injury which forced him to hirple his way through the rest of the game. 'Kilmarnock were thrice in the lead and thrice were pulled back to level pegging by a plucky

Clyde team that had Mathie all the second half hirpling on the left touchline with a groin strain,' reported the *Daily Record*.

Resilience had long been a trademark of Clyde. The club's origins were, like those of Queen's Park (see Chapter 6), unsullied by professionalism but unlike their fellow Glaswegians, they did not retain that policy for long. Clyde declined an invitation to join the inaugural Scottish League in 1890, because, clydefc.co.uk recalls, they 'saw the whole exercise as an affront to their amateur pastime'. However, the challenges of competing with the vast majority of clubs who paid players soon forced a rethink. 'Professionalism was also adopted in 1893 after a fierce debate,' according to the website – a decision heavily influenced by the emergence, in 1888, of a team by the name of Celtic. Until then, Clyde had the football followers of Glasgow's East End pretty much to themselves, but Celtic's growth was immediate and immense. The history of the Bully Wee was to unfold in the shadow of big Glaswegian brothers.

Just before the Second World War came the club's finest hour so far. In front of 94,779 at Hampden Park, they beat Motherwell 4-0 to lift the Scottish Cup for the first time. The margin of victory did not tell the whole story. Clyde's Troon-born goalkeeper John Brown was the star. 'Motherwell had over 60 per cent of the play. Clyde got the goals,' reported *Daily Record* correspondent W.G. Gallagher. 'That may suggest that the Shawfielders were lucky to win. They very emphatically were not. They possessed a sting that was never the property of the Fir Parkers who, with a strong wind behind them in the first half, had the ball mostly in Clyde territory. But ram it into the net they just couldn't.'

The imposing Brown was a hot property, having recently made his Scotland debut, against Wales at Hampden. The 24-year-old drew high praise from Mr Gallagher who also took the liberty of giving himself a nice pat on the back, quoting himself at length, 'In writing of the match in the Spotlight on Saturday, I said that goalkeeper Brown's "dominating influence is bound to have a two-fold effect. It will give his mates confidence, in addition to making the opposition wonder if there is any chance of reward in shooting from outside a distance of 12 yards. This latter point is vital, for if Motherwell take it into their hands that a score can only be secured from close quarters then they may be led into mix-up that will see the Clyde defence succeeding in clearing their lines." That is exactly what happened. The big fellow was unbeatable. Time and again in that first half he stepped out to intercept, clutch and clear corner kicks and cross balls in a manner that must have been heartbreaking to the Motherwell attack.'

A superb career beckoned for Brown only for what would have been his peak footballing years to be spent serving his country in the Royal Navy. His first game for Scotland transpired to be also his last.

By 1946, the team that powered Clyde to Scottish Cup glory seven years earlier had scattered far and wide – Brown was at Hibernian – but that redoubtable club spirit still beat strong. 'And what of Clyde?' pondered a *Daily Record* columnist. 'Gone in its entirety is their prewar cup-winning team. Manager Pat Travers and his directors have the difficult job of rebuilding, and no football team worth its salt was built overnight. It will take time before there is at Shawfield a team to compare with the 1939 lot, but there is one thing not lacking in the ranks of the Bully Wee – a grand fighting spirit, evidence of harmony behind the scenes. When you have a happy atmosphere in the dressing room, you are on the direct route to success on the field.'

Travers, it was reported in the Aberdeen match preview, 'was also on the job with pen and ink yesterday. He fixed up, as an amateur, 18-year-old Alex Russell, inside-left of St Mungo. This news will certainly cause disappointment in some quarters, for Russell was fancied by several other clubs, including some of the more prominent junior combines.'

The Dons, in form and eyeing up a serious title challenge, proved too strong for Travers's transitional side. Both goals came from centre-forward Tony Harris, signed in July, part of the exodus from still-amateur Queen's Park as the lure of professional football increased with the league's resumption. Harris was destined to make history as the only member of the Aberdeen team which won the Scottish Cup in 1947 to practise dentistry in the city's King Street. For now, he pounced once in each half to sink Clyde: on 29 minutes he headed home a cross from young winger Alex Kiddie, and seconds into the second half he accepted a simple chance set up by another rapid run down the right by Kiddie.

A solid away win to back up the victory over Hibernian sent Aberdeen to the top of the table, Hibs having lost at Motherwell (see Chapter 46). They were, it appeared, credible contenders for the title. 'REAL DANDY DONS' was the headline in the *Sunday Post*, 'The jinx that has so long haunted Aberdeen at Shawfield played turncoat. What breaks there were they got. Yet there's no denying they had a better, sweeter brand of football offerings. It was, in many ways, a great game, worthy of the occasion and the 30,000 crowd. Dons earned their win and confirmed their status as title challengers. It is equally true Clyde missed several chances of the "snipe" variety, Galletly and Johnstone being particularly remiss. Most of the victory credit must rest on the shoulders of a brilliant half-back line equipped with the essential solidity in defence and displaying a delightful variety of attacking ideas. Dunlop and Taylor linked as well with each other as they did with their forwards. Waddell was master in the middle. Bouquets, too, for Stan Williams, the best outside-left I've seen this season; for Tony Harris making his brightest contribution since joining the Dons; and for George Hamilton whose quick thinking so often switched defence into attack. Nor forget that young Kiddie supplied both the goal passes. Clyde's main merit lay in their ability to keep trying. Hugh Long was a dandy at left-half. Galbraith was very good. Hepburn a consistent forager. But David Mathie was sadly missed. And the defence was often jittery.'

One of the less popular characters in the stadium as the afternoon advanced was referee A.M. Campbell, from Johnstone. Mr Campbell had a trying afternoon, especially during a free-for-all described by the *Post* as 'a second-half miniature donnybrook that might have had more serious repercussions. As it was, at least one name was taken. Dons' first goal was a Harris header from a Kiddie cross I thought Sweeney should have punched. The second, 30 seconds after the restart, was a close-in Harris prod that sealed the issue. Afterwards came the ten-minute free-for-all, in which fouls were more frequent than attempts to play football. The referee was highly unpopular with the crowd. I thought they often had cause for complaint.'

Aberdeen Press and Journal writer Norman MacDonald was cautiously and eloquently upbeat about the Dons' prospects, under the headline 'ANYBODY'S LEAGUE AT THE MOMENT': 'Four weeks of the season gone, and no Scottish League club can claim immunity from defeat. It's anybody's league at the moment. Partick Thistle, the last of the undefeated, suffered their first reverse, against Third Lanark. The Cathkin team "arrived" with a 4-1 victory. The Dons' 2-0 success at Shawfield ended an eight-year-old lean spell against Clyde. Aberdeen are now established at the head of the league table along with Morton. What a build-up for Rangers' visit to Pittodrie on Wednesday! The champions are a point behind the Dons with a game in hand. An Aberdeen victory will open up the title race more than ever. And the Dons can do it on the form they showed against Clyde on Saturday. They were confident from the moment they took the field at Shawfield. Gone was the hesitancy in defence. The tackling was sure and the backs cleared their lines without delay. The half-back play was good, too. Waddell was never at a loss. He invariably got the ball in the air and on the ground. Taylor "made" the left-wing triangle. His service to Williams and McCall enabled this pair to wage a "nerves" war on the Clyde defence. My happiest recollection of the game was a bewildering draughtboard movement by this trio which ended in Taylor smashing the ball against the crossbar with a left-foot drive. Even more emphatic was Aberdeen's superiority in attack. They played cool, calculating football, and the forwards weren't afraid to shoot.'

The good news for the Granite City from 31 August 1946 did not end there. While the Dons were sailing to two points at Shawfield, back in the north-east equally exciting scenes were unfolding at Aberdeen Fish Market as onlookers clamoured to see the 'LONG-RANGE MOTOR FISHING VESSEL'. 'A motor fishing vessel, the *Christian*, which may be the boat of the future for North Sea fishing, attracted attention at Aberdeen Fish Market on Saturday,' reported the *Aberdeen Press and Journal*. 'She has just been built at Peterhead and is 75ft in length. She is fitted with a diesel engine of 150 hp. The outstanding feature is her range of action. The *Christian* can proceed to Great Yarmouth, fish for six weeks, and return to Aberdeen without having to refuel. Her owner is Mr A. Robertson, Aberdeen, who intends putting her on the Seine net fishing.'

Four days later, Mr Robertson shared the Aberdonian delight when George Taylor's goal secured the Dons a 1-0 win over Rangers at Pittodrie where the bumper crowd included royalty. 'Among the 35,000 spectators at the Aberdeen-Rangers game last night was The Kabaka of Buganda, an under-graduate at Cambridge,' revealed the *Press and Journal*. 'He was accompanied by Baillie Raffan.' His Majesty no doubt monitored the Dons' fortunes throughout the months ahead and shared their angst when, having moved three points above Rangers in his regal presence, they finished the season seven behind them, in third place, albeit 12 points ahead of tenth-placed Clyde.

Wolves provided one of the stories of the day when they thrashed Arsenal 6–1 at Molineux

Sir Matt Busby's first Football League match as Manchester United manager was the 2–1 win over Grimsby at Maine Road on 31 August 1946

Ivor Broadis: player-manager of Carlisle United, aged just 23

Spectators pour towards Stamford Bridge to watch Chelsea play Bolton Wanderers

Stan Mortensen was among the stars and the scorers for Blackpool at Huddersfield

Manchester City supporters enjoyed their team's strong start away to Leicester City

Sunderland legend Raich Carter made an emotional return to Roker Park as captain of Derby County

Southampton manager Bill Dodgin and his team endured a wasted journey to south Wales

Born in Chile, honed in Barnsley: George Robledo started the season with a hat-trick at home to Nottingham Forest

Wilf Mannion scored a late winner for Middlesbrough to disappoint most of a huge crowd at Villa Park

Charlton Athletic legend Sam Bartram received an emotional visitor at The Valley in the days leading up to the big kick-off

Gil Merrick was in fine form as Birmingham City scored the first goal of the new era on the way to victory over Spurs at White Hart Lane

Cape Town-born Berry Nieuwenhuys helped power Liverpool to an opening-day win at Bramall Lane – and then to the League title

Joe Harvey, a £4,250 signing from Bradford City, starred on his debut for Newcastle in their 4-1 win at Millwall

Fuelled by good wishes from the inaugural guest on Desert Islands Discs, *the charismatic Dave Mangnall (back row, right) led QPR to victory at home to Watford*

Charlie Mitten scored Manchester United's first Football League goal under Matt Busby, in their 2-1 win over Grimsby

26

Football League Division Two
Bury 7 Fulham 2 (HT: 2-0)
Scorers – Bury: Kilshaw, Meaney (2), Carter (2), Moss (2); Fulham: Rooke (2)
Attendance: 12,847

'Craft was allied to power in adequate proportion and when such an amalgam is achieved, goals are bound to accrue.'

THE NOBLE town of Bury, which was first served by coal barges in 1796, five years after the opening of the Manchester, Bolton and Bury Canal Company, was hammered as much as anywhere by the wet week leading up to Saturday, 31 August 1946. Mrs Howarth could testify to that. At noon that day, while the Shakers' supporters were starting to think about making their way to Gigg Lane for the Division Two opener with Fulham, Mrs Howarth got a bit of a shock. 'MAROONED ON KITCHEN TABLE' reported the *Bury News*, 'Occupants of a house in Harwood Road, Tottington, were temporarily marooned on their kitchen table, while furniture swirled around the floor during the torrential rains which swept the district during the weekend. Mrs Howarth, of Harwood Road, opening her door at Saturday noon to find a two-feet deep stream of rainwater flooding into the kitchen and cellar; while in a nearby house in Turton Road, Mr C. Midgley also found his cellar flooded.'

On this very soggy Saturday, almost a million people around the country braved the elements to relive that precious experience, setting off to watch a Football League fixture. Most made it safely to the respective grounds but for an unfortunate few who set off for Bury v Fulham, the journey ended with a jolt a couple of miles before Gigg Lane.

'HURLED OVER HEDGE' was the headline in the *Bolton Evening News*, 'Michael Flatley, Egyptian-st, one of nine Bolton men injured on Saturday afternoon when the lorry in which they were travelling to Bury Football Ground crashed into a lamp standard, is detained in Bury Infirmary "still very poorly" with fractured ribs and head and face cuts. Two others, Joseph Fleetwood, Oak-st, suffering from concussion, and Wm. Green, Denvale-ave, with a broken leg, are reported to be comfortable. The lorry was completely wrecked by the impact, which occurred near the Jolly Carters in Bolton-rd, Bury. The driver, Thomas Schofield, Oak-st, escaped with superficial injuries. Two men were hurled over a hedge, five yards into an adjoining field, and others were scattered about the road.' It is to be hoped that Mr Flatley and his friends made a full recovery. Their spirits would certainly have lifted when they heard how the match went: Bury began the season with a mighty bang.

The Shakers had spent all their 52 years in the Football League in its top two divisions. FA Cup winners in 1900 and 1903, they were relegated from Division One in 1929 but nine years in Division Two then yielded four top-five finishes. Norman Bullock's side looked ready to challenge for promotion and an opening-day win appeared likely against opposition which joined the league in 1907 but was still to reach the top flight.

Bury News reporter Ranger began his preview by referencing an issue bubbling under the surface as footballers prepared for the league's return, 'Amid rumours of threats of determined action by the professional footballers to achieve their demand for increased wages, the first normal soccer season since the war begins today. It is to be hoped the differences of view will not lead to open conflict, for there is every promise that the campaign will be eventful and interesting.' It was an issue monitored with great interest by 18-year-old Balham boy Jimmy Hill, who had played briefly for Fulham juniors during the war. Hill would join them as a professional in 1952 and, a further nine years on, as head of the footballers' union, lead the successful fight to end the maximum wage.

Turning his attention to the match, Ranger expressed confidence in the rear and middle departments of the Shakers' team, 'The Craven Cottage side will field a strong combination, which includes Jack Watson, the erstwhile Bury centre-half who went south last season. Bury will have to fight hard for whatever reward is gained. After last Saturday's practice game, it was obvious that the Bury defence and middle line would be chosen along familiar lines at least in the early games. What queries there were concerned the attack. Manager Bullock has decided to give Meaney an early chance of showing his talents as leader of the attack and he will have on his right, Wyles, the former Everton player who was signed during the close season from Blackburn Rovers. Moss will be at inside-left and Kilshaw and Carter on the wings. It is to be hoped this formation settles down into a workmanlike and effective unit, for the defence should give a good account of itself.'

The unit proved highly effective. Ranger's concerns about the attack were blown away by a scintillating performance from the rampant Shakers, who led 2-0 at half-time through goals from Eddie Kilshaw (19 minutes) and Terry Meaney (35) and doubled their advantage by just past the hour mark through Don Carter (53) and Jack Moss (62). Bury's dominance was interrupted only briefly, midway through the second half, by two goals from a player who had hurt them before.

Ronnie Rooke joined Fulham in October 1936, signed by manager Jack Peart from Crystal Palace for £300. It was perhaps the best £300 the club has ever spent. The Guildford-born striker started with a hat-trick on his debut, a 5-0 win over West Ham United. It was an impressive introduction, but he doubled that achievement when Bury visited Craven Cottage for an FA Cup tie in January 1939. On a bone-hard pitch, Fulham won 6-0 and Rooke scored all six, three in each half. It remains a Fulham club record for a player in one match. Rooke scored Fulham's last goal before the war, against Luton Town on 2 September 1939, and bagged 212 goals in 199 wartime games for the club. He was a hero to the Cottagers' fans, although, as they cheered his double at Gigg Lane, they had no clue that he was soon to depart.

Rooke needed to bag another six at Gigg Lane to turn this match round. Instead, Bury blew hot again with three goals, from Meaney,

Moss and Carter, in the last six minutes. The storming finish earned the Shakers a huge ovation at the final whistle, though it was at the other end of the afternoon that some innovative thinking from Mr Bullock had prepared the feast for the fans. 'A few minutes before the start of the game the Bury players came out with four balls,' reported the *Bury News*. 'Mr N. Bullock, the Bury secretary-manager, told me that he considered it a better way than "shooting in" as a means of loosening up. It will be remembered the Moscow Dynamos introduced this feature during their tour of this country last winter.'

The groundbreaking strategy was picked up by the national press. 'RUSSIAN IDEAS HIT FULHAM' was the headline in the *Daily Express*, 'Bury took a tip from the Russian Dynamos. Before the kick-off they had four balls to kick at, warming up idea. Result: seven goals against Fulham.' Charles Buchan, writing in the *Daily News (London)*, was sniffy about the concept, 'Bury, leading goalscorers of the day, adopted, I understand, the Dynamo practice of a few minutes' kickabout before the game with Fulham. I don't suppose it helped a lot, but they did score seven times.'

'BURY OVERWHELM FULHAM IN NINE-GOAL CURTAIN RAISER' was the headline in the *Bury News* underneath which was Ranger's report, an elegant and balanced blend of celebration and analysis, 'Bury's 7-2 win over Fulham at Gigg Lane on Saturday, in the opening match of the Second Division season, fully merited as it was, set the whole football world agog. Rarely have the Shakers carried off the distinction of being the biggest goal-getters in the country, but this honour fell to them on Saturday. The query concerned the development of finishing power in attack, and all doubts were revealed to be unfounded. Even those who were generous enough to suggest that Bury might draw – and they included most of the newspaper prophets – were confounded. At all phases of the game were Bury superior to their opponents, for the Fulham machine was never allowed to run into gear.

'This was an achievement to send the crowd home happy and hopeful. Goals, especially when intelligently obtained, are the lifeblood of the sport, and the spectators' appetite was surely satisfied on Saturday. There was virility and power allied to the needed basic understanding, and the Fulham defence was repeatedly torn asunder by the speed and effectiveness of the home forwards. Craft was allied to power in adequate proportion and when such an amalgam is achieved, goals are bound to accrue. Seven goals is a ready-reckoner of the success of the attack. All five played their part, even though Wyles was not so nippy as his colleagues, and Meaney's lack of experience was at times apparent. Fulham were not so good as expected. Their defence had no counter to the thrusts of the home forwards. Ill-served in goal, their whole defensive scheme was cut to ribbons. Their forwards, when well-placed, fiddled about too long, and only Rooke had the finishing power to cause Bury any concern.'

A lovely evocation of a memorable game. Ranger had clearly seen plenty of football in his time and would not be getting carried away by one big win. In an era when local newspaper reporters, if respected and trusted, were allowed close to managers, it is easy to picture Ranger popping down for a post-match beer with Mr Bullock and his colleagues. 'Those who saw the game will not, I am confident, have persuaded themselves that all is well in the best of all worlds,' he continued as thoughts turned towards Bury's visit to Manchester City on Wednesday. 'Certainly, the Bury management have not. Yet, along with their supporters, they were stimulated by the excellence of the display. A good start by any team, provoking a confidence in their own ability, is always welcomed, but the glow produced by a handsome victory must not be allowed to become a screen for even the limited shortcomings in the play of the team. There is little danger of the victory lifting the management into the realms of make-believe. For it is recognised that in this campaign only the best will be good enough to put Bury among the leaders.' Ranger added that, for the visit to Maine Road, 'Bury will field an unchanged side if Carter, who is in the army, is able to attend.' Wednesday, 4 September 1946 promised to be an important day for sport in the town. At 6pm, the Shakers would face Manchester City. At 8pm, the Bury & District Table Tennis League would hold a meeting at the YMCA, The Rock, to see if there was sufficient interest to restart the competition.

Ranger's caution was vindicated by a 3-1 defeat at Maine Road. Carter did play and scored the Shakers' goal, but City continued their excellent start after their opening-day 3-0 victory at Leicester (see Chapter 44). Fulham suffered a second defeat, 3-1 at West Ham, on Monday but were to bounce back with home wins over Luton and West Ham. The Cottagers would finish above the Shakers in the final table – 15th to Bury's 17th.

By that time, Rooke was an Arsenal player. In December, Peart controversially sold the striker to Arsenal for £1,000 plus two players. Rooke helped the struggling Gunners to escape relegation and the following season was the country's leading scorer with 33 goals as Arsenal became champions.

A first taste of Division One was not far away for Fulham – in 1950 they went up as Division Two champions – but Bury would never reach the top level again. Engulfed by financial crisis, in 2019, having failed to show that they could pay off their creditors and survive the season, they were expelled from the Football League altogether.

27

Football League Division One
Portsmouth 3 Blackburn Rovers 1 (HT: 3-1)
Scorers – Portsmouth: Reid (2), Crook (og); Blackburn Rovers: Rogers
Attendance: 30,962

'Two policemen waded out to sea with a rope and secured a live mine washed up by the gale.'

EVERY CLUB entered the new Football League era with a clean slate. This fresh start was perfectly illustrated by the front page of the programme for the Division One match between Portsmouth and Blackburn Rovers at Fratton Park. Supporters who shelled out two pence for the publication were greeted on its front page by a bang-up-to-date Division One table. Pompey occupied a worryingly low position, 17th, albeit level on points with the leaders. Blackburn sat a promising third. Arsenal were top and Wolverhampton Wanderers bottom, though those positions were to be spectacularly reversed by five o'clock after the Gunners were routed at Molineux (see Chapter 2).

A former Arsenal player was high among the talking points as Blackburn's fans looked ahead to an attractive opener. Making his debut in goal for the visitors would be George Marks, who had arrived from the Gunners for £5,000 just a few days earlier. Marks had spent a decade at Arsenal, having joined as an apprentice and then served mostly as understudy to George Swindin and Alex Wilson. His first-team chance finally arrived late in the 1938/39 season when he played the last two games. He then played all three at the start of

1939/40 before its abrupt early conclusion, just as his career was at last taking flight. For few players can the outbreak of war have been more professionally frustrating.

After wartime service with the Royal Air Force, Marks moved to Ewood Park in search of first-team football. The £5,000 fee was a hefty one for a goalkeeper and his signing underlined the determination of Rovers, one of the Football League's founder members, to re-establish themselves among English football's elite. The former champions and FA Cup winners had hit some turbulence in the late 1930s, with relegation to Division Two and an embarrassing FA Cup defeat to Division Three North side Accrington Stanley.

The appointment of Bob Crompton as manager turned things back round. A true Rovers legend, having first played for them in 1896, Crompton led them back to Division One in his first season in charge, the last before the war. Sadly, in 1941, Crompton collapsed and died hours after watching Rovers play Burnley in a regional league fixture. The club entered the new era in very different hands, those of former Arsenal and England star Eddie Hapgood, for whom it was a first job as manager. Fans wondered what lay ahead for their team with its cleanest of clean slates: a rookie boss with a newly composed side blending new signings with veterans from 1939.

While Hapgood prepared for his first Football League match as a manager, it was all very familiar for his Portsmouth counterpart, Jack Tinn. Secretary-manager since 1927, Tinn had led Pompey to their first FA Cup triumph in 1939 when they beat hot favourites Wolves 4-1 in the final. He attributed the success to the lucky spats he wore for every round of the competition. The spats saw off Lincoln City, West Bromwich Albion, West Ham United, Preston North End, Huddersfield Town and finally Wolves at Wembley where, just after five o'clock, they climbed the steps to meet King George V who, parking his disappointment that Clapton Orient went out to Walsall in the second round (see Chapter 20), offered congratulations.

Tinn's spats did not survive the war which is almost certainly why Portsmouth's defence of the cup ended at the first hurdle when it returned in 1945. They lost 1-0 on aggregate to Birmingham City over two legs and also endured a moderate league season, finishing

19th of 22 in the League South. Ahead of the Football League's return, however, anticipation and interest among Pompey fans was still sky-high. 'FOOTBALL FANS STRAINING AT THE LEASH' was the eve-of-season headline in the *Hampshire Telegraph*. Their correspondent, The Ranger, expanded upon the theme, 'Tomorrow, hundreds of thousands of football fans all over the country will be shouting themselves hoarse at the first real league matches they have attended for seven years. During the war they had to be content with makeshift competitions, which did little more than maintain an interest in the game and keep the players in trim. There was little to win and less to lose. True, the FA Cup competition was restored last season but even that had a touch of the war about it in that the early ties were decided on the aggregate score from home and away matches.

'All that has now disappeared. The cup ties will be on the old nerve-straining knockout principle and in the league competition some teams will be fighting for championship honours and promotion while others will be struggling to avoid relegation. All this will restore much of the old lustre which we have missed so much during the war years, and there is bound to be a tremendous revival of enthusiasm for the game. There was an indication of this at Fratton Park last Saturday when 13,000 Pompey supporters attended a trial match. The demand is there and it is up to the clubs to supply the goods. If they do and serve up what the public want, I do not think they will have much to worry about on the financial side. The football public are thirsting for the game to get under way again and clubs with enterprising managements have a great opportunity in front of them.'

Tinn was cagey about the coming season. The wily Geordie plumped for a strategy often deployed by managers keen to lower expectations – he got his retaliation in first. 'Few clubs have made greater effort than Portsmouth to get new players,' he told the paper. 'I have travelled all over the country but first-class players are not to be got. Those clubs which have good players to spare are refusing all offers. They are nervous about injuries in the first few weeks and no money will induce them to part. I shall be very content to finish in a safe place in the league but several clubs will have to fight hard to avoid relegation.'

The manager's assertion that first-class players were not to be got may have raised the eyebrows of Tim McCoy and Duggie Reid, who had just signed for the club. 'McCoy is 6ft tall and weighs 13st 2lb,' revealed The Ranger. 'He belongs to the Birmingham district but at present is working at Brighton in the sheet metal industry. He has played in Egypt and Germany and it was while playing for his unit that he came under notice.' Scottish inside-forward Reid had arrived from Stockport County earlier in the year. He moved south from his native Ayrshire as a 15-year-old to take up a plumbing apprenticeship and was picked up by the Hatters in 1936. In March 1946, he relocated even further south with a £7,000 move to Pompey but took time to settle in a makeshift team. Tall, slightly ungainly at times, and plucked from a lower level, Reid entered the 1946/47 season with the Pompey fans' jury very much still out on his merits.

The jury was not to remain out for long. Reid would become a true Portsmouth legend, not least for his ferocious shooting which earned him the nickname 'Thunderboots'. One penalty, which he converted against Manchester City at Fratton Park, burst through the net and reportedly struck the mayor of Westville, Durban, standing among the spectators behind the goal, on the left shoulder. Reid's progress to the heart of Pompey fans' affections was to be rapid and it started just 18 minutes into the new season.

The storms of the week had lashed the south coast as violently as anywhere. To the west, in Devon, 'beach huts, bathing tents and deckchairs were swept into the sea and smashed at Teignmouth' reported the *Western Mail*, while 11 miles east of Portsmouth came heroism. 'Two policemen waded out to sea with a rope and secured a live mine washed up by the gale off Bungalow Town, Hayling Island,' the paper reported. 'They were watched by hundreds of holiday-makers.'

On Saturday morning, George Marks linked up with his new colleagues at a wet railway station in south London. In the afternoon, the Fratton Park pitch was deemed playable despite the deluge and from three o'clock the Blackburn debutant was soon hard at work. 'Marks, this week's big capture, joined his new colleagues at Waterloo and appeared in goal,' reported Rover for the *Lancashire Evening Post*. 'Twice in the first minute, Marks impressed the crowd. The remarkable length of his kicking, first from a backpass from Pryde, travelling fully three-quarters of the field.'

While the debutant's footwork impressed, his ball-handling skills did not start so well. After ten minutes, Reid got the season going, and the Fratton End roaring, with the first goal. Marks rose to collect a cross but, under pressure from Reid, dropped the ball. Bert Barlow was first to it and when his shot was cleared off the line, Reid netted the rebound. 'It seemed that Marks was a trifle late in going down, but he may have been unsighted,' commented Rover.

Those 'thunderboots' then struck in the 18th minute when Reid hammered a 20-yard free kick directly past the helpless Marks. That got the Pompey Chimes chiming and it was 3-0 before the half-hour mark when Bobby Nutley, a winger signed from Hibernian, crossed from the left and Wally Crook turned the ball into his own net. Rovers didn't deserve to be 3-0 down and pulled a goal back before half-time when Billy Rogers pounced on a rebound off a post. The visitors pressed hard in the second half but failed to take their chances. Hapgood's reign began with defeat in the Hampshire rain. 'Blackburn Rovers had a luckless opening but the general quality of their football was not discouraging' was journalist Rover's verdict. 'They were inferior to Portsmouth only in the immediate covering of goal, and there were excellent touches in their approach play. Portsmouth's four first-half raids produced three goals, whereas the Rovers, in a courageous second-half rally, misused hard-earned chances that would have saved a point. It was not a happy start for Marks, but wing-half strength was promising and the wingers were in good form.'

The *Hampshire Telegraph* correspondent was realistic, his thoughts echoing the pragmatic views offered by Tinn before the game, 'From the statistical point of view it was a good win and it gives Pompey a good start in what is bound to prove a tough campaign, but few will shut their eyes to the fact that there must be an improvement if Pompey are to achieve anything during the next eight months. And when I talk of achievement I mean holding on to what they have rather than attaining higher prizes.'

The pragmatism was justified. It was a middling season for Portsmouth. They finished 12th, kept out of relegation trouble largely by 29 goals from Reid, but glory lay just around the corner. Tinn's 20-year tenure had run out of steam and ended in May 1947 when he announced his retirement. He was succeeded by Bob Jackson who steered the team to successive Football League titles in 1949 and 1950, successes to which Reid was integral.

Blackburn finished 1946/47 in 17th place, the position Portsmouth occupied in the match programme on the opening day. You wouldn't make it up.

28

Football League Division Two Newport County v Southampton: match postponed due to a waterlogged pitch

'Mr Davies added that the creature appeared to be wearing a blue suit.'

IF SATURDAY, 31 August 1946 was a momentous day for football, it was also a significant day in the world of cricket. And the mayor of Southampton was at the heart of it.

It was the day on which England's cricketers, captained by Wally Hammond, set sail from Southampton on a three-week voyage to Australia where they would contest the first Ashes series for eight years. In 2025/26, England's Ashes series lasted for 48 days, between November and January. It was rather different in 1946/47 when the team departed on the first day of the football season and returned when it was nearly over. Hammond's side reciprocated the mayor's valedictions in August knowing that they would not see England again until April.

Hundreds of cricket lovers gathered in the rain at Southampton docks to watch the *Stirling Castle*, carrying Hammond and his team, disappear into the murk. England's quest to reclaim the urn, which Australia had possessed for 12 years, was under way. 'The great adventure to Australia has started,' *The People* reported. 'Yesterday the English cricketers left these sunny (!) climes to battle for the Ashes down under, and rarely has a tour started with such interest and controversy. The mayor of Southampton led a quayside crowd at Southampton docks in three cheers for the MCC party when the cricketers sailed away in the Union Castle liner, *Stirling Castle*. The mayor had earlier wished the team a successful tour and, as the liner drew away, Wally Hammond, the English captain, leant against the rail of the boat deck and responded to the cheers. Hammond was in confident mood and, just before he left, he said, "I am very proud to be going out as captain of this team, and I think we are going to do well. You can rely on one thing – we shall not let England down." A full-length matting cricket pitch has been laid out on the Stirling Castle's promenade deck.'

Hammond was no doubt sincere but proved to be entirely wrong. Despite the benefit of seven first-class warm-up matches, England lost the first Test, in Brisbane, by an innings and 332 runs. From Brisbane they moved to Sydney and lost by an innings there too. Australia went on to retain the Ashes by a 3-0 margin in front of huge crowds. Just as football supporters flooded back to their beloved sport after the war, so did cricket fans: the Ashes series was attended by 846,263 people.

The mayor of Southampton was not one of them but, on that murky morning in August, he did his bit by turning up in the rain to wave the team off and wish them well on behalf of the nation. Then he toddled off to dry out, find a nice, warming cup of tea and switch his attention to his city's other big sporting matter of the day, the footballers having also embarked on an international mission that morning – not quite as exotic as England's, but also eagerly awaited. The Saints had travelled to Wales for an intriguing Football League Division Two fixture at Newport County.

Newport were at the zenith of their existence. If Accrington Stanley felt aggrieved, on a football level, by the arrival of the Second World War (see Chapter 16), then no less so did Newport. Founded in 1912 by a bunch of blokes from the West Midlands, mostly Wolves supporters, to provide an association football option in a rugby football hotbed, the Ironsides had found it hard going. They suffered recurring financial problems and dips in and out of the Football League but then, out of nowhere, in 1938/39, came promotion. Under former Rangers left-back Billy McCandless, County finished top of Division Three South, three points clear of Crystal Palace and six ahead of third-placed Brighton. It was a triumph built upon a superb defence. Thirteen clubs in the division, including relegated Walsall, scored more goals, but they conceded only 45 times in 42 games. Division Two football awaited for the first time and the achievement was celebrated by a banquet at the Lord Raglan Hotel and the manufacture of souvenir pencils.

County's momentum spanned the summer. They started Division Two life with a flourish with a 3-1 win over Southampton at Somerton Park, and a solid 1-1 home draw with Tottenham Hotspur followed, but war clouds were gathering. Newport's new adventure was truncated after its third instalment, a 2-1 defeat at Nottingham Forest in a match already impacted by the impending cataclysm. 'Newport County made their first appearance at the City Ground on Saturday and they are not likely to forget it,' reported the *Nottingham Journal*. 'They arrived 40 minutes after the match was due to commence, having changed into football kit in the train which was delayed owing to the evacuation scheme.' Into abeyance went the Football League. Could the Ironsides' momentum span a seven-year interruption?

On Friday, 30 August 1946, the *South Wales Argus* furnished County fans with match information. Admission to the grandstand would be 4/6, to the enclosure 2/6 and to the field 1/6 and 1/3. Service personnel in uniform and boys aged under 16 would pay 9d. Newport Corporation Transport would run special buses to the match from Clarence Place for a fare of 2d. The *Argus* also brought its readers an intriguing tale under the headline, unusual for a Friday, 'HALF MAN, HALF HORSE', 'An amazing story of a strange creature, half man and half horse, said to be haunting Blaenavon in the early hours of the morning, has been reported in detail to the police at Blaenavon. Mr William Henry Davies, aged 34, a miner at Kays Slope Colliery, who lives at 1, Forge Row, Cwmavon, has made a signed statement describing how he saw the creature running at terrific speed, apparently frightened by the light from his bicycle. The incident occurred at 4.50am on Tuesday, while Mr Davies was cycling home from work. On Cwmavon Road, near the turning to Twynmawr road, he saw in the half-light of dawn and with the aid of the light of his cycle, a creature which appeared to be a man except that it had a head similar to a small horse, and a flowing mane.

'Until Friday he was reluctant to tell anybody except his wife of the experience, but on Friday morning he decided to make a statement to

Blaenavon police. Mr Davies said, "I have not the slightest doubt about what I saw. I was riding down the hill and was only five yards from the creature when I saw it. It was running very fast, and my attention was drawn by the long hair which flowed over its shoulders. It had a small horse's head, just like that of a colt. It ran up a side street, apparently to avoid me, and as I pulled up, I heard a neigh. It was not loud but it was unmistakeable." Mr Davies added that the creature appeared to be wearing a blue suit.'

The *Argus* also revealed, in a prophetic filler, 'Early morning rain at Newport today threatened to make August 1946 the wettest August on record. At 9am today, a fall of 1.5in had been recorded for the previous 24 hours, bringing the total rainfall for the month to 6.9in, three more inches than the average figure for August.'

The two teams had met recently. They were drawn together in the 1945/46 FA Cup, Southampton winning 6-4 on aggregate. They had joined the Football League at the same time, in 1920, but their fortunes soon diverged. While County struggled, Southampton settled to life much more quickly. They won promotion to Division Two the following season and solidly remained there through 17 years and 16 mayors – Walter Mouland, Thomas McDonnell, Joseph Silverman, Percy Bowyer, Lucia Welch (the first female to hold the office), Maurice Pugh, Hector Young, Edward Cross, Fred Woolley, William Buck, George Waller, Thomas Sanders, Harry Chick, George Prince, Arthur Powdrill and Robert Sinclair – until the outbreak of war.

Bill Dodgin (senior) had not long taken over as Saints manager and an intriguing opening-day tussle was in prospect. Intriguing, though surely not of the magnitude to be a candidate to make headlines in the Sunday papers. That's what happened, though. *The People*'s back page led with 'MATCH RAINED OFF ON FOOTBALL'S OPENING DAY!'

It reported, 'Newport, due to play Southampton in their first serious Second Division match since they set all Wales talking by pocketing promotion from the Third Division (South) in 1939, found their ground waterlogged after overnight torrential rain. But although they called in the local fire brigade, more rain in the morning completely flooded the pitch, and the game had to be postponed.'

'There is always something new,' wrote the *Southern Echo* correspondent. 'Who would have thought we would be rained off in August? The Saints footballers squelching their way over the Somerton Park pitch on Saturday looked glumly at the flooded ground and just as glumly as the sun shining out of a clear sky. For, after the last midday shower, it was a perfect afternoon at Newport.

'Manager Bill Dodgin and I had a preview of the pitch for we visited the ground early after breakfast when the shadow of the afternoon's disappointment was already apparent. There was a big pond around the top left-hand corner flag and other "distressed" areas. A fire pump was already busy pumping out of a sump – with 20ft of water in it. We suggested to manager Tom Bromilow that it might help if pails and buckets were brought into action to bale the surface water off the pitch. We were assured that it would not do any good – and so the pumping went on as the only hope of play in the afternoon. But when in the afternoon the match was postponed and the Saints left the ground, the ponds were just as wide and deep as in the morning.'

Monday's *South Wales Argus* offered more details, 'Saturday's cancellation was a big disappointment to County's supporters, and some have protested that there was unnecessary delay in calling the match off. In an official statement, Mr F. Lionel Watkins, secretary of Newport County AFC, said. "We had no right to cancel the match before the arrival of the referee. It is entirely the responsibility of the referee to decide whether a ground is in a fit condition. The referee is not due to arrive on the ground until an hour before the match. Mr G.H. Hann, the referee, arrived at two o'clock on Saturday. He spent some time inspecting the ground and consulting with the National Fire Service officials and at 2.20pm decided the match could not be played. The announcement was then made to the crowd outside the gates."'

Also revealed was a circumstance unlikely to be replicated in 2026. During the morning, the manager had dealt with numerous inquiries from fans on the phone. 'Mr T.G. Bromilow, the manager, explained that throughout the morning he received many telephone enquiries about the match. "At that time," he added, "there was no suggestion that the match would be postponed. The last torrential storm just before one o'clock put the finishing touch to it."' The Somerton Park pitch was to remain a swamp for days but former Liverpool and England left-half Tom Bromilow, who was to sadly pass away at Nuneaton railway station in 1959, resourcefully arranged for the players to train indoors at the Drill Hall.

While Bromilow dealt with the storms in Wales, for England's cricketers the early progress was serene. 'MCC PARTY HAPPY', reported the *Yorkshire Evening Post* on Monday, 'The Stirling Castle, carrying MCC tourists to Australia, today passed through the Bay of Biscay in perfect weather and in comparatively calm sea. All members of the team, most of them passing through the bay for the first time, avoided sea sickness.' The serenity ended quickly after their arrival in Australia. Those team members were a weary, beaten lot when they returned home in April to find Newport County also in deep strife. The Ironsides' prewar glory was a fast-fading memory as they finished bottom of Division Two, having lost 29 of their 42 games. Southampton beat them twice: 2-1 in the rearranged game in October and 5-1 at The Dell on 28 December.

County returned to Division Three South and would never regain Division Two status. Oblivion beckoned. Evicted from their Somerton Park home, the club was wound up in 1989, the year in which Norman Best became mayor of Southampton.

29

Football League Division Three North Doncaster Rovers 2 Rochdale 1 (HT: 2-0) Scorers – Doncaster Rovers: Maddison (2); Rochdale: Cunliffe Attendance: 8,279

'Ind. Coope & Allsopps Burton Ales on draught and Double Diamond in bottle – telephone 2261.'

AUGUST 1946 brought football fans across the country clamouring back around their beloved clubs. For plenty of those supporters, football being the wonderful, emotion-threshing, mean old moose that it is, the following months were to bring frustration, misery and ire. Followers of Leeds United, Newport County, Brentford, Swansea Town, Halifax Town, Southport, Mansfield Town and Norwich City in particular had cause to wish the Football League had stayed dormant for another year. Doncaster Rovers fans, on the other hand, had a blast.

Great days and happy memories piled up for Donny during a record-breaking, goal-packed thrill-fest of a season. The team's success delivered immense joy and, as with any successful football club (as sagely pointed out by the *Barnsley Chronicle* – see Chapter 15), a very welcome economic boost for the town.

The architect of all this was manager Jackie Bestall. A Grimsby Town legend as a player (a road in the town is named after him), Bestall moved into management at Doncaster in 1945. He was appointed as assistant to Bill Marsden who divided his time between managing Rovers and running a pub in Sheffield. In March 1946, the board decided they wanted a full-time manager and when Marsden declined to give up the pub, they gave the gig to Bestall. A brilliant decision.

A month into his reign, Bestall negotiated his team through one of the strangest games in the history of English football. Rovers visited Stockport County for the second leg of a League Three North Cup match and, after both legs finished 2-2 and extra time was scoreless, referee Mr Baker from Crewe ordered the game to continue under the trial 'play to a finish' rule (known on playgrounds up and down the country as 'next goal wins'). The players carried on. And on. And on. There were 203 minutes on the clock when Mr Baker at last decided enough was enough. 'Finally in the dusk and with a haze of smoke from the railway settling over the ground, Mr Baker decided the light was too bad to continue,' reported the *Yorkshire Post*, 'and 22 weary players and three tired officials hobbled off the field.'

Footballers of 2026 would need at least six months' rest to recover from such an ordeal. The players of Stockport and Doncaster met again four days later when Bestall's side, having won the toss to host the replay, won 4-0 thanks to a hat-trick from Donny-born Ralph Maddison. The homegrown winger was also to be the star of the winning start to Rovers' momentous 1946/47 campaign.

While Bestall was busy building his magic in South Yorkshire, 60 miles away across the Pennines, Ted Goodier had his work cut out. Rochdale manager since September 1938, except for a six-month stint as caretaker boss of Birmingham City between November 1944 and April 1945, Goodier's primary mission was simply to keep Dale above the two re-election places.

Rochdale AFC was born on 14 May 1907 at a public meeting in Fleece Street. 'At a meeting convened by Mr Harvey Rigg in Central Council Schools, Fleece Street, Rochdale, last evening, with Mr. H. [Herbert] Hopkinson in the chair, it was decided to form a club to be called The Rochdale Association Football Club,' reported the *Rochdale Observer*. Dale had faced their share of challenges ever since. In 1910, having finished top of the Lancashire Combination, they applied to join the Football League, but received just one vote. When the league expanded in 1921, they were accepted and started in style with a 6-3 win over Accrington Stanley, but that existence proved gruelling. In nine seasons leading up to the Second World War, in the 22-club Division Three North, Dale finished 21st, 21st, 18th, 22nd, 20th, 20th, 18th, 17th and 15th. They started the aborted 1939/40 season well, though, and, with Goodier still in charge seven years later, there was some optimism around the club.

Under the headline 'QUIET CONFIDENCE AT SPOTLAND', *Rochdale Observer* correspondent, Scrutator reported, 'In all, 22 professionals have been signed and every position is duplicated with the exception of outside-left, and Mr Goodier will probably remedy that in the near future. Not given to exaggerated statements as to what his men are likely to accomplish, the Rochdale manager prefers to let results speak for themselves as they come along. It is a wise policy, for a balloon inflated with too much hot air at the beginning of a season bursts all the more loudly if it does burst. At Spotland this week, I found none of that, just a quiet air of confidence about all the pre-season preparations.

'Every one of the nine forwards seems ready to take his place in Third Division football. Dave Robbie is again trainer and Hilbert Barnes, the Crompton cricketer and former Oldham Athletic player, is assistant trainer and groundsman. Newly mown this week, the pitch looked better than it has done for years and the whole atmosphere around the ground is one of far greater efficiency and method than used to be the case. Ground improvements are still continuing. The biggest improvement has been made in the players' accommodation, which has a cleaner and healthier look about it and there seemed to be no lack of enthusiasm about the players themselves during ball practice which was in progress this week. Swimming at the Riviera is an aside to training while the weather lasts.'

From his more distant vantage point, Eric Thornton of the *Manchester Evening News* opined, on the eve of the big kick-off, 'I am sanguine about Rochdale and Southport's ability to win on tour. However, you never know. That's the very reason why the game maintains its strong hold.'

Thornton withheld his opinion on the most fraught and life-affecting issue of the day – bread rationing – but his paper carried news of a further twist to the tale. 'YOUR OWN BREAD – AND

3 COURSES' was the front-page headline, 'Anybody eating in a restaurant who takes his own bread is still entitled to be served with three other courses. This decision has been reached by the Ministry of Food following advice given to its members by the Hotels and Restaurants' Association that, pending a decision, they should regard bread, whether supplied by the restaurant or the customer, as one of the three courses entitled to be served. The ministry has issued a notice saying, "There is obviously no offence if a customer takes bread out of his pocket or bag and eats it with his meal. We do not think it reasonable to say that if he first gave it to the waiter to put on a plate for him, an offence is thereby created."'

The ministry's ruling was of interest to two of the four businesses which showed their support for Doncaster Rovers by taking out advertisements on the front of the programme (priced two pence) for the opener. The front page bore a picture of Rovers' Belle Vue ground above adverts for: the Danum Hotel in High Street ('Ind. Coope & Allsopps Burton Ales on draught and Double Diamond in bottle – telephone 2261'); S.M. Wilson & Sons Ltd, Luxury Coach Proprietors ('Let us quote you for the Football Match or the Panto – telephone 53259'); Co-Operative Cafe, Station Road ('Good Food, Quick Service, Reasonable Prices – telephone 2455/8') and Pennells Seedsmen & Nurserymen ('Everything For The Garden … Doncaster Rovers Football Ground is treated with Pennell's Lawn Restorer – tel. 3674-5').

Rovers supporters were soon contemplating a celebratory Double Diamond or two in the Danum. 'PICTURE HEADERS BY MADDISON HAVE ROVERS CROWD THRILLED' was the headline in the Saturday night 'Green 'Un'. 'Maddison thrilled the crowd with a clever dribble past three opponents, but Birch succeeded in turning his centre away for a corner,' readers were informed. 'Then, in the tenth minute, Sterland put the ball over from the left wing and MADDISON, racing past Roberts, scored Rovers' first goal. Rochdale replied with a low drive from Makin, brilliantly saved by Ferguson, but gradually, Doncaster got the upper hand and the referee got in the way of a hard drive from Thompson which was well on its way to goal.'

Five minutes before half-time, Rovers doubled their lead when Clarrie Jordan chased a lost cause down the right wing, retrieved the ball when a goal kick seemed inevitable and crossed for Maddison to score. A Rovers stroll seemed nigh, but the visitors' response was impressive. The 'Green 'Un' continued, 'Towards half-time, Rochdale pressed strongly, Hallard and Hargreaves trying hard ground shots, but Ferguson handled them safely. Cunliffe, who was an almost incessant cause of trouble to the Rovers' defence, suddenly cut in and fired a shot across goal, but it went wide.' Five minutes after the break, 'a skidding ball shot between Archer and Swallow, leaving CUNLIFFE with a clear field. He raced away and shot into the net as Ferguson advanced.'

There, due to pressing deadlines, the detail from Donny ended, though there was news of a goal fest at Grimethorpe, 'A muddy field and a greasy ball did not allow good football at Grimethorpe, where a young Wath team were equal to the task of keeping out the home side. Scorers for the home team were LAW (2) and HALLIDAY. Wath replied with goals from WILLIAMS and JACKMAN. Half-time; Grimethorpe Rovers 3 Wath Wanderers 2.'

There was also a plea from the editor, 'DON'T BLAME THE NEWSAGENT': 'Please tell your friend, if he has been unable to get the "Green 'Un", not to blame the newsagent. Circumstances over which we have no control necessitated temporary limits – but they are only TEMPORARY. Tell your disappointed friend he will get his copy regularly if he places an order before September 28, by which time all irksome restrictions will have been removed.'

Rochdale were defeated but far from disgraced and the eve-of-match optimism expressed by Scrutator in the *Rochdale Observer* was undiminished, 'Mr Jackie Bestall, the Doncaster manager, and his directors were probably the most nervous people on the Belle Vue enclosure during the last ten minutes. Rochdale were doing their utmost to snatch an elusive equaliser. It did not come, however, and Doncaster managed to hold their slender lead, yet had the ball run just a little better for the Rochdale forwards, the game might easily have ended in a draw. Doncaster were a smart and workmanlike side with an extremely dangerous forward line. The fact that they were playing on their own enclosure with the vociferous support of their own supporters weighed the scales just sufficiently in their favour. But Rochdale were their equals in the football sense, and the visitors' work, no less than Doncaster's, was instrumental in keeping most of the play of a high standard considering it was the first game of the season and the disadvantages of heavy rain and a greasy ball.'

Scrutator's positivity proved justified as Rochdale enjoyed a strong campaign, finishing in sixth place. For Bestall's side, the season just got better and better. They won 33 of 42 league games, losing just three, and scored 123 goals to finish eight points clear of runners-up Rotherham and 16 clear of third-placed Chester. They won 11 of their first 12 games and went on to secure the most wins ever in a league season, a record which stood until Birmingham City broke it in 2024. Their 18 away league victories was also a record. Donny failed to score in only two of 42 games, scoring four fours and eight fives and beating Barrow 8-0 and Carlisle 9-2. Jordan scored 42 league goals to attract the interest of Sheffield Wednesday for whom he signed the following season for £6,000 plus Arnold Lowes.

Mao Tse Tung, who never attended a match at Doncaster Rovers (although it has been suggested that, during a clandestine visit to England in late 1926, he was among the 4,487 crowd at Sincil Bank for Rovers' goalless draw at Lincoln City), famously said that 'every great march begins with a first step'. Rovers' great march to the Division Three North title had begun, with a humble first step, a narrow victory over unlucky Rochdale.

30

Football League Division One
Aston Villa 0 Middlesbrough 1 (HT: 0-0)
Scorers – Middlesbrough: Mannion
Attendance: 50,000

'The football season's here again, thank goodness, so we've something more to think about than the Paris Conference and the Nuremberg Trials.'

RESIDENTS OF Birmingham had a cornucopia of leisure options at their disposal on the afternoon of 31 August 1946.

At 3pm, Aston Villa would meet Middlesbrough at Villa Park in a much-anticipated match between two teams regarded in some quarters as potential Football League champions. The home team enjoyed a massive supporter base – Villa's FA Cup quarter-final against Derby County five months earlier attracted 76,588 – so the stadium was likely to draw the biggest crowd in the Second City that day. But there was plenty else going on.

An alternative football option was presented nearby, at The Hawthorns which hosted a Central League fixture between the reserves of West Bromwich Albion and Manchester United. Those craving a broader spectrum of sports entertainment could head for Henry Road Playing Field, near the Swan, Yardley. Here, the Grand Sports and Fete organised by the Daily Worker, Communist Party and Young Communist League promised races, tug-of-war, revolving horse, beat the goalkeeper competition, music, dancing and a baby show.

Murder Without Crime, 'a thrilling play by J. Lee Thompson', was the matinee at the Alexandra Theatre while the Theatre Royal hosted

Good-night Vienna, a romantic musical, starring James Etherington, Marjorie Brown, Teddie St Denis and Jackie Hunter. The Odeon cinema enticed movie fans with George Bernard Shaw's *Caesar and Cleopatra* 'in Technicolour with Vivian Leigh and Claude Rains'. At Edgbaston Reservoir, Butlin's Amusement Park, open from 2pm to dusk, offered roller skating, boating lake, 'kiddies paddling pool and all latest amusements'. Bearing in mind the poor weather, a safer bet was perhaps 'House & Furniture 1946 – A Demonstration', arranged by the Bournville Village Trust at No. 5 Charfield Close, Bournville. The good people of Birmingham mulled over all these options while also looking forward to more pleasure in the pipeline. Coming down the track in seven days' time was Stourport-on-Severn Land and Water Carnival. This would include a jazz band competition, illuminated boats and firework display and culminate in 'the crowning of the carnival queen by Big Bill Campbell'.

On the day in question, 50,000 people, perhaps including Big Bill Campbell, plumped for Villa Park. Into Aston they poured, as they had since Villa's glory days when Queen Victoria was on the throne, in celebration of the return of proper football and the hope of excitement and goals. Supporters of both teams harboured recent happy memories of golden, goal-laden seasons. Middlesbrough's Division Two title triumph of 1926/27 was powered by 122 goals, a divisional record, of which 59 were scored by George Camsell. Villa's 1930/31 campaign brought them a Division One record 128 goals (although they still finished only second to Arsenal) including 49 from Tom 'Pongo' Waring. Camsell, signed from Durham City, went on to score 345 goals in 453 games for Boro. Waring, a £4,700 purchase from Tranmere Rovers, scored 159 goals in 215 games for Villa. Great strikers. Great days. Could the Villa and Boro 'Class of 1946/47' evoke the magic of George and Pongo?

The *Birmingham Daily Gazette* correspondent was not so sure. He voiced excitement at the arrival of the big kick-off but also reservations about Villa's attack, 'Tomorrow afternoon is football's D-day. Millions of soccer enthusiasts, eager for a glimpse of big-time football after seven drawn-out years of "regional fare", will make their way to grounds all over the country ready for the kick-off that will herald in the greatest season of soccer since that fateful first Saturday in September 1939. Villa start off with a home game against Middlesbrough whose forward line was fast making a name for itself towards the end of last season. Surprisingly enough, Villa have decided not to play Ashton, their close-season capture from Wolves. He will not be turning out at all tomorrow, but will be standing by in case of injuries for the match with Everton at Aston on Monday evening. Fellow townsmen Dixon and Dodds fill the inside-forward positions. In defence, Villa are undoubtedly strong, but the chief question is whether the halves can combine with the attack to produce soccer fast enough to cope with the speed-up in the game that is bound to come. Key to Villa's forward line is Dixon. Towards the end of last season, he was the player who, by his sheer enthusiasm, fine ball control, and intelligent scheming, put some zip into a Villa front line that had lost some of its sting.'

Villa had secured inside-forward Johnny Dixon from close to Middlesbrough territory in the north-east, signing him as an amateur from Spennymoor Town. The Geordie was to become a Villa great and lead them to FA Cup glory in 1957, but his Football League debut proved forgettable. The Villa hordes were left wondering if they'd be better off with Big Bill Campbell up front, as their attack palpably failed to show that sting. The match took 88 minutes to yield a goal and then it came for the visitors, from a scrambled effort from Wilf Mannion.

'BORO HAD STAR TRIO' was the headline in the *Sunday Sun*, 'Middlesbrough inside-forward trio Mannion, Fenton and Dews were the stars at Villa Park. Their persistent beating of the Villa offside traps made them always a danger and in the last 20 minutes or so when they were right on top, it was a wonder they didn't score more often. There is little doubt they would have done if the Villa had had anyone in goal but Rutherford. He was the acme of security and yet at the same time took chances that nine goalkeepers out of ten would never take.

'The Villa's inside three, Edwards, Dixon and Dodds, were not the equals of Middlesbrough's. Dixon and Dodds, the Hebburn boys, who have been seen frequently as guests in north-east football during the war, lacked the experience of the Middlesbrough attackers, and it was in this department that Villa really failed. Hardwick and Gordon played grand defensive football for Middlesbrough, and so did Cumming, though he had a lot less to do than Rutherford. The goal that decided the issue was scored by Mannion in the 88th minute.'

That Mannion was the match winner provided a happy twist to the powerful story of a man who had heroically served, and suffered heavily for, his country. Middlesbrough-born Mannion was among more than 338,000 soldiers evacuated from Dunkirk in 1940 – a local newspaper reported that he had been killed. Happily, that wasn't the case and he then fought in Italy where he was wounded. Sent to Cairo to convalesce, he developed malaria, but having been challenged by serious illness as well as injury, Mannion had shown the strength to recover completely enough to play football at the very top. After making his Boro bow at Villa Park, his excellent early season form earned him an England debut, against Northern Ireland at Windsor Park, Belfast, on 28 September. He scored a hat-trick in England's 7-2 win.

While Boro fans rejoiced at a winning start, the pleasure was even greater for those who had the confidence to mark their team down for an away win on the coupon. The Churches Committee on Gambling's lecture (see Chapter 1) notwithstanding, the pools coupons remained an integral part of the fun for many football fans and *Sunday Sun* columnist John Polwarth tapped into this affection, 'The football season's here again, thank goodness, so we've something more to think about than the Paris Conference and the Nuremberg Trials. While hundreds of poor footballers are jumping up and down and sideways, under the watchful eyes of the trainers, thousands of even poorer punters are standing patiently at street corners, getting into training for the postal order queue. Not that we have anything but praise for the pools. In pre-pool days, hundreds of illiterates could sign their names only with an "X". Today they can also do a "1" and a "2".

'The coupons have changed a bit this year. We see the famous line, "Winnings payable at ..." is missing. There's no place for sarcasm on a pool coupon – though they still call us "investors," we notice. We think the promoters could improve things even more. For a long time we've felt that the seamen of Shields have an unfair advantage in this matter of football forecasts. With a wife in every port, it's too easy to find eight homes.'

While *Sun* readers chuckled away at Mr Polwarth's witticism and basked in Boro's win, back in Birmingham the inquest began into

Villa's anticlimactic start. Under the headline 'WASTED EFFORTS AT VILLA PARK', the *Birmingham Daily Gazette*'s report spared only goalkeeper Joe Rutherford (another north-easterner) from criticism, 'Few reputations were enhanced at Villa Park where 50,000 spectators went away cheered only by Rutherford. Even Middlesbrough, winners through a Mannion-scrambled goal two minutes from time, never produced football above the mediocre, and it was more hard work than skill which gave them the points. Quick tackling and prompt switching of the ball gave early promise of things to come, but they never came. Instead, speed in the tackle persisted, and defeated its own purpose, both teams parting with the ball too hurriedly – and aimlessly. There was too much wasted effort and too little of the smooth, concerted movement. Villa gave more than they took in the first half and promised better when the second half opened and Dixon led hectic assaults on the Boro goal. They then faded out till they had only Rutherford to thank that the deficit was confined to a single goal. He thoroughly deserved the ovation the crowd stayed to give him.

'Dixon was the best of a ragged front line; debutant Dodds not impressive. He worked hard but his passing was faulty. The halves were more destructive than constructive, and even at that wilted under pressure and left too much to Potts and Cummins. They would have done better to keep the ball close to the ground. Hardwick, Shepherdson and Mannion were Middlesbrough's best.'

Ahead of both Villa and Boro lay solid, if unspectacular, campaigns, culminating in top-ten finishes – eighth and tenth respectively – though, for Villa, things got worse before they got better. Two days after losing to Middlesbrough, they were at home again, to champions Everton. Again they lost 1-0 and again it was an uninspiring spectacle. 'It was a pathetic sight to see two sides, whose names are rich in tradition, play ragged and unmethodical football,' reported the *Gazette*. 'Before the season began both these sides were freely tipped as possible First Division title challengers but on last night's display it is obvious that, if this is to happen, drastic changes will have to be made. Early season impressions can often be false but Villa's weaknesses are all too glaring to demand cautious diagnosis. Summed up in a word, they are slow – much too slow and cumbersome for most of the First Division opposition that lies ahead.'

31

Football League Division Three South
Exeter City 1 Torquay United 1 (HT: 0-1)
Scorers – Exeter City: Wright; Torquay United: Kernick
Attendance: 11,468

'A good footballer, he played the typical Scottish game and controlled the ball as well as any player on view.'

IT HAD been a busy week for the mayor of Torquay. While the players and supporters of Exeter City and Torquay United looked forward to starting the season with an enticing Devon derby, Alderman Courtenay Thomas Bowden was hosting his socks off as his counterparts from around the country dropped by. Some years would elapse before John Cleese, a six-year-old boy growing up in Weston-super-Mare, incubating an early passion for Bristol City, delivered the immortal line, 'That is Torquay, madam,' to a grumpy Mrs Richards. But the town was already charming visitors from far and wide and, most enthusiastically, Oldham. 'The past ten days have been notable for the number of mayoral colleagues Alderman Bowden has received at the Town Hall,' reported the *Torquay Times*. 'First came the lord mayor and lady mayoress of Leeds, then the mayor and mayoress of Oldham, followed by Alderman J. Cochran JP, of Leyton. All of these expressed their great admiration for Torquay – the mayor of Oldham, I am told, was almost lyrical – and also for its Town Hall. The last visitor was the socialist mayor of Poplar – a lady – who travelled down by car. No doubt Alderman Bowden is looking forward to the days when he will have enough leisure time to return these courtesy visits!'

It was also a busy week for the chairman of Exeter City, but then, for Sidney Thomas, it had been a busy few decades. The history of every professional football club includes great figures, central to its creation, survival and prosperity. Nowhere was anyone more integral to the existence of a club than Thomas at Exeter. As a 15-year-old, in 1900, he started playing for St Sidwell's United, whom he helped to win the Exeter and District League title. Thomas was a good player on the field (he scored 40 goals in the 1901/02 season) but a powerhouse off it. He became secretary in the club's second season and in 1904, while still a teenager, assisted with the administration when St Sidwell's became Exeter City. He played in the Grecians' first match, a 2-1 win over the 110th First Royal Artillery on 10 September 1904, and scored the winner.

Thomas remained club secretary for 31 years, overseeing the club's entry into the Football League in 1920, before stepping up to join the board. He was a natural choice as chairman, in which capacity, on 27 August 1946, he addressed the Grecians' supporters about prospects for the coming season. The *Western Times* reported, 'A meeting at Exeter Guildhall on Tuesday, convened by The Grecians' Association, in support of Exeter City Football Club, was addressed by, among others, Mr S.H. Thomas (chairman of the directors) who said that in the year ahead the directors had budgeted for an expenditure approaching £8,000 on wages, and to that amount had to be added travelling costs, hotel expenses, and other commitments which would bring the total liability to about £12,000. It was evident, therefore, that the club would need an average home gate of £600 clear to pay its way and provide for next year's summer wages. The club was out to build a team for promotion.'

A promotion challenge appeared realistic. Since joining the Football League, Exeter had more than held their own in Division Three South and knitted in a few highlights. In 1931 they reached the FA Cup quarter-finals, holding the mighty Sunderland to a 1-1 draw at Roker Park before losing the replay 4-2 in front of 20,984 at St James Park. Two years later they were tantalisingly close to promotion, finishing second to Brentford at a time when only one club went up. When the 1939/40 season was aborted, the Grecians had started well, placed second in the table with five points from three games. They aspired to join fellow Devonians Plymouth Argyle in Division Two as soon as possible.

The one point that Exeter dropped in the snippet of the 1939/40 season was in an opening-day 2-2 draw with Torquay. The visitors were pleased with the result. They were the south-west's newest Football League entrants, having replaced Aberdare Athletic in 1927. The Welsh club's six seasons in the league ended after a second re-election ballot. The first vote ended 21-21 but Torquay won the second 26-19 and on 27 August 1927 played their inaugural Football League fixture, against Exeter at Plainmoor. That was a draw too, 1-1. Torquay thereafter resided largely in the bottom half of Division Three South until the war arrived, at which point, having drawn all three games, they were on course to become the first Football League side ever to draw every league game in a season.

In 1946, Exeter went into the opening-day derby as favourites in front of a full-house crowd which, reported the *Torbay Express,* included an illustrious guest, 'Football League secretary Mr Fred Howarth, at present holidaying in the west country, will be at St James Park, Exeter, tomorrow afternoon to see the game between Exeter City and Torquay United. Today's report from the Park was that, with the exception of 80 seats, all the reserved stand accommodation has been taken up. The game will start at 3.15 and Exeter will be represented by their Probables 11 which was so surprisingly beaten in last week's trial fixture. Plainmoor will stage a friendly fixture between the United Reserves and a team from the Royal Naval Barracks, Devonport.'

The chaps who made up the Exeter Possibles team seven days earlier, having beaten the Probables 6-4, might have felt slightly aggrieved that manager George Roughton stuck with the Probables. Their angst may well have then manifested itself in some chuntering as the match wore on. Despite sustaining a first-half injury which reduced them to ten fit men and a hobbling passenger, Torquay looked the stronger team.

The visitors took an early lead when Exeter goalkeeper Bert Hoyle came out for a cross and didn't make it. The ball ran loose to blacksmith's son Dudley Kernick, who had guested for the Grecians during the war, and he shot into the empty net. Exeter responded with some first-half pressure but with veteran goalkeeper Phil Joslin in fine form, Torquay held firm despite taking a blow just before half-time when centre-half Bert Head was crocked. Head came out for the second half but could do little more than limp around the left wing. When Exeter equalised soon after the break, through a sharp turn and shot by Ray Wright, victory appeared to beckon them. Instead, it was beleaguered Torquay who finished the stronger.

'INJURY KEPT UNITED FROM BEATING THE CITY' was the headline in Monday's *Torbay Express*, 'Torquay United have every reason to be fully satisfied with their opening performance of the season, at Exeter on Saturday, when they shared the points after a hard-fought game. Exeter were superior in the first half but were foiled over and over again by Joslin, still one of the best goalkeepers in the Third Division. He was grandly supported by resolute full-backs in Keeton and Calland. While Exeter were in the ascendancy before the interval, a vastly different tale was told afterwards. The more youthful Torquay side lasted better and played fast, trustful and intelligent football, frequently harassing the uncertain Exeter rearguard. Twice in the final minutes, the United came within an ace of snatching victory when a couple of corner kicks led to hectic scrambles on the home goal mouth and it was only by desperate packing that Exeter survived. If Head, the Torquay centre-half, had not sustained an injury just before the interval, the United would probably have started the season with a win. Head played in the outside-left position throughout the second half and the reshuffled Torquay team fought courageously and with surprising pace to give the City many frights.'

In the *Western Morning News*, Exonian extolled the virtues of Joslin. The 30-year-old was much loved by Torquay's supporters for his sense of fun, shown by impromptu gymnastic displays on the crossbar during pre-match warm-ups. His goalkeeping skills also appealed, 'Honours of a grimly contested first half between Exeter City and Torquay United at St James Park went to Joslin in particular and his defensive colleagues. For it was Joslin, a brilliant goalkeeper, Keeton and Markham, a resolute full-back partnership, and Phillips, Head and Markham, a trio of hardworking, tenacious and quick-tackling half-backs, who successfully defied the City's intense pressure during this period. Thereafter, a different story had to be told. Torquay lasted better than the City, and despite a reshuffle of their team, had rather more of the second half play. Taking all factors into account, the result, a draw, one goal each, was a fitting result of this Devon derby. Of the two sides, the City had the more finesse but it was polish which lacked sparkle for the movements were not carried through with sufficient pace. Without being so crafty, the younger United were every bit as dangerous. They had speed and directness to pit against an Exeter defence which was suspect under pressure. Final thrills of the match came when Ebdon ran through at speed, drew Joslin out only to shoot low and inches wide of the far upright, and then when Torquay swiftly transferred play to force a couple of corners which led to tense skirmishes in the Exeter goalmouth.'

Exonian liked the look of Bill Harrower, who had just joined Torquay from Third Lanark and was to cross Devon to join the Grecians for £1,000 in July 1948. 'I admired the clever, constructive work of Harrower, at inside-right,' he reported. 'A good footballer, he played the typical Scottish game and controlled the ball as well as any player on view. Wardle had a disappointing match and he certainly missed the chance of the afternoon through delaying his effort and allowing Joslin to advance and fluster him into slicing the ball wide from half a dozen yards range.'

It was a frustrating afternoon for Exeter but nothing that Sid Thomas had not seen many times before. Most importantly, the £600 gate receipts required to keep the club going had been harvested. The great man remained chairman until 1957 when he was appointed president of the club. The future was to bring the Grecians many vicissitudes, including a severe financial crisis when the ageing Thomas made a donation to help the club survive. A true Exeter City legend.

For Torquay, it was a highly satisfactory start and they went on to finish above Exeter in the final Division Three South table – 11th to 15th. And alongside the encouraging report in Monday's *Torbay Express*, there was more heartwarming news – 'AUSTRALIAN FOOD FOR OLD FOLK. DISTRIBUTION AT TORQUAY' – with the indefatigable Alderman Bowden at the heart of it.

The *Express* wrote, 'The second distribution of food from overseas was made at Torquay Town Hall today. The food was handed out to 250 aged and needy people and was a gift from various parts of Australia. A similar number of people will receive parcels tomorrow and on Wednesday and Thursday. The mayor and mayoress (Alderman and Mrs C.T. Bowden) and the deputy mayor and deputy mayoress (Alderman and Mrs A.J. Allams) distributed the gifts. Each person received a plum pudding or raisins, a tin of meat or sausages, and a tin of honey, cheese, jam or beans. The Mayor, addressing the recipients, said he was glad to see so many happy people. He thanked all who had given assistance, remarking that much of the food had arrived in bulk and it had to be made up into definite quantities. They greatly appreciated the kindness of people in Australia who had so generously thought of those in this country.'

32

Scottish League A
St Mirren 0 Celtic 1 (HT: 0-1)
Scorers – Celtic: Cantwell
Attendance: 12,000

'If championships were won by the mere expenditure of energy, these two teams might easily be at the top of the league. They tried all they knew. Few of them knew enough.'

THE LAST week of August 1946 was accompanied by rotten weather, better suited to November 1875, but it takes more than high wind and torrential rain to deter sports-loving Scots. The inclement meteorological conditions failed to prevent bumper attendances at St Mirren v Celtic and the Sutherland Sheep Dog Trials. 'Judging by the crowd that flocked to Love Street today, Celtic are as attractive at the foot of the league as they are at the top,' reported the *Glasgow Evening Times*. 'Of course, the Saints' recent successes had a lot to do with the attendance, which looked like being the best of the season.' A little further north, the first postwar event held by Sutherland Sheep Dog Trials Association drew a record attendance. 'The trials not only provided an excellent display of sheepdog-handling but also formed one of the chief events of the season in the county, many shooting lodges and mansion houses being represented,' revealed the *John O'Groat Journal*. 'The only setback in a day which was otherwise an unqualified success was a breakdown in the weather in the afternoon. The task set the dogs required efficient handling, the chief difficulty being in the "lift", the grass being so long that many of the dogs failed to find the sheep.'

Football fans in the vicinity were no less dogged, the *Journal* continued, '"I'm thinking your no' wise" (not wise) was a salutation bedraggled spectators hurrying home from the Thurso Pentland-Wick Academy match at Thurso on Wednesday evening could be prepared for from their women folk. The game was played in wind and rain and their choice of sheltered vantage points took some of the crowd about as far away from the pitch as late-comers to the terracing on a Scotland-England international day are to the Hampden Park pitch.' Wick Academy won 3-1 and the spectators who braved the elements were rewarded with an entertaining game. At Love Street, less so. Rarely are referees offered as candidates for man of the match – they are invariably mentioned only to be questioned or criticised – so when the *Sunday Post* correspondent at St Mirren v Celtic suggested that 'if a vote had been taken among the crowd as to the best performer on the field, there is not much doubt that they would have plumped for Peter Craigmyle', it suggested it wasn't a thriller.

For Celtic, at least it was a first win of the season, at the seventh attempt. The giant club was close to the lowest point in its history. While arch-rivals Rangers strode into the postwar landscape strong, confident and favourites to win the league, Celtic stumbled into it. To a large extent, they were the architects of their own trouble, as Graham McColl explains in *The Official Biography of Celtic*, 'Celtic had failed to match the efforts of other Scottish clubs in maintaining standards during wartime. Unlike Hibernian and Rangers and others they opted not to use the widely adopted system of playing high-calibre international footballers from the Football League who were relocated to Scotland while serving with the armed forces. Morton fielded top-notch England internationals such as Tommy Lawton and Stanley Matthews. Celtic did no such thing.'

Their emphasis on homegrown players, laudable up to a point, left a thin and inexperienced squad. To tackle the crisis, in July 1945, they turned to one of their greatest former players: Jimmy McGrory, scorer of 468 goals in 445 games for the club. McGrory was an integral part of the teams which won the league in 1926 and 1936 and the Scottish Cup in 1925, 1931, 1933 and 1937. In the summer of 1945, he took on the manager's job with a mighty mission ahead. Another blow soon followed when star winger Jimmy Delaney joined Matt Busby's Manchester United for £4,000 following a dispute over wages.

Celtic arrived in Paisley on 31 August 1946 without a win after six games. Their supporters, especially those who had shelled out 40 shillings for a season ticket, were not happy. St Mirren's fans, on the other hand, were quite chirpy after a promising start. In the last week, the Saints had scored four against a strong Aberdeen side and drawn at Hearts, a brace of strong results which would have evoked great pride from Messrs Shearer, Muir and Graham.

St Mirren FC was created in 1875 when a group of young men decided to form a sports club with teams to compete at cricket and rugby. Two years later, Mr J. Shearer, from Renfrew, suggested that the club should venture into the new-fangled pastime of 'association football' which was becoming popular. The committee approved the idea, and Mr F. Muir and Mr T. Graham were charged with buying the necessary equipment. 'With money tight, the two men walked to Glasgow to visit Harry McNeil's sports shop,' relates stmirren.info. 'There they purchased a ball and other equipment. Mr McNeil, a Queen's Park man, enquired about where the men had come from and, upon hearing that they had walked from Paisley, he told them that they were the first people from the town to purchase a football and as a gesture of goodwill he gave them the money for their train fare home and wished them good luck in the venture. On 29 September 1877 a trial match was held between two teams to see who would represent St Mirren FC in their first match the following week. The two teams lined up in the 1-2-2-6 formation that was used at the time.'

By 1946, the Saints had shed the 2-2-6 formation but, after scoring six goals in two games against potential title challengers, they fancied their chances against troubled Celtic. The struggling giants arrived with only Hamilton and Third Lanark below them in the table, and the transitional nature of their team is suggested by the *Glasgow Evening Times* update, 'Lamb, the St Anthony's boy, made his debut at right-back. Cantwell was at outside-right and Rae, home on leave, at centre-forward.' It was to be Peter Lamb's only game for Celtic. Jack Cantwell made just nine appearances. Joe Rae stayed a little longer, playing 45 games, before joining Torquay United in 1948.

Of Cantwell's nine outings, just one brought a win, thanks to his winning goal at Love Street. The match, and indeed the goal, was far from pretty. 'Early indications were that it would be a needle game,' said the *Evening Times*. 'Some of the tackling was extremely wild, and twice the referee intervened. The ceremony of having players shaking hands after they had committed a glaring foul seemed oddly out of place. The players ran big risks and the trainers were very busy. In nine minutes, Cantwell scored for Celtic. Rae shoved the ball out, and Cantwell escaped a very poor attempt to tackle him. There was not much in his shot either. Newlands misjudged it completely and the ball passed under the keeper's body – altogether a bit of a gift. St Mirren were squandering chances and their power of football was to no avail. Any football there was came from Celtic.'

Sunday Post correspondent George McLachlan was very clear that the victory should not gloss over the big problems at Parkhead. Under the headline 'ONE IN A WILDERNESS', he wrote, 'Their first victory will bring a measure of pleasure to Celtic. But the more discerning Parkhead supporter will still feel anxious about the team's future. If championships were won by the mere expenditure of energy, these two teams might easily be at the top of the league. They tried all they knew. Few of them knew enough.

'The football craft of Tommy Kiernan, typical of the stuff we used to expect from the whole Celtic team, seemed almost out of place in this company. To a lesser extent, Deakin was in the same position in the Love Street line-up. He had even poorer support than Kiernan. St Mirren's main trouble is that they have too many full-backs. There were five yesterday. Although three were shown in the programme as half-backs. With all their faults, Saints brought out the best in Miller. Three one-handed saves from close-in headers were right out of the top drawer.'

Glasgow Evening Times columnist Alan Breck could see little light at the end of Celtic's tunnel, 'I saw St Mirren losing to Celtic by a Cantwell goal and, my word, how most of the fellows in both teams biffed that ball about. I doubt if I have ever seen a First League match so bereft of studied play. It was my first view of both teams and when I think of the Celtic that used to be I am almost in despair. I know the Parkhead troubles, the suspensions and the injuries. Even so, I wonder how long it will be before Celtic resume their place as a leader of

Scottish style and ways. Miller in goal and McAulay and Kiernan in the outfield were Celtic men all right, while St Mirren had real footballers in Deakin and McLaren. To most of the others, football appeared to be a game of just hitting the ball as hard as can be and hoping for the best. St Mirren had a shocking day of ill luck and wretched finishing at goal. Otherwise, they must have won handsomely.'

Breck then turned his attention to Love Street, the wider issue of what supporters want from a matchday experience and, in particular, their increasing desire to sit down, 'When I was at St Mirren's ground for the Celtic match, I noticed the progress in making the terrace accommodation up to date. At the Love Street end the terrace has been stepped and barriers erected. The stepping continues a good way round, and the enclosure in front of the stand is completed. I counted almost 100 people looking at the match from the overlooking tenement windows. They represented over £5 in gate money, or in the 30 home league games, £150. The free look will be abolished when St Mirren, as must be their ambition, build a covered enclosure or even a stand on that side. Really the clubs will have to get down to better accommodation or spectators. People don't want to stand nowadays. They want to sit and are prepared to pay a reasonable price for the privilege. It is surprising that even clubs with covered enclosures do not put seats in them. They do not require to be elaborate. The clubs which lead the way with more seating are going to reap a dividend. Rangers realise that, and they have 10,000 seats already. This lack of seating is partly responsible for the situation which has developed at Parkhead this week. There are only 4,000 seats at Celtic Park, and when the regular customers have been satisfied, there are only 2,500 available.'

Celtic rallied, to a degree, to finish seventh, but the crisis was to deepen. They ended the following season in 12th, just four points above relegation. They were to continue to flounder for a good while but, though nobody knew it at the time, a mighty seed was planted during their home game with St Mirren on Saturday, 8 December 1951. Celtic won 2-1, Jim Lafferty scoring both goals, and the *Sunday Post* reported, 'Jock Stein made a quiet debut, attempting nothing spectacular.'

33

Football League Division Three South
Northampton Town 4 Swindon Town 1 (HT: 1-0)
Scorers – Northampton Town: Heaselgrave (2), Morrall (2); Swindon: Williams
Attendance: 12,013

'The skeleton of wartime utility football has been pushed into the cupboard, and the door slammed, locked and bolted. Let it rattle its bones unheard and unmourned.'

FOR AWAY fans, a timeless ingredient of a day out at football is finding the ground. Getting lost en route to a game, on the way to the home team's town or city or, having located that, losing your bearings in the streets around the ground, can be a bind. In 1946, travelling supporters had an additional complication to tackle.

The *Wiltshire News* aired the subject in its Wiltshire Wanderings column, written by Roger Roundabout. On a recent drive into the countryside, Roger was struck by a wartime restriction that was still to be restored: 'DEARTH OF SIGNPOSTS': 'Although the war has been over nearly a year, there are numerous signposts still awaiting reinstatement. A few days ago, I was motoring in the three counties of Wiltshire, Somerset and Dorset and on many parts of all three counties I found motorists lost because signs, taken away as a defence measure during the war, had not been replaced. One has to be fair to the officials whose duty it is to see that road signs are up, by classifying which counties are the biggest culprits. I would say Dorset are the biggest culprits, although Ralph Wightman of *Country Magazine* fame is always lauding the praises of his home county. I must admit that Dorset is still able to live up to Mr Wightman's description – lovely Dorset. But that natural beauty is a poor consolation for the motorist who gets lost in the maze of endless pretty Dorset lanes. Somerset also has many crossroads not fully signposted, and I saw motorists "left guessing" in the cider county. Wiltshire has made a fair effort to signpost its roads, but I would suggest there is room for improvement on Salisbury Plain. If motorists can avoid "wild goose chasing" because they can't find their route, petrol can be saved.'

On 31 August 1946, the paucity of signposts in Dorset did not concern supporters of Swindon Town unless they erred badly at the very start of their journey and headed south instead of north. The trip across the Midlands to Northampton was relatively short and simple, and Swindon fans embarked upon it confident of finding the venue. They were less confident of seeing their team win there. Earlier in 1946, the teams met twice on successive Saturdays in the Division Three (South) Cup, and the Robins emphatically lost both games, 4-1 at home and 5-1 at Northampton.

Hit hard by the conflict, their ground taken over by the War Department and huts erected on the pitch to house prisoners, the club almost disbanded. It came through, though, and advanced into the new era with ambitious plans. 'SWINDON FOOTBALL TAKES ON NEW LEASE OF LIFE' announced the *Swindon Advertiser*'s *Football Pink*: 'DIRECTORS AND MANAGEMENT MAKING ALL-OUT BID TO GIVE CLUB DIVISION TWO STATUS'. Details were supplied, in elegantly supportive fashion, by RCE, a correspondent clearly well trusted and connected at the club, 'The skeleton of wartime utility football has been pushed into the cupboard, and the door slammed, locked and bolted. Let it rattle its bones unheard and unmourned, for today British football takes on a new lease of life, freshened with the thrills and attractions of competitive games. Swindon Town, like every other club in the country, is out to raise its reputation and its gates to as high a plane as possible. The directors realise that to attract even bigger crowds they would have to field a winning side. For this reason, they have given Mr Louis Page (secretary-manager) a free hand during the "close-season" in the matter of acquiring new blood. In addition, they signed contracts for the general brightening up of the County Ground.

'The new players look good on trial form but personally I don't give a fig for such games. They are more trouble than they are worth, and like the rest of the managers up and down the country, Mr Page breathed a sigh of relief when his men left the field last Saturday without any of them sustaining injury. Swindon's professional staff is a comparatively small one. They cannot afford to have any injuries if they are to field strong Division Three and Combination sides.

'Whichever way you look at it, and whatever the results, the men holding the reins of office at the County Ground have made courageous efforts to bring the standard of football in Swindon up to a level worthy of the town's size. It was hoped to have the ground and clubhouse entirely redecorated in time for the first match, but unforeseen difficulties have cropped up and the work will be completed at the earliest possible date. Meanwhile, construction of the new bathrooms etc., is well advanced.'

Swindon's team at Northampton included twins Alf and Bill Stephens, whose powerful story RCE had brought to his readers earlier in the week under the headline 'WAS MYSTERY MAN IN PUBLIC TRIAL. FOUR YEARS TOGETHER IN POW CAMPS', 'The identity of the mystery inside-forward who impressed in Swindon Town's trial on Saturday is disclosed as Alfred Stephens, twin brother of the new centre-forward, Bill Stephens. Mr Louis Page made this announcement this morning, and added that he had completed Alfred's transfer to the Town from Leeds United. Stephens is a progressive type of forward who can fill either inside-right or inside-left positions with equal ability. You probably guessed his identity from his natural facial resemblance, but what you wouldn't know is the story of their adventures together during the war. Both were on Leeds United's books before the war, and both joined the army. Bill was in the RASC and Alf in the Engineers. Both went out East and were captured in 1941. Within an hour of Bill being taken prisoner, he had met up with Alf and, for the next four years, they kept together, sharing the privations and discomforts of prison camps in Germany and Italy. Now, after a short separation, they are back together again in Town's colours. The parable of the inseparable twins in real life.'

Waiting for the Stephens twins at the County Ground was a Cobblers side which had signed off from the Football League seven years earlier on a low note. Their last game before the league's suspension ended Bournemouth 10 Northampton 0. 'Comment is almost unnecessary,' reported the *Northamptonshire Evening Telegraph*. 'The side was overwhelmed and the defence cracked badly in the second half.'

That was a bruising experience for Tom Smith in only his third match as manager, having just succeeded Warney Cresswell (known to Everton fans as the 'Prince of Full-Backs'). Seven years later, Smith was still at the helm and decided to pursue a strategy eschewed by most clubs. Most started the 1946/47 season with numerous debutants, some starting pretty much from scratch either by choice or out of necessity, but Smith stuck with the tried and tested.

'COBBLERS RELY ON 'OLD BRIGADE' announced the *Northamptonshire Mercury*. 'Northampton Cobblers will rely chiefly on the 'old brigade' for the opening match with Swindon Town at The County Ground tomorrow,' reported Flag-kick. 'All the team, except Jack Jones the goalkeeper, did duty last season. Jones, of course, is a prewar Cobbler who has been just as successful with the clubs he helped during the wartime seasons as he was at Northampton. One blow to the Cobblers is the news that Harry Lowery will not be available for many games this season. It is not expected that he will get time off from his business firm to play much. Another player, Hughes, has recently joined the RAF but being stationed at Melton Mowbray he will be available for most games. In the forward line, everyone will welcome the return of Gordon Roberts. Both he and Heaselgrave are now fit after their long absences last season through operations and, if these players have recovered their best form, it will make a big difference to the attack.'

Flag-kick's preview proved prophetic. Smethwick-born Sammy Heaselgrave, who scored 57 goals in 163 games for West Bromwich Albion before moving east in November 1945, was highly influential as Swindon were swept away. The visitors' goalkeeper Frank Boulton was first beaten in the 30th minute when Heaselgrave exchanged a one-two with Alf Morrall and added a slick finish. Shortly after half-time, it was 2-0 when Boulton saved from Morrall but Heaselgrave tapped in the rebound. Morrall added two late goals as the Cobblers pulled away for a commanding win, but it was the visitors' consolation, or at least the reaction to it, that was to make the headlines.

'A surprising incident followed the Town's solitary goal,' reported the *Swindon Advertiser*. 'Williams netted after the ball had been bobbing about in a melee in the goalmouth and immediately the referee (Mr G. Johnson) whistled and pointed to the centre spot almost the whole of the Northampton team rushed up and clustered around him, gesticulating excitedly and apparently disputing the decision on the grounds that one of the Swindon forwards had handled the ball. Accompanied by loud booing from the spectators, the incident continued for more than a minute, the players refusing to let the referee walk away. Eventually play resumed, but spasms of booing continued to the final whistle.'

In its celebratory account of the win, the *Northampton Mercury* mentioned, but did not condemn, the players' mobbing of the ref, 'The Cobblers' form against Swindon fully merited victory, even though Morrell's two goals came in the closing minutes. The Cobblers' declared policy of using last season to build up a ready-made side paid full dividend. Swindon, introducing seven new men, played without a plan, despite some individual talent and the valiant efforts of their skipper, the Welsh international Lucas, to weld them into a workmanlike combination. Jones, the Cobblers' goalkeeper, quickly proved he is as clever and agile as ever. Two other men made welcome returns. Roberts, whose injury had kept him out of the side since February, was a great success. Always too fast for his opponents, he centred accurately and never hesitated to cut into goal when necessary. Heaselgrave too showed that the summer's rest has brought full recovery from his knee operation, and he scored the first two goals.

'Swindon's goal resulted in a remarkable scene. So definite were the Cobblers' players that the ball had been handled before Williams scored that they formed up in one solid mass round the referee, declining to let him pass for several minutes. He refused their request to consult a linesman to the accompaniment of a storm of booing from the spectators.'

The poor, harangued Mr Johnson made it on to the back page of the following day's *People*. In a round-up of opening-day highlights, Long Acre revealed, in idiosyncratic note form, 'Disputed goal by Swindon at Northampton nearly caused ructions. The referee was surrounded by angry Northants players who grasped him by arms and shoulders, would not allow him to return to the centre for more than a minute. Disapproving crowd whistled and hooted – just like the "good" old days, what!'

For Northampton, it was a most satisfactory start – an emphatic victory and a big crowd, generating receipts of £1,023 16s 3d. They seldom hit those heights in the months ahead, finishing 13th, but did have a happy day in the FA Cup. Roberts and Morrall shared four goals to see off ambitious non-league outfit Peterborough 8-1 in a second-round second replay at Highfield Road on 23 December. Archie Garrett, soon to join Birmingham City for a club-record £10,000, scored the other four.

Swindon blew hot as the season deepened. They bounced back from losing to Northampton to win the next two games, scoring ten goals, 3-2 at home to Cardiff and 7-0 at home to Aldershot, and rose to finish the season in fourth place. Roger the Roundabout, meanwhile, continued to chug around Wiltshire and make his rye observations. What, one wonders, would he have had to say about Swindon's infamous Magic Roundabout which was installed in 1972 and surprises, intrigues and confuses drivers new to the town to this day?

34

Football League Division Three North
Gateshead 2 Crewe Alexandra 1 (HT: 0-0)
Scorers – Gateshead: Clark, Howden; Crewe Alexandra: Shaw
Attendance: 4,000

'Though we may not realise it, all of us have had hundreds of demonstrations of how electricity can bring down the rain.'

THE RETURN of the Football League was a big topic of conversation across the country at the end of August 1946, but it had a serious challenger as the main topic – the weather. The country had been swept by day after day of unseasonal gales and rain. It was the wettest August for more than 30 years and people were wondering why. Why was this month, usually so sunny, dry and holiday-friendly, so miserably wet?

That was the big question. In the north-east of England, readers of the *Sunday Sun* were presented with the answer. It was, explained the paper's columnist Boyd Ewing in a thrilling exclusive, all down to electricity.

'WAS IT ELECTRIC RAIN?' was the attention-grabbing headline, as Ewing wrote, 'Yesterday ended the wettest August since 1912. While hundreds of thousands of holiday makers waited for the rain to stop, they read in their newspapers of radio control for farm ploughs, radar for the Queen Elizabeth and the Mersey, and how Britain's grid network of high tension cables was piping the power for the export drive in the factories. How many realised that there could be any link between the rains that ruined their holidays – and electricity? Yet it is not nearly as impossible as it sounds.

'In this electrical age, in a country that becomes more dependent on electricity every month, the atmosphere has never been so crowded with electrical discharges. Television has started up again. There are many more radio transmitting masts than ever before. The RAF are still operating hundreds erected during the war. All our electrical installations mean more discharges in the atmosphere, and it is possible that a saturation point has now been reached when our weather is being affected. Though we may not realise it, all of us have had hundreds of demonstrations of how electricity can bring down the rain. A heavy black thunder cloud creeps over. We get out raincoats and umbrellas – and then wait. Surprisingly, the rain holds off, until the first flash of lightning. Then, within seconds, giant raindrops arrive. Another phenomenon, almost certainly due to electricity, though we cannot observe it, is that a light cloud will often cause a heavy downpour, while a far denser one passes over without sending down the rain.

'If a sample of a rain cloud could be trapped, and examined under a microscope of extreme power, it would be shown to consist of minute globules of moisture, perfectly formed like miniature soap bubbles. Normally, these tiny globules are always bumping up against each other but they bounce off again because of their perfect spherical shape. Only when they are pulled and distorted do they stick together and eventually grow into a raindrop. One of the main ways in which "pull" is exerted on the moisture globules is through electrical influence. How this happens has been shown in the laboratory by allowing water from a fine jet to fall as spray into a metal bath. When an electrified rod is brought near to the spray, it changes into drops of water which patter noisily into the bath. The rod acts exactly like the flash of lightning that sets off the rain during a thunderstorm.'

No way could the *Crewe Chronicle* compete with such a remarkable revelation. They did, however, bring a comprehensive round-up of Crewe Alexandra manager Frank Hill's activity ahead of their Division Three North visit to Gateshead. On the Thursday before the game, the paper revealed, Hill travelled to Staffordshire to finally conclude the on-off saga of signing of outside-right Fred Basnett from Stoke City. Basnett agreed terms with Portsmouth, then spoke to Hill, then veered back towards Pompey but finally plumped for Crewe because he didn't want to move down south. 'He will play at outside-right in Crewe's team at Gateshead on Saturday,' reported the *Chronicle*. 'The Crewe manager also visited Manchester on Wednesday and completed the transfer of Jack Stanley, half-back from Rochdale. He played in the trial game at Crewe on Saturday, and he will also assist Crewe at Gateshead. The Alexandra have also signed Arthur Rice, inside-forward, who played for them before the war and has recently been demobilised. He joined Crewe, with Stevens, from Stockport County.'

As well as the plethora of ins, there was an out as the *Chronicle* revealed that 'CREWE BOY JOINS THE VILLA', 'Aston Villa have signed on amateur forms J. Capewell, centre-forward or inside-right. He played in Crewe schoolboy football with Bedford-street Schools and more recently with Crewe Steam Sheds where he is an apprentice mechanic.'

If Crewe's team was heavily reshaped, no less so was Gateshead's, as chairman Bill Tulip confirmed in his wary comments to the *Newcastle Journal*, 'I believe we have several "finds" in the reserve team. As for the first team, we have so many newcomers that I prefer to reserve any comments until after the opening games of the season. We are hoping for the best.'

Of the 44 fixtures on the day of the big kick-off, the one at Redheugh Park was perhaps most difficult to call. There was nothing to choose between Gateshead and Crewe. They had advanced along parallel lines in the years up to the war. In 1936/37, both struggled and were separated in the final table only by goal average which put Crewe above the re-election line and Gateshead below it. The Tynesiders were comfortably reprieved by their fellow league members, polling 34 votes to fend off Shrewsbury Town (12), South Liverpool (four) and Wigan Athletic (one). In the following two seasons, both improved to finish in the top half of the table. In the first of those campaigns, Gateshead did the double over Crewe. In the second, Crewe did the double. As pools punters around the country pored over their coupons to come up with jackpot-winning draws, this was a strong candidate.

On the eve of the game, a football-related matter surfaced in the letters column of the *Newcastle Evening Chronicle*. Underneath a masterpiece of concision from Mrs A.M. Patten of Low Fell – 'Isn't it time the maximum controlled price of fruit, particularly apples, was reduced?' – Football Fan from Gateshead addressed the eternally debated subject of players' wages, 'Not many tradesmen can boast of having more than £7 after working hard for 47 hours per week, yet the footballers, who depend upon the support of these people for their living, are not satisfied with £10. Personally, I think they are very well paid and I look forward to the day when it will be possible to reduce the admission charges and restore the "bob" end. Yours, etc.' What would Football Fan from Gateshead make of players' salaries of 2026?

The match transpired to be as tight as seemed likely; Gateshead edged the first half but were denied by fine work from Ron Mawson. Back in his native terrain, the Bishop Auckland-born goalkeeper was applauded even by the home fans after making superb saves from Bill Temple, clean through in a one-on-one, and Cec McCormack. Early in the second half, the home crowd rose to applaud Mawson when he produced a masterpiece of a save, twisting low to claw a header from Temple away from the bottom corner. Pelé and Gordon Banks, aged eight and five respectively and growing up playing football in the streets of Sheffield and Bauru, would recreate the moment in Guadalajara 24 years later.

With 15 minutes left, the game remained goalless, largely due to Mawson's excellence but then, as the *Crewe Chronicle* reported, 'After the second half had been in progress half an hour, Gateshead took the lead with a beautiful goal. Clark cut in from the wing and beat Mawson with an upward drive. The lead was short-lived, however, for a few minutes later, following a goalmouth scrimmage, Shaw put the ball into an untenanted goal. Some exciting exchanges ensued. With only seven minutes to go, Howden, always a thorn in the side of Crewe's defence, flashed down the wing and worked his way to within shooting distance to beat Mawson with a curling shot. It was a fine solo effort but poor consolation to Crewe who, at that stage of the game, had, at least, hoped to earn one point. True, Mawson brought off some capital saves and was the hero of the first half but, as a team, Crewe were every bit as good as the north-easteners.'

That assessment was not shared by Alf Groomley, beavering away in the Redheugh Park press box on behalf of the *Sunday Sun*. 'Gateshead were full value for their 2-1 victory over Crewe Alexandra at Redheugh Park,' wrote Alf under the headline 'VALUE FOR VICTORY', 'and had it not been for some inspired first-half goalkeeping by Mawson the score might easily have been doubled. The first half was all Gateshead with McCormack, Clark and Howson forcing Mawson to bring off saves which earned him deserved applause. McCormack, despite the close attention of Hayes, held the forward line together well and in the first half fully tested Mawson with a hard low drive. Clark's was a picture goal. He sidestepped two players, cut in and beat Mawson with a terrific drive, while Howden's effort, to restore Gateshead's lead, curled just inside the upright.'

Groomley then gave his readers, and the home players, the benefit of his opinion on some individuals, 'Callender (T.) was the stalwart of the home defence with Cassidy better in promoting attack than defending. Both full-backs did well but Dawson was uncertain under pressure. Franklin was the better of the backs but only Boothway and Shaw seriously troubled the home defenders.'

Both teams deserved great credit for serving up such an entertaining game despite all the electricity-driven rain. Such weather did, of course, make life difficult for all – players, officials, spectators and also members of the noble profession of football reporter. Back in Cheshire, at Sandbach, the Manchester Amateur League fixture between Fodens and Ferguson Pailin was played in 'torrential rain, hail, thunder and lightning'. The *Crewe Chronicle*'s correspondent reported, 'Had the referee abandoned the match, no one would have been surprised, indeed the players would have welcomed such a decision. However, the man in charge decided otherwise and the game was, more or less, of an aquatic character.' And the hostile conditions did not deter the ultra-diligent, unnamed reporter from seeking out the ref in the deluge, post-match, to get to the bottom of a mystery, 'Many spectators had an optical delusion when they thought that a cross-shot from Roberts had penetrated the goal. They thought it was disallowed for some infringement. The *Chronicle* reporter, however, ascertained from the referee that the ball fell on the top of the net close to the cross bar and not inside.'

For Gateshead and Crewe, contrasting futures lay ahead. The latter was to unfold a long and productive Football League existence, enjoy time in the second tier and become renowned as a production line of talented young players. Gateshead were far less fortunate, dropping out of the league in 1960 when they lost a re-election vote in favour of Peterborough United. This despite Gateshead having an average placing of ninth in 21 seasons in Division Three North and having only applied for re-election twice. The decisive factor was their northern location as votes were swayed towards the more accessible Cambridgeshire club. Gateshead was too far north for some. For others, it was not far enough north – they applied to join the Scottish League but were unsuccessful there too.

35

Football League Division Three South
Queens Park Rangers 2 Watford 1 (HT: 1-0)
Scorers – Queens Park Rangers: Mallett (2); Watford: Robertson
Attendance: 22,000

'Queues for 607 trolley buses formed at every stop and often it took a 15-minute wait before you could get on a bus. Queens Park Rangers were beginning the new season with unparalleled support.'

QUEENS PARK Rangers approached the 1946/47 season with ambitious plans, a dynamic manager, sky-high levels of local enthusiasm and felicitations from the inaugural guest on *Desert Island Discs*. Dave Mangnall, manager since April 1944, was building something special.

In the 1945/46 season, Mangnall steered the club to the Division Three South (North) title and through a thrilling FA Cup run in which they beat Barnet (8-3 on aggregate), Ipswich Town (6-0), Crystal Palace (1-0 in a replay at Craven Cottage after both legs finished 0-0) and Southampton (5-3) before losing to neighbours Brentford (3-1) in the fifth round. Mangnall, born in Wigan and formerly a miner at Doncaster Colliery, was a confident, combative character. His playing career as a striker with Leeds United, Huddersfield Town, Birmingham City, West Ham United and Millwall appeared to have ended in 1938 following a wages dispute with the latter. However, as the *Acton Gazette* reported, 'In 1939, he received a telegram from the Rangers, asking him if he was aware that he had been given a free transfer from Millwall. He wasn't aware, but soon after that telegram came, he signed for the Rangers.'

Mangnall played for QPR and scored many goals throughout the war before accepting the role of player-manager. His vivacious Lancastrian passion was soon driving the team forward and after such a strong 1945/46 season, the club aspired to its first promotion. Five days before the big kick-off, and Rangers' opener at home to Watford, Mangnall was among those to address supporters about the club's plans. The *Acton Gazette* was there, 'A lively meeting was held at Ellerslie Road School, Shepherds Bush, on Monday when the Queens Park Rangers Supporters' Club combined with the development association in calling fans together for a pep talk. The meeting was opened by Mr R.A. Starnes, leading light of the development association, who presided jointly with Mr Stone of the supporters' club. Queens Park Rangers are out to raise £25,000 to build themselves a new double-decker stand, and to do this they must be sure of a 15,000 gate at their first-team matches and at least 6,000 at reserve matches. They are asking for 5,000 life members, who will pay a fee of £5 on joining and then been sure of their seat at matches. For those who can't afford to pay the £5 outright, they have a modified scheme. This consists of a 2/6d entrance fee to matches, until £5 5s is paid – this way it works out 5/ dearer.

'Dave Mangnall, Rangers' cheery north country manager, said that every member of the team had had an offer made for him recently. A full-time scout was employed by the club, and he was at the moment in Scotland with instructions to buy where he could. Mangnall appeals to supporters not to go off to away matches in the coming season but to support the reserve team at home, where he would like to see a 6,000 gate each game. "It's very nice to hear two or three hundred of you in the crowd shouting for us at an away match," said Dave, "but we can get by, I think, and we need your support at home." Rangers' manager also made an appeal for furnished "digs" for some of his married players, and for bachelor quarters too – travelling expenses are proving considerably higher than rents!'

Alongside Mangnall's down-to-earth northern magnetism, some southern showbiz sophistication was then stirred into the mix. The microphone was passed to London-born music journalist and composer Ray Sonin, a scriptwriter for radio comedian Vic Oliver, a huge star who was the first castaway on BBC Radio's *Desert Island Discs* programme, in January 1942.

'A surprise speaker at the meeting was Mr Ray Sonin, who writes the script for Vic Oliver's radio shows. Mr Sonin said that he imagined that most people were wondering what right he, who worked for the BBC, had to address a football gathering. The secret was that he formerly earned an honest living as a football reporter and was a keen Rangers supporter. Vic Oliver, though he supported Brentford, had signed an autographed photograph of himself, signed "Good luck to QPR, best wishes for speedy promotion, Vic Oliver". Mr Sonin put the following resolution to the meeting and then stepped down amid deafening applause, "This meeting pledges its wholehearted encouragement and unswerving loyalty to take Queens Park Rangers through to the Second Division and beyond."'

Facing this tide of positivity on the opening day of the season was an improving Watford team led by Bill Findlay. After joining the league in 1920, the Hertfordshire club endured some tough times, on and off the field, in the 20s, but settled in the following decade to string together a sequence of decent seasons. Up to the war, they recorded five successive top-six finishes in Division Three South, the last two under former Third Lanark, Liverpool and Leicester City half-back Findlay who was appointed in January 1937. Within months of taking over, he guided the team to a share, with Millwall, of the Southern Section Cup, the two-legged final ending 3-3. In stormy west London, could Findlay's men rain on Rangers' parade?

Inside a packed and buzzing Loftus Road, QPR almost had the perfect start. They were awarded an early penalty but skipper Alf Ridyard, a £625 signing from West Bromwich Albion in 1938, put it wide. Rangers had the better of the first half but were thwarted by a combination of the goal frame and Watford goalkeeper Tommy Rigg until three minutes before the break. Then a flowing move created an opening for Joe Mallett and he planted a sweet header past Rigg.

To the delight of his wife, Bertha, and the rest of the Rangers fans, Mallett made it 2-0 soon after half-time but Watford responded with strong pressure and Rangers keeper Reg Allen, who spent three years in a Japanese prisoner-of-war camp, was called upon to make several fine saves. Allen was finally beaten by a late goal by Len Robertson, and then again when Watford netted, only for the effort to be disallowed for offside. Rangers held on to give most of the big crowd the perfect start – an entertaining game and a win.

'In spite of the slippery ground both sides showed surprising speed and accuracy in an evenly divided first half,' reported the *Weekly Dispatch*. 'Inside-forwards Hatton and Mallett combined well for Rangers, and Ridyard, who missed a penalty during the first five minutes, also kept the attack moving. Rigg, Watford's goalkeeper, made several clearances, but Mallett put Rangers ahead just before the interval when he headed in a corner from McEwan. Queens Park Rangers found their men better after the resumption and Mallett put them further ahead with a low shot. Robertson replied for Watford with ten minutes to play.'

With more space at his disposal than the *Dispatch* stringer, the *Acton Gazette* scribe did full justice to the joy of the occasion. Football was back and brought immense colour, cheer and exuberance to a wet afternoon in west London, 'Saturday afternoon shoppers in Acton knew something was happening eastwards on the Uxbridge-road. Queues for 607 trolley buses formed at every stop and often it took a 15-minute wait before you could get on a bus. Queens Park Rangers were beginning the new season with unparalleled support. A 22,000 gate for their first match of the 1946/47 season, against Watford, made the directors at Loftus-road rub their hands – even the Press box was full. The gales of last midweek had died down to breezes by kick-off at 3.15pm. Cheering crowds packed the stands. It was like the 1930s over again to hear the familiar cry, "Up the Rangers", echo round.

'Despite the fact that one felt there should have been many more goals – there were enough opportunities on both sides – the game was a good one, and supporters went home well satisfied from this first game of the season.'

The relative shortage of goals was a resounding tribute to the skills of Allen and Rigg, and they were not the only goalkeepers from the locality to shine that afternoon. Fred Hunt also took star billing as Acton Town opened their season with a thrilling 5-3 win over Staines at the Staines Greyhound Stadium. As the home team poured forward in the closing minutes, Hunt saved two penalties.

While the *Gazette*'s ebullient report from Loftus Road evoked golden memories of the 1930s, the paper's front page looked forward. It brought sporting news of a futuristic nature and arrow chuckers were at the heart of it as the very latest technology was displayed at Acton Town Hall. 'DART BROADCAST FROM ACTON': 'A darts match between Joe Hitchcock and Jim Pike, captains of the St Dunstan's and *News of the World* teams, was broadcast from Acton Town Hall on Monday night. Stewart MacPherson, the BBC commentator, joined the teams on the stage and stood just behind the microphone which relayed the match to the loudspeakers around the hall. Mr MacPherson's microphone was a tiny portable which he held very close to his mouth and into which he spoke so softly that even the spectators in the front row could not hear, although they could see his mouth moving. Radio listeners could hear the slap of the darts on the board, and the voice of the other announcer calling scores out to the spectators.

'Very interesting to watch was the electric scorer. This consisted of a replica dart board covered in push buttons, and wired to a huge canvas dart board above it. As the darts found their marks, the operator at the electric scorer pressed the appropriate button on the corresponding part of his board, and on the giant score board above his head an electric lamp lit up the corresponding spot.'

Exciting times – and plenty more excitement lay ahead for Rangers fans as their promotion aspirations were soon to be fulfilled. Mangnall's side finished second to Cardiff City that season, with only one club promoted, but the following year that club was QPR after they finished top, four points clear of Bournemouth. They also enjoyed a brilliant FA Cup run, beating Gillingham, Stoke City and Luton Town to reach the quarter-finals where they took Derby County to a replay.

Reg Allen was a huge part of that success before joining Manchester United in 1950 for £11,000, then a world-record fee for a goalkeeper. He made his United debut, against Fulham at Old Trafford on 19 August 1950, 11 days after Phil Parkes entered the world in Sedgley, Staffordshire. Parkes was to become another record goalkeeper sale from QPR, to West Ham for £565,000 in 1979.

Tommy Rigg left Watford to return to his native north-east and play for Consett before joining Gillingham in August 1951. He played 201 games and kept 43 clean sheets for the Gills. Fred Hunt's future appears to be undocumented.

For Watford, a thin decade lay ahead. 'The next 12 years might be classed as the least remarkable in the club's history,' writes Geoff Wicken on the club website, watfordfc.com. 'There were few highlights for fans to celebrate as Watford failed to challenge regularly at the top end of Division Three South in the way that they had in the late 1930s. The FA Cup offered the chance to escape the humdrum, but only one campaign delivered anything to recall fondly – a victory away to second division Preston in 1950, followed by a narrow and controversial home defeat to Manchester United. Otherwise, results were disappointing, especially the three defeats to non-league opposition within four years.'

No one at Watford could possibly know, as they tasted narrow defeat in west London on 31 August 1946, that the seeds of unforeseeably great days for the club were in the process of being sown. On 15 September 1944, a baby boy was born in Worksop, his family soon to move to Scunthorpe where his wonderful football life would begin. That was Graham Taylor. On 25 March 1947, in Pinner, meanwhile, along came Reginald Kenneth Dwight – Elton John. Taylor would one day be manager of Watford and England. John would become the only chairman of a Football League club ever to attend Lincoln City's Sincil Bank ground in sequinned purple tights.

36

Football League Division Three South
Brighton 0 Port Vale 0
Attendance: 11,000

'A ding-dong duel had provided a number of incidents sufficient to keep a crowd of 11,000 continually on the qui vive.'

'A goalless draw at Hove was a fitting result to a game which was almost entirely lacking in incidents.'

MAYBE IT was something in the south-coast air, but Brighton & Hove Albion emulated Portsmouth in publishing, in their opening-day programme, the very latest league table. It listed all 22 teams in the Division Three South, locked together on no points, of course, but the Seagulls' programme editor took the liberty of including his club as Albion, rather than Brighton. This tweak put them top of the table, rather than second behind Aldershot Town. It was an endearing gesture of loyalty. Less clear were his motives for dumping Walsall on the bottom of the table, below Watford, and putting Mansfield Town beneath Northampton Town, Norwich City and Notts County.

The programme as a whole (number one in the series, price two pence) bore the hallmarks of testing times for the football club and surrounding business community. Several pages contained blank areas with the message, 'For advertising in this programme and on the ground, apply Frank Mason & Co. Ltd. Tel. Hove 2750.' Some space had been sold. On page two, readers were informed that 'The best way is the electric way' by Brighton Corporation Electricity Department, Electric House, Castle Square, Brighton. If only Brighton Corporation Electricity Department knew what *Sunday Sun* writer Boyd Ewing knew (see Chapter 34), it might not have rained so much in the days leading up to the big kick-off.

On page three, supporters were reminded, 'DON'T FORGET'. The Brighton and Hove Omnibus Company are running Omnibuses to and from the Ground every match.' Plenty of fans took advantage of the facility on 31 August as more than 12,000 packed into the Goldstone Ground to see the Seagulls launch their quest for a first promotion since joining the Football League in 1920.

'New hopes arise in the hearts of the Albion supporters this afternoon,' wrote Victor Champion, who covered the club as Crusader for the *Brighton Evening Argus*. 'There is every good reason for those hopes, for there is a feeling of confidence in the Albion camp. The first reason for this was last Saturday's trial match when most of the newcomers were on view. They gave a good impression, and the general opinion is that with their available resources, the executive have done a good stroke of work during the close season. Of course, it is much too early to clinch on to an 11 which will produce that consistent form necessary to emerge out of the Third Division where we have been members far too long. Changes in the composition of the side are bound to come, and we should not be too concerned about them, for I can never recollect when the Albion had the material for such a good reserve side. No team can progress unless they have that standby, for every position in the senior side should be duplicated and, if at all possible, triplicated.

'For this our first match of the season we welcome old friends in Port Vale. Like ourselves, they have undergone many changes since 1939. Under practically a new directorate, they have hardly a player who did service with them on prewar days, and with the Second Division in view they have got together quite a useful number of players. However we shall be able to get a line on their future hopes by their performance this afternoon.'

Crusader was correct. Vale had experienced considerable transition which was very much ongoing, particularly in terms of their home ground. The club had withdrawn from regional competition after 1940, continuing as a junior team to keep the club in existence, until restarting in 1944. That year, to alleviate some of the financial pressure, they sold their ground in Hanley – the Old Recreation Ground, now the car park of the Potteries Shopping Centre – to the local council for £13,000. They continued to play there but as tenants rather than owners, and drew up ambitious plans for a new 70,000-capacity stadium in Burslem. That scheme would be seriously modified before Vale Park became a reality but, under the shrewd stewardship of chairman Thomas Flint, the club weathered all the war adversity. Two days before the visit to Brighton, Flint, having just handed over the chairmanship to Thomas Holdcroft, funded a slap-up spread for the staff and players.

'PORT VALE PLAYERS ENTERTAINED', reported the *Staffordshire Sentinel*, 'An eve-of-the-season dinner to his fellow directors and staff and players of Port Vale Football Club was given by Mr T.W. Flint at Burgess' Café, Newcastle, last night. A very pleasant prelude to tomorrow's opening of the new football campaign, the gathering was a happy thought on the part of Mr Flint in appreciation of the presentation made to him by the club and players some time ago on his retirement from the chairmanship.

'Alderman W.A. Holdcroft (chairman of the club) presided and with him at the top table were Mr J. Diffin (vice-chairman), Alderman A. Hollins and Messrs F.W. Burgess, A.E. Wilbraham and G. Dodson (directors). Mr P. Cooper, another director, was unable to attend. A company of over 40 was present. The chairman said it was a very happy thought on Mr Flint's part to arrange the gathering. It was on the eve of another season on which very much depended. They attached very great importance to what happened at Brighton next Saturday. We believe (went on the speaker) that every one of the players is as keen as we are to put Port Vale back in the division to which they belong – the Second Division. We are of the opinion that we shall have 90 minutes triers seeking to give us the result we want.

'Referring to the club's ground improvements, Alderman Holdcroft declared that no effort had been spared. The club had gone to much expense, and the ground was better today than ever before in meeting Home Office and other requirements. In his opinion, they wanted £750 home gates to carry on as it ought to be. Last season they paid out over £250 a week on travelling expenses and tax before there was a penny for wages. The expenditure would be far more this season. Mr W. Frith (manager) said Mr Flint was going on holiday, and if the team could get a point or two on Saturday, it would increase Mr Flint's enjoyment of his holiday and would be the best way of repaying him for his hospitality.'

Awaiting Billy Frith's side in Brighton was a Goldstone Ground which had taken its share of damage and disruption. In August 1942, a bomb landed on the North Stand, fortunately not on a matchday so no one was hurt. Three wartime games were abandoned due to air raid alerts. Chelsea's visit in October 1940 lasted just five minutes before players and spectators fled for cover. Understandably, just a few minutes in, the game was still scoreless.

On 31 August 1946, Brighton and Port Vale played the full 90 but also failed to produce a goal – one of only two 0-0 draws that day – thanks largely to the excellence of George Heppell. The Vale goalkeeper's finest moment of the afternoon arrived late on, though his brilliant save from Ernie Marriott's penalty in the closing minutes did not even earn him a name-check in the *Sunday Express*. 'A goalless draw at Hove was a fitting result to a game which was almost entirely lacking in incidents,' *Express* readers were told. 'Brighton should have opened the season with a victory but Marriott, an excellent full-back, failed to profit by a penalty kick. Defenders generally controlled the play: Trainer and Cheadle, the opposing pivot, who was injured late in the game and carried off the field, being very workmanlike. The forwards, however, seldom excelled, although Hindley, the Brighton leader, often made some good individual efforts. In the Port Vale forward line, Bellis, at outside-left, carried off the team honours.'

Press box opinion was divided on the merits of the match. While the *Sunday Express* scribe was so unimpressed, Placer in the *Staffordshire Sentinel* found plenty to enthuse about, 'There were moments of high drama in the match in which Port Vale, in a goalless struggle, took a point from Brighton and Hove Albion at Hove on Saturday. They occurred in the second half, though before the teams changed ends, a ding-dong duel had provided a number of incidents sufficient to keep a crowd of 11,000 continually on the qui vive. Midway through the second stage of the game, when it was very much touch-and-go who would get a goal, Brighton moved in from the left. Cheadle seemed to have successfully dealt with the threat by getting the better of Hindley, the Brighton inside-left, in a tussle for possession, but suddenly the centre-half's attempted clearance was deflected by Hindley's leg towards the Vale goal. In a flash, Hindley was on the ball and, although at an angle to the goal, did everything he could in accuracy and power of shooting to bring about the Vale goal's downfall. Heppell, however, who had already distinguished himself in the first half, was not disposed to fall victim this time. With a fine effort, he flung himself at the ball and punched it away. The hovering Bloomfield on the Brighton right wing got it, and the danger was still there. And then calamity! As he closed in, Butler, in the anxiety of the moment, fouled him, and it was the inevitable penalty. Even then, Heppell refused to be beaten. Magnificently, he got up to Marriott's rocketing shot before it sped under the bar and turned it over the top.

'Considering the Vale's superiority, it would have been a tragedy had they found themselves behind as a result of this incident. Yet they were not to go scot free. When the drama was continued, events were not without a touch of tragedy for the Hanley team. In jumping to head the ball at the same time as Hindley, Cheadle was severely cut across the forehead, and was taken off to have four stitches inserted in the wound. Cheadle, with head bandaged, made an appearance at outside-left a few minutes before the end.'

It took more than a head cut to topple Tommy Cheadle. He was made of stern stuff, as shown by his Port Vale provenance – a hand grenade. 'In 1944, on a battlefield in Holland, Cheadle threw a faulty grenade which went off almost in his hand,' relates the club website, port-vale.co.uk. 'Tommy woke up in hospital, where he met Ken Fish, PT instructor and Vale trainer. After being demobbed, Tommy went to see Ken and got a trial at Vale, which led to him signing professional forms in May 1946. Solid as a rock, he soon held down a regular place in the Vale defence and became captain. He was known as Wooden Head because of his toughness.'

Port Vale owed their opening-day point in part to the steel of 'Wooden Head'. Back in the Potteries, meanwhile, the police were perplexed by the actions of a sieve head. 'Somebody went without the Sunday joint yesterday, for it is lying in cold storage, together with a quantity of bacon, at Stoke Police Office,' reported the *Sentinel*. 'The meat and bacon were found in a canvas bag in London-road, Stoke, on Saturday, and were taken to the police office where they now await their owner.'

For Wooden Head and for Vale, great days lay around the corner. The club finally moved into Vale Park in 1950, a crowd of 30,196 watching the first competitive match there, a 1-0 win over Newport County. In 1953/54, captained by Cheadle and managed by Freddie Steele, they enjoyed a glorious season, romping to the Division Three North title, 11 points clear of second-placed Barnsley, and coming thrillingly close to making history as the first Third Division side to reach the FA Cup Final. In the semi-final against First Division opponents West Bromwich Albion, in front of 68,221 at Villa Park, they led 1-0 before succumbing to a controversial 2-1 defeat. Albion's winning goal came from a penalty dubiously awarded when Gordon Lee collided with Cheadle in the box. Albert Leake, who scored Vale's goal, then netted what he thought was a late equaliser but it was disallowed for offside – another far from clear decision. The 25,000 Vale fans headed home disappointed but proud. They were soon celebrating promotion.

Brighton supporters had to wait a little longer, but the Seagulls finally escaped Division Three South in 1958 when they went into their last game of the season, at home to Watford, needing a draw to seal the title and promotion. They won 6-0 thanks to five goals from 20-year-old reserve forward Adrian Thorne in front of a crowd of 31,038 which included a 15-year-old Des Lynam.

37

Football League Division Two
Burnley 1 Coventry City 1 (HT: 1-1)
Scorers – Burnley: Kippax; Coventry: Bett
Attendance: 16,971

'The ex-Wolves player was demobilised on Thursday from the Tank Corps, in which he has seen some of the fiercest fighting of the war, including D-Day and the subsequent drive through to Germany.'

FOOTBALL REPORTERS have different types of relationships with the clubs they cover. Most are cordial, founded on a flow of information which is mutually beneficial. Some are fractious, when the reporter or manager, or both, are difficult. Other reporters are very close to the club, pretty much embedded, and to judge from his preview of Burnley's opening-day fixture with Coventry City in 1946, it is safe to say that *Burnley Express* correspondent Sportsman was in that category. He was clearly on good terms with Burnley's manager, the former Everton and England right-half Cliff Britton. 'I expect a big crowd at Turf Moor this afternoon for the visit of Coventry City (kick-off 3.15),' reported Sportsman under the headline 'CLARETS FACE NEW SEASON WITH HIGH CONFIDENCE'. 'It may well be an historic occasion for the Burnley club. A win may mean a great deal towards setting the Clarets on their hard task towards promotion. If team spirit counts – and it is a valuable factor in the success of every side – then Burnley are happily placed. There need be no anxiety on that account, as those privileged to meet the men have been quick to realise.'

Sportsman then waxed lyrical in a way of which Britton and the Burnley board no doubt approved, 'Keenness is a keynote and this has been fostered by the training tactics introduced by Mr Cliff Britton, the manager. Let me again congratulate the Burnley directors on their discernment and enterprise in engaging one who has such an intimate knowledge of football theory and practice. Mr Britton has not only won high honours in the game, at Burnley he is passing on that knowledge for the betterment of the Burnley players. Since they reported for training, in addition to the usual fitness and ball control exercises, they have had talks on tactics and have put them into practice on the ground. They will be putting them to a sterner test today.'

Sportsman rounded off his preview with a bit of housekeeping and a nod to the generosity of Burnley's supporters as he listed the beneficiaries from the previous Saturday's trial game at Turf Moor, 'Spectators are asked to note that the entrance from Belvedere-road, behind the cricket field, will be open for first-team matches. This will be an advantage to those living in the Burnley Lane district. The £136 6s received as a result of the public trial has been allocated as follows: Burnley Victoria Hospital £50 12s; Burnley Nursing Association £20; Reedyford Hospital, Nelson £15 15s; L.F.A Benevolent Fund, Burnley St John Ambulance Association, Burnley Society for the Blind £10 each; League Secretaries and Managers Association, Dr Barnardo's Home and Burnley Police Welfare £5 5s each; Lancashire Referees Association Benevolent Fund, and Burnley House of Help £2 2s each.'

While Britton and his players were busy preparing in north-east Lancashire, down in the west Midlands, Coventry manager Dick Bayliss was simply trying to get a team together. 'Coventry, journeying to unknown Burnley, have only 16 professionals on their full-time playing strength, but for all that they are a useful side and should make their mark,' reported the *Birmingham Daily Gazette.*

The club, like the city of Coventry, had risen again from the horrors of the Blitz. On the evening of Thursday, 14 November 1940, Coventry was hit by the most concentrated attack on a British city in the Second World War. On that clear, moonlit night, German bombers unleashed a firestorm in which 554 people were killed, 865 were injured and more than 4,300 homes and 75 per cent of the city's factories were destroyed. As historian and author Jim Brown relates in his wonderful book, *Ghosts of a Vanished Stadium*, 'On 23 November the *Midland Daily Telegraph* reported, "There will be no football at Highfield Road for a long time, Hitler having done a spot of ploughing up the playing space with a series of bombs, besides knocking a large-sized hole in the new stand. In addition to that, nobody knows the exact whereabouts of the players. It is thought they are all safe, but at the moment it would be impossible to guarantee the raising of a team." The club's directors had no alternative but to suspend operations.'

The city responded with incredible strength. The spirit of Coventry people is unbreakable, and a manifestation of that was the return of the football club. The Bantams (to be renamed the Sky Blues by the visionary Jimmy Hill in 1962) returned to Highfield Road on 25 May 1942 when 5,491 watched a 4-2 friendly win over Birmingham City. Coventry rejoined the regional leagues for the next four seasons, after which Bayliss's mission was to cobble together a team capable of competing in Division Two of the Football League. Players had dispersed far and wide in the preceding years and, on the eve of the visit to Burnley, the *Coventry Evening Telegraph* supplied a vivid example of the astonishing pathways that some had taken, 'George Ashall, Coventry City's wing-forward, became a civilian again on Thursday, and yesterday was signed again at Highfield Road as a full-time pro. Tomorrow, this popular winger, who is equally at home on either wing and will undoubtedly help to strengthen the City side, will be in football boots once more – in the A team. Ashall told the City manager he wanted loosening up and was quite willing to have a run with the young players in their Birmingham Combination match against Stourbridge. The ex-Wolves player was demobilised on Thursday from the Tank Corps, in which he has seen some of the fiercest fighting of the war, including D-Day and the subsequent drive through to Germany. He came from Trieste to get his "ticket" – and to be fitted with a new pair of football boots.'

How would the reconstructed Bantams fare at Turf Moor? Could they record their first win there, their previous four attempts having brought three defeats and a draw with an aggregate score against them of 11-3? These questions were debated by City fans in Canley and Kenilworth, Bell Green and Bedworth, Walsgrave and Warwick, along with another vexing matter: the 'ICE CREAM QUESTION'. 'Recent criticisms of ice cream, amongst them being one from Warwickshire County Council, have led the Ice Cream Alliance Ltd, a trade association with a membership of over 5,000 manufacturers and vendors, to issue a four-page pamphlet in answer to its critics,' revealed the *Warwick and Warwickshire Advertiser*. 'The Ice Cream Alliance is in full agreement with health authorities that the present legislative position can be improved by the laying down of certain agreed standards for ice cream. This would be in the interests of the trade no less than in those of the community, for the trade at present suffers considerably from the uncertainty of the position and the wide divergence in opinion on the part of health authorities.'

Ice cream weather it wasn't when the players took the field at Turf Moor. Steady rain left the surface slippery and the ball greasy – tricky conditions, especially for goalkeepers, but the home side was to encounter a masterclass from Coventry keeper Alf Wood. Aldridge-born Wood was on his way to making 260 consecutive appearances for City between 1945 and 1951 and this was arguably the best of them all. 'Wood, the City goalkeeper, although hampered by a first-half knee injury, played one of the greatest games of his life at Turf Moor today,' related the *Coventry Evening Telegraph*'s Saturday sports edition.

The afternoon didn't start well for Wood when Peter Kippax gave Burnley the lead after only ten minutes. Wood was not deemed culpable by the *Telegraph*, however, as they pointed the finger instead at winger Emilio Aldecoa. One of thousands of Spanish youngsters who sailed from Bilbao to Southampton in 1937, seeking safety from the Spanish Civil War, Aldecoa became the first Spaniard to play professional football in England, for Wolves in 1943. He joined Coventry in August 1945 and carried the can 12 months later, 'The goal provided an object lesson in the fault of a player running the wrong way. Aldecoa, in attempting to beat a man, went back with the ball and tried to pass to Coen, who was blamelessly beaten. Chew went down the wing and shot, the ball was blocked and went out to the waiting Kippax who scored with a fine shot.'

Another tough day at Turf Moor beckoned the Bantams, especially when, a few minutes later, Wood dived at the feet of striker Jack

Billingham and was left limping heavily with a wounded knee. But Coventry hit back before half-time when Ted Roberts's long pass into the box reached Fred Bett, an inside-forward signed that summer from Sunderland, who sent a rising shot into the net. From then on, Wood towered. He was beaten only once, in the closing minutes, when Billingham's shot hit the inside of a post late but the ball was hoofed to safety by Tommy Crawley.

'Burnley had the greater part of the play but Wood's brilliance – it was nothing less – combined with fine defensive work by Mason, Elliott and Crawley, stopped them from getting more than one goal,' wrote Nemo in the *Coventry Evening Telegraph*'s Saturday sports edition. On Monday, he cranked up the goalkeeper's performance even further, 'Hurt in the first half when he made a daring, diving save from the toe of Billingham, the Burnley leader, Wood played better than brilliantly in the second. He saved low shots and high shots, hard shots and soft shots, expected and unexpected shots – he saved them all.'

In the *Burnley Express*, meanwhile, Sportsman showed that, while well connected to the club, he was certainly not afraid to be critical. 'Over-elaboration in front of goal cost Burnley both points at Turf Moor,' he reported under the headline 'FORWARDS' DILLY-DALLY METHODS LOST A POINT'. 'It was a game of more vigour than skill, with the Burnley defence pinning the Coventry attack down to isolated attempts to challenge the home goal and the Burnley forwards persistently getting the City rearguard – and sometimes themselves – into a muddle. Strong had an easy afternoon in contrast to Wood, who was kept constantly on the alert, but made some of Burnley's scoring attempts look insipid by his coolness and anticipation. Indeed, his yellow jersey seemed to have an irresistible attraction for the Clarets' inside men, for they made it their target often enough!'

After describing Coventry's equaliser, Sportsman took the liberty of giving Britton some advice, 'This reverse meant that the forwards had again to build up a lead. They tried hard enough, they were clever enough, but their methods were wrong. There was too much overcrowding in the centre which at times looked like a congested area. Most of the danger came from the wings where Chew and Kippax did what little they were required to do with an efficiency which might have led to goals had they been used better. More full-blooded, first-time shooting and a little less tip-tap might have brought a handsome dividend in goals.'

With such sage counsel, how could the manager fail? Burnley won their next game, 2-0 at Birmingham City, and in the months ahead rose to the challenges of the 'hard task towards promotion' to which the reporter referred in his preview. The Clarets had a wonderful season. They won 22 of their 42 games to gain promotion as runners-up behind Manchester City and reached the FA Cup Final where they lost 1-0 to Charlton Athletic. In their first season back in Division One, they finished third, a level of success which earned Britton a crack at the manager's job at his beloved Everton. He had played for the Toffees when they won the First Division and the FA Cup, but his time there as manager was to be less happy: they finished 18th in each of his first two seasons in charge and, in his third, they finished bottom and were relegated.

That was all far in the future on Monday, 2 September 1946, as Britton leafed through the *Burnley Express* with its copious food for thought. On the back page, readers enjoyed the opinions of Sportsman. On the front sat a scoop of giant proportions – 'PAINTING OF LAMP STANDARDS. SOCIETY'S PROTEST' – delivered in a sentence of giant proportions: 75 words.

'Following the protest by the North-East Lancashire District Committee of the National Society of Painters against the painting of lighting standards by street lighting attendants in the Gas Department, the Gas Committee has replied that it proposes to continue the practice carried out before the war of bona-fide painters undertaking the painting of all the steel lighting standards on the main roads, and employees of the Gas Department undertaking the painting of all cast-iron lampposts.'

38

Football League Division Three North Darlington 4 Southport 2 (HT: 2-1) Scorers – Darlington: Clarke (2), Stubbs (2); Southport: Clough (2) Attendance: 8,913

'I suggest that you deliberately charged this girl 2s for the tomatoes.'

ON SATURDAY, 31 August 1946, the Darlington and District Football League was all prepped and good to go. Pitches marked out, players champing at the bit and referees allocated for the long-awaited opening-day Division A fixture list: Darlington RA v Cockerton (G. Davison), Middleton Wands v Rocket (J.R. Cherry), Barnard Castle v Celtic (E. Dixon), 59th RAC v 62nd RAC (N. Telford) and Bank Top Loco v Rolling Mills (S.R. Bates). Could the Wands cast their spell over Rocket? Would Bank Top loco start the season like a train and roll over Rolling Mills? Who would take the bragging rights in the RAC derby? Exciting times.

One venerable resident of the north-east, however, was not happy. James Welford had just had a bad result in Guisborough. With food shortages still a highly emotive issue, the 75-year-old had copped a conviction and significant fine for selling overpriced tomatoes. Readers of the *Cleveland Standard* were furnished with the full story, 'LINGDALE PENSIONER AND HIS TOMATOES: I WISH I HAD DIED', from which they could decide: was Mr Welford a callous rogue seeking to exploit customers already struggling to make ends meet? Or was he just a well-meaning, short-sighted old boy himself a victim of entrapment by the authorities?

'A 75-year-old Lingdale pensioner appeared at the Guisborough Magistrates Court on Tuesday on a charge of selling tomatoes at a price above the controlled price,' the *Standard* reported, at the top of its front page. 'He was James Welford, of Hillcrest, Stanghow, Lingdale. Welford, defended by Mr J Askew, pleaded not guilty.

'Mr R. Beckwith, prosecuting on behalf of the Skelton and Brotton Food Control Area, said, "This man has committed an offence under the Defence Regulations by selling tomatoes at 2s per pound when the controlled price was 1s 7d. The Order states that no person shall sell tomatoes in excess of the controlled price applicable at the time."

'Mr James Watson, deputy food executive officer for the Skelton and Brotton Food Control Committee, gave to a food office clerk, Miss Waller, half a crown and instructed her to go to Mr Welford and purchase one pound of tomatoes. She got them and handed Welford the half-crown for which she received a sixpenny piece change. She took the tomatoes together with the change to Mr Watson. Mr Watson weighed the tomatoes and found there was one pound, he then went round to see Welford who admitted supplying Miss Waller with the tomatoes but denied having charged her 2s for them, saying, "She gave me two-and-six but I thought I had given her 1s change. It is my eyesight." He offered to refund the money.

'Mr Dodsworth, the food enforcement officer for the area, interviewed Welford and asked him if he knew what the proper price of tomatoes was. Welford said 1s 7d a pound. "If he thought he had given Miss Waller 1s change, that would have meant he was charging below the controlled price which was hardly likely. This man knew full well what the controlled price was. In my submission the mere fact of him saying that he thought he gave her a shilling is no defence at all."

'Mr Watson, deputy food officer, stated that he went to see Mr Welford and told him he was making enquiries resulting from complaints that had come to the Food Office. He told him the matter would be reported. Welford again offered to refund the money.

'Miss Vera Waller, of 23 Oxford-street, Boosbeck, a clerk in the Skelton Food Office, in her evidence, said, "I went to Welford and asked if he had any tomatoes. He said, 'Yes, a few.' I gave him the 2/6 and he gave me 6d change. I then took the tomatoes and the change to Mr Watson."

'Mr Robert Dodsworth, the food enforcement officer, "I went round to see Welford and asked him if he had sold a pound of tomatoes to Miss Waller for two shillings and he replied, 'She asked for a pound of tomatoes. I told her I had a few, I thought I had given her 1s change. I offered to give them a shilling back but they would not take it. I have told the truth.'"

'Mr Askew, on behalf of the defendant, "Mr Welford is a little too old. If Miss Waller had brought up the matter at the time, I suggest that Mr Welford would have immediately put the matter right. He is an old-age pensioner and is not a retailer of tomatoes, he does it merely as a hobby."

'Mr Welford, "I do not reckon to sell tomatoes as a shop, it is at home. I got talking to her and said, 'Where might you come from?' and she said Boosbeck. I said, 'Can't you get any tomatoes there?' and she said no. I did not know I had made a mistake until the officer brought her back. If Miss Waller had said to me, 'Is this the correct change?' I should have immediately given it to her. What I have said is the honest truth."

'Mr Beckwith, "I suggest that you deliberately charged this girl 2s for the tomatoes."

'Welford, "I did not sir, I did not."

'Mr J.E. Watson, in stating the decision of the magistrates, after a short retirement, said, "The court has very carefully considered your case and we are quite satisfied that you are guilty. You will be fined £3 and will also have to pay £2 2s solicitors charges and 10s witnesses' costs – that is £5 12s altogether."

'Welford, "I am an old-age pensioner. I have nothing. I have twice been to the doctors and wish I had died."

'Mr Watson, "You will have four weeks in which to pay the fine."'

Watson was clearly not a man to allow compassion to compromise the course of justice. Welford returned to Lingdale with a hefty fine to find and pondering whether he could spare 1/3 for admission to the Division Three North fixture between Darlington and Southport on Saturday. Boys and forces in uniform would pay only 9d but he qualified on neither count.

Plenty of people did find the requisite 1/3. Almost 9,000, a record league crowd for Feethams, passed through the Twin Towers, walked around the cricket field to the football pitch and took their places for what turned out to be a cracking game.

During the regional wartime competitions, Darlington benefitted from having a big army base nearby. Some fine footballers were stationed at Catterick and sometimes guested for the Quakers, but the ramshackle arrangements of padding out teams with guest players had passed by the Football League's resumption. Darlington approached the big kick-off with some intriguing selection issues to unravel, reported the *Northern Despatch*, 'Darlington open their Third Division programme next Saturday with a home match against Southport and the selection of the side for that match is not going to be an easy matter. In Saturday's practice match, the potential first 11 (Hoops) was beaten 3-2 by the reserves (Whites) and several young players gave displays which suggested distinct possibilities. Allison, a young inside-left from Fence Houses, showed promise and made an excellent partner for Simpson, while other young amateurs to show up well were the 6ft full-back Edgell, from Newcastle, and Saunders, centre-half. Stubbs, the fastest man with the Darlington club, was very much at home at inside-right, and both Bates and Sinclair gave satisfactory performances on the wings.

'Though practice matches cannot by any means be regarded as the final word, Saturday's match had many satisfactory features, and with last season's players showing good form and the promise of the young players, prospects look reasonably good. Chief interest will be centred on Darlington's three new players, Bates from Sheffield Wednesday at outside-right, Sinclair from Chesterfield at outside-left and Barron, formerly of Blackburn Rovers, in goal.'

Southport arrived in the north-east with two new players and a new strip; Bill Hall (an outside-right from Liverpool), Peter Burke (a centre-half from Luton Town) and shirts of green and white hoops instead of the familiar black and white stripes. None of the newcomers were to have great longevity. Green and white was ditched in 1948, Hall was to play just 16 games for the Sandgrounders and Burke's career was as brief as can be. The Darlington game, which pitched him against one of the division's sharpest strikers in Harry Clarke, proved to be his debut and his farewell.

'Burke, the new centre-half from Luton, had a hard time against Clarke,' reported the *Lancashire Daily Post*. 'Southport's other newcomer, Hall, provided most of the openings for the inside men. Clough, too, had a successful match with two goals and more shots than any other player.'

Jimmy Clough – a prisoner of war for five years, after being captured near Dunkirk in May 1940 – opened the scoring in the eighth minute when given freedom in the box to net from 12 yards. The home side replied with heavy pressure and a plethora of corners and equalised five minutes before half-time. 'Darlington got their reward for consistent attacking,' reported the *Daily Post*. 'Clarke shot hard and low into the corner of the net from 20 yards out. Grimsditch flung himself across the goal but had no chance. A minute from the interval, Stubbs put Darlington ahead with a grand header – a first-rate effort.'

Darlington led 2-1 after a first half which was entertaining, though not as goal-laden as another on which the *Post*'s Saturday edition reported. At half-time on the north-west coast, it was Fleetwood 3 Morecambe 2 and 'among the 2,500 spectators present when play opened were over 400 from Morecambe who had travelled by sea'.

At Feethams, the second half brought more goals for the bumper crowd to enjoy. 'A DARLINGTON RECORD GATE. 8,913 THE BEST FOR HOME THIRD DIVISION GAME' was the headline in Monday's *Northern Echo*, 'Darlington started out with a good win in their home match and, in addition, created a new record attendance for a Third Division match at Feethams with a gate of 8,913. The previous best was 8,895 against Wolverhampton in 1924. All three new men, Barron, goalkeeper, Bates, outside-right, and Sinclair, outside-left, did well. The last-named, though he missed an easy chance, did some excellent work. The defence gave the Southport attack little scope. Clarke scored two of the goals, one from a penalty, while the others came from Stubbs, who fully justified his inclusion. Varty also met with much success at inside-left.'

After Halifax referee Harold Moore blew the final whistle, Darlington fans filed back out between the Twin Towers (built in 1913 but still standing proudly when the club departed Feethams in 2003) with two points and a terrific game to toast. Those of a certain vintage also recalled that famous occasion back in 1924 when Wolves, relegated the previous season, arrived top of the table and heading straight back up, but were held to a 1-1 draw. 'Darlington football enthusiasts on Saturday saw what was undoubtedly one of the best games of the season at Feethams, when the Skernesiders entertained Wolverhampton Wanderers, prospective Third (Northern) League champions,' reported the *North Star (Darlington)*. However, the paper gave greater precedence to the Division Two tussle between Crystal Palace and South Shields, 'The playing pitch at Selhurst is a long way from being ideal,' lamented the reporter after Shields' 1-0 defeat. 'It is bumpy, and the ball bounces at awkward angles.'

Southport's 1946/47 season was to evolve into a familiar struggle. With a constantly changing team (they did not field an unchanged line-up until 15 February, the 28th game), they finished 23rd in the table with only Halifax Town below them. Life in the Football League was always a grind for the Sandgrounders, who were there from 1921 to 1978 but never climbed higher than the third tier. The club will, however, always retain a unique place in the history of English football. In the 1918/19 season, having been taken over by the Vulcan Motor & Engineering Company, it competed, for one season only, as Southport Vulcan, the first time a club's name incorporated that of a sponsor.

39

Football League Division One
Manchester United 2 Grimsby Town 1 (HT: 1-0)
Scorers – Manchester United: Mitten, Rowley; Grimsby Town: McGowan
Attendance: 40,000

'Mr Sykes, pedalling quite easily, reached 18mph then drove into the canal without slackening speed.'

'SPIDER MEN WANT 3D AN HOUR MORE AND DEMAND MORE HEIGHT MONEY' announced the headline in the *Manchester Evening News* of Friday, 30 August 1946, 'The "human spiders" who work at heights up to 120ft erecting the steel structures of big modern buildings want a 3d-an-hour pay rise and a new scale of "height money". They have put their case for a new charter before the National Wages Tribunal. The men belong to the Construction Engineering Union, the Manchester branch of which has a membership of 1,000.'

Tense days awaited the human spiders and the families they had to sustain as they awaited the tribunal's verdict. Another citizen of Manchester, meanwhile, had other matters on his mind. Most immediately, for Alexander Matthew Busby, recently appointed as manager of Manchester United, the next day's Division One opener against Grimsby Town at Maine Road.

Busby made his Football League debut as a player at Maine Road, for Manchester City against Middlesbrough on 2 November 1929. With Tommy Johnson away playing for the Football League against the Scottish League, young Busby deputised at inside-left. He did OK as City won 3-1 but was dropped the following week when Johnson returned for the visit to Grimsby. 'Blundell Park is worth a goal lead to Grimsby,' reported the *Manchester Evening News* after the 2-2 draw. 'The City players complained after the match that they felt cramped and could not develop their natural game.'

Busby watched that game from the windswept touchline as a 20-year-old rookie midfielder. On the opening day of 1946/47 at Maine Road, he watched United v Grimsby from the rainswept touchline as a 37-year-old rookie manager. Nobody could know it at the time but, while the bold spider men erected their hardy structures, Busby had commenced building arguably the greatest managerial reign in football history.

The Red Devils were moving forward again after almost going out of existence at the start of the previous decade. In 1930/31 they lost their first 12 league matches, including back-to-back home defeats to Huddersfield Town (6-0) and Newcastle United (7-4), and conceded 115 goals across the season. After relegation, the opening home match of the following campaign, a midweek 3-2 defeat to Southampton, drew a crowd of 3,507. Bankruptcy loomed. Extinction was a real possibility until local businessman James W. Gibson, a supplier of military uniforms, heard about the club's plight. He was intrigued, got involved and pumped in money to save the club. Everything that Manchester United has achieved since – and is now – began with Gibson.

Among his shrewdest moves was the appointment of Busby. The Scot was to bring the club unimaginable levels of success, kudos and glory, and it all began against Grimsby on a wet afternoon at Maine Road, United's Old Trafford home having been devastated by wartime bombing.

On 30 August, *Manchester Evening News* scribe Eric Thornton looked ahead to the big kick-off, 'When the clock strikes three tomorrow afternoon, we shall be off again to a new season of English soccer – a season which promises to draw the greatest crowds the game has known. Excluding the weather factor – and how well do Manchester people appreciate the importance this plays in sport! – it is confidently anticipated that more than a million will go through the turnstiles at the 44 matches. Chief point of interest about United's curtain-raiser at Maine Road will be the performance of young Billy McGlen who makes his Football League debut at left-back. If he succeeds against a young Grimsby attack, the position may be his for the rest of the season.'

While United were stabilising again through the 1930s, 100 miles due east Grimsby Town were enjoying their golden era. In eight seasons up to the war the Mariners were an established Division One club and reached two FA Cup semi-finals, against Arsenal in 1936 and Wolves in 1939. The latter, at Old Trafford, was watched by 76,962, still a record crowd for the stadium. On 30 August the *Grimsby Daily Telegraph*'s match preview evoked memories not of that visit to Old Trafford, however, but the Mariners' next, four months later, at the start of the season that wasn't to be, 'Grimsby Town, as members of the First Division, begin the new season by playing Manchester United away, as they did on 26 August 1939, though the match will not be played on the same arena. The United's own ground at Old Trafford suffered during the "blitz" and is not in a condition for staging league football, so the club is occupying a temporary home – as guests, not as squatters – at Maine-road, the ground of the Manchester City club.'

Busby was working to a financial backdrop very far removed from United's wealth of today. In the close season he paid out just one transfer fee – £4,000 to Celtic for winger Jimmy Delaney. New training kit was acquired with clothing coupons collected from a dressing-room whip-round reinforced by donations from fans in response to an appeal by the manager. In his programme notes for the Grimsby game, Busby asked the fans to show patience. 'A player is a human being,' he wrote, 'not a mechanical engine which, when you press a button, goes through its work.'

As three o'clock approached, Busby was in familiar terrain. He went to work as a manager in the Maine Road dressing room in which, 17 years earlier, he had prepared for his debut as a player. There was no time for nostalgia. Just before kick-off he was forced into a reshuffle. Joe Walton, a right-back who combined professional football with his job as a plumber, strained an Achilles, so captain Johnny Carey switched to right-back and Jack Warner, formerly of Swansea Town, came in to patrol the right-half beat.

The Busby era at Manchester United was officially launched by the whistle of George Appleyard, from Rotherham. United started well. Jack Rowley sent an early header against the bar and the home side dominated the first half, assisted by the visitors' misfortune with injuries. Even with several players limping, with goalkeeper George Tweedy in fine form, the Mariners held firm until just before half-time when winger Charlie Mitten scored. 'A dazzling midfield movement wove through the Mariners' defence,' reported the *Grimsby Daily Telegraph*, 'and if the ball had not been greasy, Tweedy might have prevented it slipping through his hands.'

Grimsby fought gallantly after half-time and former Celtic inside-right Jimmie McGowan equalised with 'a nicely placed shot well out of Crompton's reach'. United regained the lead when another header from Rowley took a wicked deflection off Stan Charlesworth past the helpless Tweedy. Still, the bruised Mariners battled valiantly and were inches away from another equaliser with the last kick off the match when Jack Johnson's shot hit the foot of a post.

'TOWN NEARLY SNATCHED AWAY POINT. DOGGED BY BOGEY OF INJURY AT MANCHESTER' was the headline in Monday's *Grimsby Daily Telegraph*, 'Against a team which included in its forward line two of its four internationals, Grimsby Town lost their opening game of the new season when they were defeated by Manchester United by two goals to one at Maine Road on Saturday. Their performance, however, against a strong United side, was a creditable one in view of the handicaps which they had to overcome. That they were not beaten by a greater margin of goals was due to the splendid performance of the Town defence. Apart from a fairly long spell after the interval, in which the Mariners combined excellently to pen the United in their own half, little was seen of the Grimsby attack, except for a brief thrust in the closing seconds when Johnson (J.W.) hit the foot of the post with the United goalkeeper well out of position.

'Though Manchester were the better team, had Johnson equalised with that last kick of the match, it would have been just reward for the gallant display put up by the Mariners. Tweedy was solid as a rock. He brought off many excellent saves, much to the admiration of the 40,000 spectators. Misfortune befell the Town team on three occasions as far as injury to players was concerned. In the opening exchanges, Hodgson (J.V.) had to receive attention, followed soon after by Charlesworth who had a spell on the wing with a knee injury and finally, to end the run of bad luck, Clifton had to be assisted off the field almost 15 minutes before the interval. However, when the bonds of ill-luck were severed immediately after the interval, the Mariners, back at full strength with Clifton in the attack again, played like a winning team. Passes were accurate and well-placed and for some time a polished Town attack had the United defence working at full pressure.'

Curiously, Monday's *Manchester Evening News* ('the MEN') carried no report of the match, just a small piece of speculation about the team for the midweek visit to Chelsea. However, the paper did bring welcome news for one local pigeon owner. 'I have in my possession a racing pigeon with the following ring – NUHW 45/W4523 and E741,' wrote James Aldridge, 30 Sheringham Drive, East Lancs Road, Swinton in the letters column. 'I picked this bird up in Winsford on Sunday.' How noble of Mr Aldridge to go to the trouble of collecting the bird, keeping it and writing to the paper about it, rather than simply leaving it or, a tempting option in the light of rationing pressures, cooking it for his dinner.

The *MEN* also carried a world exclusive unearthed by a staff reporter who had visited Norman Sykes and returned with a scoop. '18MPH PEDAL CAR IS AMPHIBIOUS. YOU CAN EVEN GO TO BED IN IT', 'Amphibious pedal cars invented by a Sale (Cheshire) scientist to help his wife do the shopping may soon be marketed by a Manchester businessman who wants to mass produce them. The car is made of wood as the inventor, Mr Norman Sykes, believes it will be offered to the public at a low price. It has three wheels, seats four and works by pushing two large pedals. When the seat is lifted there is room on the floor for two people to sleep and it is proposed to add a hood as extra cover. I saw the car in action today when Mrs Sykes took her first water trip. On land, Mr Sykes, pedalling quite easily, reached 18mph then drove into the canal without slackening speed. The single front wheel was used as a rudder and sharp turns were made by pedalling one wheel only. The car floated well and was submerged for only six inches.'

Back on dry land, next up for United were two games in London for which, the *MEN* revealed, they would stay down south, 'Manchester United, who have two London engagements next week – Charlton on Wednesday and Chelsea at Stamford Bridge the following Saturday – have decided to set up a temporary training camp in the village of Twyford, in Berkshire.' Busby's planning was rewarded: United won 3-0 at Stamford Bridge and 3-1 at The Valley (the *MEN* got the games the wrong way round) then, back at Maine Road, thumped Liverpool 5-0. The new manager had hit the ground running.

A little further down the line, in late December, United and Grimsby met again, at Blundell Park, and again Walton missed out against the Mariners, this time due to a fractured wrist sustained when he fell off a ledge on a plumbing job. The game, which ended 0-0, was not attended by the manager who was away on a scouting mission. 'Matt Busby might have turned his Irish quest for a goalkeeper into a search for a sharp-shooting forward if he had seen the game at Grimsby, where the defence took all the honours,' reported the *MEN*. 'United cannot afford to throw away goal openings if they are to maintain a title challenge.'

'A singularly uninteresting but hard-fought duel' was the take of the *Grimsby Daily Telegraph*, which gave greater precedence on the same page to 'SANTA CLAUS CAME VIA THE CHIMNEY', 'Father Christmas came down in the chimney in traditional manner during a Christmas party for the children of members of the Royal Air Forces Association (Grimsby branch) at The Abbey on Saturday.'

United went on to unfurl a strong first season under Busby, finishing runners-up, just a point behind champions Liverpool. It was the first of four second-place finishes in the next five seasons before they took the title in 1952. By then, Grimsby were down in Division Three North having finished bottom of Division One in 1948 and Division Two in 1952. United's Golden Age was under way. Grimsby's was gone.

40

Football League Division One
Huddersfield Town 1 Blackpool 3 (HT: 1-3)
Scorers – Huddersfield Town: Glazzard; Blackpool: Mortensen, Blair, Munro
Attendance: 14,378

'Town presented the spectators with a ground looking a picture. It is a pity the team did not do justice to it.'

THERE WAS a cosmopolitan air to the Huddersfield Town coverage in the *Huddersfield Daily Examiner* on the eve of the big kick-off. While Town prepared for a tough game against Blackpool, one of the most successful clubs in the country during wartime competition, there was news to interest those with a passion for the Netherlands, Denmark and Egypt. 'Two continental teams will be seen at Leeds Road this season,' the *Examiner* reported. 'On 27 November, the Town ground will be the venue of the international match between England and Holland, and on 9 October the Town team will entertain a side representing Copenhagen. On their tour of Denmark at the close of last season, Town played in Copenhagen three times against sides selected from the five Copenhagen clubs, and the game on 9 October will be in the nature of a return visit by such a combined side.'

Huddersfieldians with North African connections, meanwhile, had their interest piqued by the prospect of one of Egypt's star players parking his boots in the Leeds Road dressing room. Abdel Karim Sakr, fresh from considerable success in Egyptian domestic football, was pondering a move to Yorkshire. 'EGYPTIAN WANTS TO

RETURN TO TOWN' was the *Examiner* headline, 'Abdel Karim Sakr, 25-year-old Egyptian inside-forward who, with Mohamed El-Guindi, left Leeds Road at the beginning of last month and returned to Egypt, appears to have changed his mind about playing in English football. He has cabled the Town club, who signed him as an amateur towards the end of last season, to the effect that he would like to come back, and has also written to a friend saying that he is desirous of returning to England.'

An intriguing prospect, but uppermost in the minds of Town fans was the visit of star-studded Blackpool, a tough opener having just encountered mixed fortunes during the war years. Like most clubs, they struggled to field a settled and successful team in the face of the era's makeshift and sometimes bizarre schedules. In successive years, Town played two matches on Christmas Day. In 1940, they won 5-0 at Bradford City then lost 4-3 to them at home. In 1941, a Christmas day tour saw them lose 2-1 to Leeds United at Elland Road and win 3-1 at Bradford Park Avenue.

On 31 August 1946, manager David Steele had the luxury of preparing for just one game, but the Scot had plenty to think about. As a member of the team that was league champions three seasons running in 1924, 1925 and 1926, he was a Huddersfield playing legend, but he was finding management quite a challenge. The *Examiner* prepared its readers – wisely, it transpired – to expect a stern test from a strong set of Tangerines, 'Town's First Division season opens with a visit from Blackpool who have occupied an illustrious place in the wartime competitions. While Town, over that period, have been successful in winning the North-Eastern Section (1939/40) and the League North championship (1944/45), the Lancashire club won the League North in three successive seasons and took the North Cup as well in 1942/43. In this wartime football, Blackpool were materially assisted by guest players, Stanley Matthews among them, and while they must now rely on their own players, it would be prudent to reckon that the influence of such skilled men will have left some mark on those who are left.'

Blackpool were a rising force in English football under the leadership of Joe Smith. A former Bolton Wanderers striker, Smith scored against West Ham in the first FA Cup Final at Wembley in

1923. Calm, measured and direct, he took quickly to management and steered Blackpool to promotion to Division One in his second season in charge, 1937. They consolidated there in the following two seasons before starting the 1939/40 campaign brilliantly. A 1-0 win at Huddersfield and 2-1 home victories over Brentford and Wolves left them as one of only two teams in the country with a 100 per cent record when the campaign was halted. Further success having followed during wartime, Blackpool's fans travelled to Huddersfield in a confident mood.

Whether that travelling support included Albert Forty is undocumented but, if so, he had a tale to tell on the train, having just been accused of perhaps the most symmetrical crime in legal history. The *Lancashire Evening Post* reported the case of Mr Forty, aged 40, accused of driving at 40, 'Albert Percival Forty, aged 40, of Lytham-road, Blackpool, said to have been followed by a police patrol who checked his car's speed over a measure half-mile, as 40 to 43 miles an hour, was fined 20s plus £1 1s advocate's fee, in his absence at Preston today for exceeding the speed limit in a built-up area.'

The match at Leeds Road started at high speed. Four goals arrived in the first 20 minutes. After Stan Mortensen gave Blackpool a tenth-minute lead, Jimmy Glazzard equalised before Jimmy Blair on 17 minutes and Alec Munro after 20 put the visitors 3-1 up. The early scoreline was harsh on Huddersfield, commented Hermes, the *Lancashire Daily Post* reporter, 'The sun was shining when Harry Johnson, who has been appointed the Blackpool captain for the season, won the toss before a crowd of about 12,000. The Town were soon attacking and, after Bateman had swung the ball across the Blackpool goal, Sibley cleared just in time. The visitors were right up against it in these early moves, and when Price burst through in brilliant style again, it was only Wallace's brilliant save, as he tipped a high cross over the bar, that saved the lead. Time after time the Town attacked and it was all against the run of the play when Mortensen put Blackpool in front by screwing the ball past McManus from six yards out.

'The Town came again and after they had forced a corner, the ball swung right across the goalmouth and Glazzard equalised after 15 minutes. He lifted the ball over his head with his back to the goal, and though Wallace fell to it, he was not quick enough as it twisted and twirled. Blair restored Blackpool's lead within a minute. After 20 minutes it was 3-1 after Mortensen's ferocious shot was blocked but Munro gave McManus no chance. Town were far from shaping like a losing side. Quite the contrary, in fact. Once, for instance, there was a tremendous tussle on the Blackpool goal line and there were appeals by Huddersfield that the ball was over the line, but a free kick followed instead. Huddersfield, in a magnificent rally, ought to have evened the score, so fast and forceful were their many moves forward, but they failed to close in and once Price missed an open goal.'

The *Yorkshire Post* correspondent was less enthused by Town's performance. Never mind the joie de vivre generated by football's return, he did not hesitate to crank up the pressure on Steele, 'It will be surprising if Town's officials remain content unless form improves quickly and significantly. If the inside-forwards Price, Carr and Glazzard had taken all their chances, the team might have won. If an appeal for a penalty had been favoured, or if the referee had agreed with Town's forwards that the ball was over the goal line before Blackpool bundled it away, the team might have drawn. However, none of these ifs came out to Town's satisfaction. Blackpool had a sounder defence, the best wing-forward on the field in Munro and three high-class inside-forwards – Blair, who produced two skilful dribbles from which goals came, Buchan, whose fine run and shot was one of the outstanding incidents of the day, and Mortensen, a hard and determined worker in the centre. Town presented the spectators with a ground looking a picture. It is a pity the team did not do justice to it.'

Key to Blackpool's victory, agreed reporters connected to both clubs, was the impact of Blair. The mercurial, much-travelled Scot, born in Glasgow and brought up in south Wales, started his career as an amateur with Cardiff City before moving to England, and Blackpool, in 1935. He played for Wales Schoolboys but his excellent early season form in 1946 was to earn a full Scotland debut, ironically against Wales. On 19 October, Wales won 3-1 in front of 30,000 at Wrexham and Blair's Scotland career began and ended that night.

'Blackpool's star at Huddersfield was that astute, baffling inside-forward James Blair who, when he faded out in the last 20 minutes, had done all that was necessary to give the visitors a welcome opening away win,' reported the *Lancashire Evening Post.* 'He scored a grand goal and was the architect of those scored by Munro and Mortensen in a hectic period which yielded most of the thrills in a generally attractive match.' The *Examiner* added, 'The dribbling moves of Blair were vital.'

If the hosts were disappointed by the result, they could take no consolation from the attendance. While grounds around the country were at, or near, capacity, Leeds Road attracted only 14,378 – the lowest crowd in the top two divisions. The wet weather didn't help, but other factors also combined to keep people away. The usual matchday special trolley-bus service was not operating due to a drivers' work-to-rule. There was serious competition from rugby league, which also took place on Saturday afternoons. Huddersfield, a top team with several high-profile Australians in their ranks, were playing at nearby Dewsbury while Wakefield, from which Town drew support, faced a big derby at Leeds.

The transition of Huddersfield's team was far from over. In goal against Blackpool was Brendan McManus, signed from Newry Town ten months earlier. It proved to be his only first-team appearance. Abdel Karim Sakr decided that English football wasn't for him – he never played for Huddersfield or any English club. Steele used 32 players during 1946/47 as Town finished 20th, just one place, albeit a relatively comfortable eight points, above relegated Brentford. They were kept up by the high class of Irish inside-forward Peter Doherty, signed in December for £10,000 from Derby County, along with the skills of winger Harry McShane, later to become a Manchester United star and father of actor Ian McShane.

Blackpool were entering a great era. An established Division One club, they reached three FA Cup Finals in five years, losing to Manchester United and Newcastle United in 1948 and 1951, then beating Bolton Wanderers 4-3 in 1953 – known as 'the Matthews final' even though it was Mortensen who scored a hat-trick. Three years later, they finished second in the league, only the brilliance of Matt Busby's United denying them the title. The other end of Division One that season saw Huddersfield enduring harder times. They finished second bottom and were relegated, agonisingly by a sliver of goal average which saved Aston Villa.

Ahead for both Huddersfield and Blackpool lay thin times and happy chapters in proud histories which include their first meeting on 4 February 1911, a cold, grey afternoon at Leeds Road. The game finished 2-2 and among the audience was the *Examiner* correspondent, extravagantly bylined Pierre Noire. Clearly free from the space restrictions which tormented 21st-century football reporters, Monsieur Noire (Peter Black?) wrote, 'To effect only a draw after being clearly the better team for the greater part of the game was disappointing, but a side which throws away chances does not deserve victory, and I am not in agreement with the writer who states that Huddersfield were unlucky in having to divide the points. The lead should have been regained with the penalty kick, but once again was demonstrated the inability to take advantage of the award. Nor was this the only time that the home team failed to clinch matters, an old weakness – lack of steadiness in front of goal leading to wretched shooting – being prominent several times in the closing stages of the game. Unlucky is surely the wrong word to use in extenuation of a comparative failure, for as such a draw must be reckoned being but half a victory.'

41

Football League Division Three South
Norwich City 2 Cardiff City 1 (HT: 0-0)
Scorers – Norwich City: Furness, Walker; Cardiff City: Richards
Attendance: 21,725

'Since 8 August, beef sausages have been put up in price from 10d to 11.5d per lb and housewives have been wondering what caused the jump.'

WHILE THE size of Huddersfield Town's crowd was affected by a trolley-bus dispute and the rival attraction of rugby league, another factor trimmed a few off the attendance at Norwich City. 'When the teams came out, there was plenty of room on the terraces,' reported the *Eastern Football News* 'Pink 'Un', 'and the attendance was probably affected by the urge of the people of the countryside to get in the harvest.'

How much they could get in as the rain poured down was uncertain, but the noble farmers of Norfolk braved the elements, even if it meant missing the start of what appeared to be an exciting new chapter in the history of the Canaries. After treading water in Division Three South for much of the time since joining the Football League in 1920, the club had just appointed as manager the highly rated and experienced Cyril Spiers. His first match pitted him against opposition he knew well. When Norwich and Cardiff met on the opening day of the 1939/40 season, Spiers was Cardiff manager, which he remained until April 1946. A fallout with the board then triggered his resignation and a few weeks later, he joined Norwich.

His appointment at Carrow Road clearly excited one member of the *Eastern Football News* staff. 'You cannot meet Cyril Henry Spiers, secretary-manager of Norwich City, without gaining the impression that here is a man of cool, unruffled judgment, a trained mind, with an unexcelled background of playing and administrative experience to guide him to his goal,' gushed Wanderer in the 'Pink 'Un'. 'Now only 44, Cyril Spiers came to Norwich to tackle a tremendous job, with 30 years of football experience behind him. He kept goal for three of the greatest clubs in the land, Aston Villa, Tottenham Hotspur and Wolverhampton Wanderers. When he went back to the Midlands – he was born at Birmingham and married a Coventry wife – his one objective was to study the administrative side of the game under Major Frank Buckley. The pupil, the ardent admirer of Frank Buckley, now reigns over the club which gave Buckley his first insight into the administrative side.

'No man in football today has passed from field to office with a clearer perception of what he is doing than Cyril Spiers. His has been a planned football career. He signed for the Villa when he was 14 and, immediately he could do so, he became a professional. It was not his seeking that he left the Villa – injury, which threatened his future, kept him idle for a time, and he left Villa Park when the specialist view was that his damaged leg would not allow him to play again. He went through an experimental operation, and the man the Villa thought to be done for made 130 consecutive appearances for Tottenham. In six seasons, Cyril Spiers missed 12 matches in Tottenham's first team – a record for the White Hart Lane club. Such a brilliant record came to a sad end, for it was in a practice match that Spiers broke his wrist, stopping a Willie Evans drive.

'At Wolverhampton, the main purpose of Mr Spiers was the coaching of the Buckley boys, no mean task. During his six years with the Wolves, Cyril Spiers not only took a leading part in the training of the astonishing succession of youngsters who won fame for themselves and Major Buckley, but he made an intensive study of club management. He is a prodigious, methodical worker, up early in the morning, and burning the midnight oil in keeping abreast with all the details of club affairs.'

Wanderer's hagiology of Mr Spiers went on. 'At Cardiff he faced a Herculean task,' he continued. 'The bank overdraft was at its limit of £15,000 and there were sundry other debts. He organised the Football League (West), making the fixtures and the referees' appointments, and instituting the War Cup (West). Last season he made the whole of the fixtures for the Third Division (Southern) League Cup which carried the clubs through the second half of the season. He left Cardiff with the overdraft reduced to £2,000, many other claims satisfied, and £60,000 or £70,000 worth of players on the books.

'Now he has complete freedom in his task of building up the Canaries. "I do not believe in rash prophecy," he told me. "I am satisfied with what I have seen of the Canaries in training. The lads have got down to their work and start the season 100 per cent fit. I feel fairly confident that we shall not have a bad season – I will not go further than that."'

Spiers was wise to not go further than that. All the early rising and burning of midnight oil notwithstanding, the Canaries had a terrible season. They finished next to bottom and had to apply for re-election.

The opening fixture at Carrow Road effectively pitted Spiers's Canaries against Spiers's Bluebirds. The Brummie had been appointed at Ninian Park in April 1939 on a mission to reconstruct a team which had declined spectacularly since the triumphs of the 1920s when they were runners-up in Division One and won the FA Cup. During the war years, with an emphasis on youth, Spiers moulded a talented, energetic side, supplemented occasionally by accomplished guests. These included, on 3 October 1942, a 29-year-old Scottish midfielder based at nearby RAF St Athan. Cardiff beat Lovells Athletic 3-1 in Bill Shankly's only appearance for the club.

The ultra-diligent Spiers put in place a highly promising foundation for Cardiff's return to the Football League – then abruptly departed. On 31 August, he took his place in the home dugout at Carrow Road while Billy McCandless, who had just left neighbouring Newport County, parked himself in Cardiff's.

Before heading for Norfolk from the Welsh capital, McCandless and his team were enlightened by hot sausage news from Friday's *Western Mail.* Under the headline 'SECRETS OF SAUSAGE

PRICES', Our Woman Correspondent reported, 'Since 8 August, beef sausages have been put up in price from 10d to 11.5d per lb and housewives have been wondering what caused the jump. It is due to the increased cost of sausage casings. To offset the cost, the quality has been improved and the meat content has been increased from 40 to 50 per cent minimum, the same standard as for pork sausages. The increased cost of casings also affects pork sausages, but these have not gone up to the consumer and are still 1s 2d per lb.'

Next day, the Bluebirds returned west with a 2-1 defeat to digest but their performance was encouraging. They played some lovely football before succumbing to a late winner which was, depending on which report you believed, a nifty opportunist strike or 'the luckiest goal Norwich are likely to get this season'.

'They're off,' reported the *Eastern Football News* 'Pink 'Un'. 'Football interest, rising rapidly during the last few weeks, reached fever pitch this afternoon, when, after the longest break in Football League history, the 88 teams jumped off once more in the old-time promotion and relegation struggles. Nowhere has the rising temperature been more apparent than in Norwich where the planning of the City directorate had aroused tremendous interest. New players, new officials and a new director – City enter the postwar era with quiet hopes of a happier future.

'On the first day of the ill-fated 1939/40 season, Cardiff, in [the] charge of Mr Cyril Spiers, gave City a shock by winning at Carrow Road, 2-1. Their visit today coincided with the Canaries' first match under Mr Spiers' stewardship. Cardiff's young and clever side was built by Mr Spiers who is now starting on the big job of reviving the fortunes of the Canaries. The Welsh club begin the season with a team patiently developed during the war years; Norwich, on the other hand, handicapped by the exclusion from competitive football during the war, are still in the process of team construction.'

After a goalless first half, Norwich took a 62nd-minute lead through Billy Furness, 'Plunkett gave Walker a short pass and the inside-right promptly sent the ball to Furness who shot into the net from ten yards' range. Furness had been playing a grand game and the crowd cheered with delight when he registered the first goal of the season at Carrow Road.'

Norwich goalkeeper Fred Hall protected the lead with several fine saves as Cardiff pressed hard but, ten minutes from time, was beaten when Stan Richards finished off a flowing move. Then came that late twist. 'Two minutes before the end, when a draw seemed a certainty, and some of the spectators were beginning to leave the ground, Walker regained the Norwich lead,' reported the 'Pink 'Un'. 'There had been some desultory play round about the Cardiff goal when Walker, taking advantage of a loose, bounding ball, connected with a neat twist of his head, and the ball went into the net wide of Poland's left hand.'

It was, according to the *Sunday Express*, 'The luckiest goal Norwich are likely to get this season. A bouncing ball looked for all the world as though it were going by. Cardiff defenders just stood in one side and waited for it to go when Walker, appearing from nowhere, raced up to nod it into the goal.'

The *Western Mail* took a more generous view of the decisive strike, despite it having scuppered their team, 'The Welshmen were a goal down, shot by Furness, after one hour's play, but retaliated splendidly to score a fine equalising goal through Richards in the 76th minute. Over 21,000 spectators cheered this effort, sufficient proof that Cardiff's point was deserved. Then, two minutes from the end, when a draw seemed inevitable, Walker netted an opportunist winning goal for Norwich.'

The knowledgeable *Mail* reporter knew a good side when he saw one, 'Several times the Welshmen completely outwitted the home defence, but their finishing efforts were not sufficiently powerful to beat Hall, the confident Norwich goalkeeper. The Welsh inside-forwards worked the ball well in midfield, especially Rees, but apart from Richards' goal, following clever combined play, they did not possess a winning shot among them. Cardiff has the makings of a good team and will win many matches when their forwards improve their shooting.'

That assessment was spot on. They did improve their shooting, led by Cardiff-born Stan Richards who rattled in 30 league goals as the Bluebirds charged to the Division Three North title. Their 66 points was a record for a season with two points for a win. Goalkeeper Danny Canning's 24 clean sheets was also a record. 'The local lads recruited by Spiers during the war years, like Fred Stansfield and Alf Sherwood, shone as the Bluebirds romped to the third tier title,' reports the club website, cardiffcityfc.co.uk. 'A brilliant 21-match unbeaten run, including 19 wins, helped them to amass 66 points, going undefeated at Ninian Park all season in front of an average crowd of 28,604.'

For the Canaries, difficult times lay ahead. Despite starting with a win and a crowd which, even with the absence of those bringing in the harvest, generated receipts of £1,614 12/10, the season soon deteriorated. They lost the next four games, conceding 15 goals, then drew with Bristol City but conceded three goals in each of the following five games, all of which they lost. Spiers's side kept just one clean sheet before Christmas and conceded 100 goals on the way to finishing in the re-election zone. They were grateful that, as it was the first postwar season, the Football League waived the re-election vote.

Spiers departed halfway through the following campaign and returned to Cardiff to resume the excellent job he had begun before the war. He took them up into Division One in 1952. Norwich finally escaped the third tier in 1960. Two years later, they won the League Cup in the competition's second season after a 4-0 aggregate victory over Rochdale in the final. 'Norwich are the new League Cup holders,' reported the *Daily Mirror* after the Canaries, already pretty much home and hosed after a 3-0 first-leg win at Spotland, won the second 1-0 at Carrow Road. 'Throughout a tedious first half, Norwich were generally in command, but they showed little interest in pressing home attacks. Norwich's goal came after 74 minutes. Inside-left Jimmy Hill smashed in a shot from a narrow angle and it flashed home through a ruck of defenders.' Possibly the lowest-key cup final win ever?

42

Football League Division One
Sunderland 3 Derby County 2 (HT: 2-1)
Scorers – Sunderland: Burbanks, Whitelum (2); Derby County: Stamps, Doherty
Attendance: 53,000

'In the most thrilling start to a football season I can remember, the "Roker Roar" inspired the home team to pull out a little better than their best.'

PERHAPS THE standout match of the entire fixture list of 31 August 1946 was at Roker Park. Five-time league champions and recent FA Cup winners Sunderland faced FA Cup holders Derby County who arrived in the north-east led by Sunderland legend Raich Carter. Described by Stanley Matthews as 'bewilderingly clever, constructive, lethal in front of goal, yet unselfish', Carter had captained the Rokerites to the title in 1936 and the FA Cup the following year. His ineffable skills at inside-forward were transferred to Derby early in 1946 and, immediately, he helped them lift the FA Cup. The Rams' 4-1 win over Charlton in the final at Wembley secured them the cup for the first (and still only) time and elicited a gloriously verbose intro to the match report in the *Nottingham Journal.* Having come up with five potential angles for his intro, Our Own Correspondent decided to pile them all into an 84-word beast: 'Because Charlton could not maintain the pace of extra time after right-half Bert Turner had created a record by scoring the only two goals of full time against and for his own club within two minutes, Derby County took the FA Cup northwards, victors for the first time in their fourth attempt after a game of omens, surprises and missed chances, which provided a parallel with the postwar final of 1919/20 when Aston Villa beat Huddersfield by the odd goal at Chelsea during extra time.'

Carter, a huge factor in the triumph, did not make it into the intro, but his presence in the Rams' team at Sunderland was the crowning ingredient in a potential cracker. Nowhere on this momentous day did a match promise more and, amid one of the great atmospheres in English football, fuelled by the 'Roker Roar', it delivered.

Two days before the game, the *Sunderland Echo and Shipping Gazette* tapped into the rising anticipation. Under the headline 'NEARLY £4,000 TAKEN IN SEASON TICKETS. NO INFERIORITY COMPLEX AT ROKER PARK', reporter Argus passed on a message from beleaguered club secretary George Crow, 'Sunderland's sale of season tickets will probably be a record, for the 900 mark has been passed – and almost £4,000 is in the bank. Mr George Crow asks me to say that season tickets will not be on sale on Saturday. He will have sufficient to do looking after the gates. The gates will open at 1.30, and given a fine day, the turnstiles ought to "click" round about the 50,000 mark. It is a nice little compliment on Derby County's part to appoint Raich Carter as captain for the day when he returns to his native town to play for the first time against the club which made him. I am certainly not one of those people who have Sunderland beaten before the game, and I can assure you that in the dressing room at Roker Park there is nothing approaching a feeling that they cannot beat Derby – rather the reverse. Roker has sufficient players of experience to face up to players with reputations.'

Down in the East Midlands, meanwhile, Friday's edition of the *Derby Daily Telegraph* focused on two big issues of the day. 'FEW BANANAS – BUT MORE TOMORROW' was first, 'Few bananas were ripe enough for sale at Derby market today, but dealers expect more to be available tomorrow and early next week. Those on sale were costing 1s 1d 1lb. Plums were rather more plentiful.' Then it was over to 'RAMS' TEAM FOR FIRST MATCH': 'Derby County will include Carter in their team at Sunderland tomorrow. There are two changes from the Rams' cup-winning side. With Duncan and Harrison, Carter has been suffering from muscle strains, and all three were given a test at the Baseball Ground today. Duncan and Harrison were found to be unfit, and their places will be taken by Morrison and Walsh.'

On matchday, Sunderland fans awoke to some hyperbole from the *Sunderland Echo and Shipping Gazette.* The press release issued by the Churches Committee on Gambling (see Chapter 1) had evidently landed on the desk of *Gazette* writer Robert Stoker who went to town on it under the headline 'BRITAIN'S BIGGEST BETTING BOOM BEGINS TODAY', 'With the start today of England's first postwar season of football, the curtain rises on what is expected to be the biggest gambling boom the country has ever known. The turnover of the pools promoters in their last prewar season, before the players of the country exchanged their playing kit for battledress, was no less than £35,000,000, but by comparison with the "target" for the season just beginning, that was a modest figure indeed. Before the season ends next May, pools organisers expect to have handled between them coupon stakes amounting to more than £100,000,000. So the astronomical figure is equal to the 1938 takings of the LMS and the GWR put together. Even at that, however, the picture is incomplete. When we add to that the estimated public expenditure on other forms of gambling, the total amounts to something like £500,000,000, representing more than a shilling for every pound of national income. Of this total – nearly twice as much as was spent in this country last year on lighting and heating our houses, five times as much as was spent on furnishing them and very much more than was spent on cinemas – £230,000,000 will go to bookmakers on horseracing bets and £150,000,000 to dog-track "totes".

'A capital expenditure of four shillings a week for every man, woman and child in the country, which this total represent, causes gloom and despondency in no small measure among orthodox economists. Such a revenue without any accompanying import, export, purchase or sale, finds no place in their planned economy.'

Warming to his subject, Stoker outlined his lack of confidence in the ability of the authorities to tackle the issue, 'Almost automatically, therefore, the new boom in uncontrolled expenditure in Britain is being met by the long-haired intellectuals with more and more lack of restrictive legislation. Could the nation's gambling laws be made any more chaotic than they already are? It seems doubtful. It is still in order to go to a racetrack to bet in pounds, but a man who goes to the street corner to gamble in shillings is a criminal. Newspapers may no longer print pools coupons, but advertisements of pools promoters are as legal as roulette in Monte Carlo. And how would the legislators and planners define the subtle difference between the punter and the "bulls" of the Stock Exchange? These are days of consumer goods in short supply, say they, and while wages continue high and goods are either rationed or unobtainable, money will find its outlet elsewhere. When Mrs Sunderland is again able to go into the shops of the town and buy as many curtains as she likes, she will no doubt have something to say on the subject of weekly postal orders. If, instead of Mr Grindon spending money on the dogs and his weekly coupon, Mrs Grindon is able to buy furniture again, she will no doubt do so. Will the bubble burst in the days of plenty? That is the question which moralists, economists and social students alike are asking?'

That was not the question on the lips of most Sunderland supporters as they headed for Roker Park. At the stadium gates, they were offered a more edifying way to part with a few coins, a collection for the Roker Volunteer Life Brigade, but a different and more immediate question soon arose – will we get in? Thousands didn't as George Crow and his under-resourced turnstiles team struggled to cope with the huge throng.

'The most disappointing thing about the game is that so many failed to secure admission,' reported the *Gazette*. 'Yet there were not 15,000 in the Roker End Stand. There were just about 50,000 in the enclosure – and about 5,000 disappointed supporters outside who never got in. There will be some grousers but I think it ought to be borne in mind that many of the turnstiles were manned by men new to the work, and the entrances which were not available were closed because there were not attendants for them. To man the gates is a problem these days.'

Those spectators who did gain entry were treated to a match which fully lived up to expectations. Sunderland started brilliantly and soon led after Rams defender Jack Howe handled in the box and Eddie Burbanks netted the penalty. Carter, given a huge ovation by the home supporters, then combined cleverly with Peter Doherty to set up Jackie Stamps to equalise. The game was exhilarating and evenly poised as half-time approached, but then Sunderland seized it, as the *Derby Daily Telegraph* reported, 'With the game in the hollow of their hands, however, the Rams slackened their hold, and Sunderland, with a goal in the last minute of the first half and another in the first minute of the second, knocked it out of their grasp. Both of these goals were scored by Whitelum, a dashing opportunist centre-forward.'

The double strike by Cliff Whitelum, later to become a legend at King's Lynn for whom his 237 goals in 218 games included six in a 10-2 Norfolk Senior Cup victory over Thorpe, proved decisive. Sunderland needed the breathing space as Doherty pulled a goal back with a 73rd-minute penalty, but held on for a breathless and breathtaking win.

'ROKER PARK HAD 90 MINUTES THRILLER' was the *Sunday Sun* headline, 'More games of the calibre staged at Roker Park, Sunderland, and seen by about 60,000 supporters, and we can say with emphasis that Wearside football is back to all its former glory. Sunderland defeated Derby County in a titanic struggle, fought out in a sporting manner and in a see-saw nature that held the crowd in its grip until the last blow of the whistle.'

Charles Mann, reporting for the *Derby Daily Telegraph*, gave a big assist to the home fans for their side's winning start. 'CROWD ROARED – SUNDERLAND SCORED. WIN INSPIRED BY ROKER FANS': 'Sunderland were swept to a 3-2 victory over Derby County at Roker Park on Saturday on the crest of a crashing wave of sound that surged from more than 50,000 frenzied football fans with one-track minds. In the most thrilling start to a football season I can remember, the "Roker Roar" inspired the home team to pull out a little better than their best. The effect was similar to that which the famous "Hampden Roar" has on a Scots side in an international match. Neither Carter cunning nor Doherty dexterity could give balance to the Rams' forward line, which was severely handicapped by the absence of wingers Duncan and Harrison. The substitute wingers – Morrison and Walsh – flapped vigorously occasionally but did not soar.'

Neither side was quite to soar in the months ahead, but they finished solidly enough in mid-table – Sunderland ninth, Derby 14th, separated by just three points. The Rams' defence of the FA Cup was ended in the fifth round by Liverpool, who beat them 1-0 at Anfield. Sunderland's cup run had ended early, and embarrassingly, in the third round with a 1-0 defeat to Division Two side Chesterfield in a Saltergate mud bath. 'When first-class footballers cannot see that a sea of mud and water is not the surface upon which to play short, passing football, they ask for what they get – and Sunderland got it' was the frank opinion of Argus in the *Gazette*. Though he did add, in mitigation, 'There is one thing I wish to say about the ground conditions. The Chesterfield club did not make any attempt to clear the three or four inches of snow off the pitch and consequently, excepting within the penalty areas, the snow had been left to melt and leave a waterlogged ground from which the surface water could not get away. I think they could have done better.'

Sunderland's aqueous cup exit was greeted with dismay by their fans in the north-east of England and, as revealed by The Cockpit, a column in the *Reveille Sporting Supplement*, in the west of Africa, 'I hear that football is flourishing in the four British West African colonies and that it is spreading so rapidly that even individual chiefdoms are taking interest! With team names Everton, Bolton Wanderers, Arsenal and Sunderland, it is obvious that they are keen followers of our clubs over here, and one wonders just how long it will be before they get the craze for filling in their weekly coupon to complete the picture.'

Robert Stoker would have no doubt urged all African sports fans: follow the football but, please, resist the coupons.

43

Football League Division Two
Chesterfield 1 Bradford Park Avenue 1 (HT: 1-1)
Scorers – Chesterfield: Booker; Bradford Park Avenue: Shackleton
Attendance: 15,000

'Hundreds of people were soaked to the skin, but it takes more than a soaking to damp the ardour of Chesterfield football supporters, and they stuck it cheerfully.'

'SUCCESSFUL SEASON ENVISAGED' was the *Derbyshire Times* headline ahead of Chesterfield's opening-day fixture with Bradford Park Avenue at Saltergate. 'Optimism was the dominant tone of the annual meeting of the shareholders of the Chesterfield Football Club Ltd, held on Monday at the Station Hotel, Chesterfield,' the paper reported. 'Last season was the most outstanding in the history of the Chesterfield Football Club.'

Excitement was high around the Spireites' prospects and their opener against a Park Avenue side including the 'Clown Prince of Soccer', Len Shackleton. Leading up to the game, however, the footballers of Chesterfield and Bradford had to compete for attention with Mrs Bird and Rev. Vesey.

'CLOCK FACE EGG LAID AT TEMPLE NORMANTON' was the stunning exclusive which Mrs Bird had taken to the *Derbyshire Times*, 'A freak egg has been laid by a fowl owned by Mrs J. Bird, licensee of The Lord's Arms, Temple Normanton. The egg is normal in shape and weight, but the shell has the striking resemblance of a clock face on it, the numbers from one to 12 being in a strict circle and resembling the normal Roman figures on a clock face. The clock face part of the shell is embossed. This unique specimen has caused much interest in the district. Mrs Bird also has another egg, laid just after by the same bird, with the numbers rotating the circumference of the egg, but are not so vivid as the other one.'

Visitors flocked to Temple Normanton to examine this extraordinary egg. Over in Bridlington, meanwhile, the entertainment on offer veered towards the raunchy – too raunchy for the liking of the Rev. H.A. Vesey. 'STRIPTEASE FILM ON A SUNDAY' was the shocking headline in the *Bradford Observer*, 'A letter protesting against a film trailer showing "striptease" girls being screened at a Bridlington cinema on a Sunday night was read to Bridlington Town Council last night, when the council decided to apply for powers for Sunday cinema opening. The Rev. H.A. Vesey, vicar of Christ Church, Bridlington, said in the letter that he did not object to Sunday pictures, but he did not like a trailer of one film, from which it appeared that 700 people were going to see a picture of scantily clad ladies fighting like cats. A letter from the Free Church Council also asked for control of the films to be shown. One councillor said that if the council closed the cinemas on Sundays, the queues for the public houses would be longer.'

While Bridlington's town councillors considered their position, and the till at The Lord's Arms rang merrily in celebration of the landlady's enterprise, Chesterfield and Bradford Park Avenue prepared to resume their long-standing rivalry. The clubs had first met back on 5 September 1908, in a Division Two fixture which Park Avenue won 1-0. 'The home team was fortunate to have choice of ends,' reported the *Bradford Daily Telegraph*, 'and this proved of great service to them, for the visitors could not make much headway against the stiff breeze and the strong kicking of the Bradford defence during the first 45 minutes, and when they had the advantage of the wind in the second half, a good deal of the sting had been taken out of their attack.'

Chesterfield remained up against the wind all that season and were ultimately blown away. They finished one from the bottom of Division Two of the then two-division league and were not re-elected, losing their place to Lincoln City. Park Avenue, meanwhile, moved in the other direction, winning promotion to the top flight in 1914, so the clubs' paths diverged. They did not meet again for eight years, by which time Park Avenue had suffered successive relegations while Chesterfield regained their league status as members of the new Division Three North.

In 1922, officers of the two clubs had much to discuss during a December double – a 2-2 draw at Saltergate on the ninth and a 1-0 home win for Bradford on Christmas Day. The hot topic was fears that adding a third tier to the league would diminish its quality but, after watching Bobby Turnbull's penalty clinch two points for Park Avenue, the *Bradford Daily Argus* correspondent expressed confidence that would not be the case, 'The Park Avenue team's sparkling play has done much to sweep away many wrong impressions as to the standard of Third Division football. There were certainly many among the 15,000 crowd yesterday who were surprised at the high quality and thrilling character of the game.'

The clubs met regularly through the 1920s in Division Three North and the 1930s in Division Two. Park Avenue's best days were behind them, it was to transpire, but Chesterfield emerged from the Second World War in a positive mood after a 1945/46 season which brought on-field success and substantial support on the terraces. 'Last season was the most outstanding in the history of the Chesterfield Football Club,' reported the *Derbyshire Times*. 'For the greater part of the early season, the first team headed the league, and then misfortune arrived – players received injuries and in a short period the whole forward line had to be changed. This created a situation very difficult to cope with because of the few players on full-time training. But the reserve players drafted into the first team did excellent work and, in spite of all the many great difficulties encountered, the team finished in the seventh position of the league table – a great achievement. The balance sheet, showing of profit of £15,367 on last season, was reviewed by the chairman, who pointed out that the large increase in expenditure was due to running four teams, increased numbers of players, matches played, and travelling expenses. Gate receipts, however, had more than doubled – £29,000 against £14,000 in round figures – and the average attendance at the first team home matches had been 15,000, which would have been larger had the team continued at the head of the league.'

Derbyshire Times reporter Casual added that the local community would benefit from the strong interest of football fans, 'The enthusiasm with which the football season is being approached in Chesterfield has been reflected in the attendances and financial proceeds of the two practice matches held by Chesterfield FC. The first produced a record crowd of 3,200 for a practice game at Saltergate, and £200 in receipts, and the second, played on Saturday in weather which was none too inviting, attracted 2,500, and £139 was paid in "gate" money, making a total of £339 to be devoted to charities to be decided upon.'

The goodwill around the club did not encompass all, however. The paper's letters column contained some trenchant views from Mr W.H. Rodgers of 16 St. Augustine's Drive, Chesterfield: 'Sir – The Chancellor fixed the admission price to football grounds at 1/3. I was informed last Friday that Chesterfield had cut the ground into portions, and left a small portion at 1/3 and the larger portion at 1/6. Is this a matter of sport or finance? After making a good profit last season, I, like others, have helped to put the club in its present position. What are other supporters' views on the matter? No more for me. Yours, etc.'

Park Avenue resumed after the war eager to recapture former glories and with a squad which included one of the great players of the era, though for how much longer was uncertain. Bradford-born Len Shackleton turned professional with Park Avenue in 1940 and was a prolific scorer throughout the war, principally for them but also as a guest for other clubs. In April 1946, he played for England in the 'victory international' against Scotland at Hampden Park, but his flamboyant skills were not to everyone's taste. 'Though frequently at the top of the scoring charts, Shackleton's antics did not always go down well with the home supporters,' recalls the National Football Museum in its Hall of Fame section. 'By 1946, the mercurial forward was complaining about the reception he received from the Park Avenue crowd. Having scored 175 goals for the club, most of which were scored in the wartime leagues, Len was angling for a move elsewhere.'

Shackleton was in his last few weeks with his hometown club but, inside a packed Saltergate, he scored his side's first goal of the new season before Ken Booker equalised from the penalty spot. The game offered plenty of entertainment for spectators, some of whom, in the stands, were nice and dry; others, out in the open, less so. 'The opening of the football season at Chesterfield on Saturday was marked by a severe thunderstorm which swept over the Saltergate ground about 20 minutes before the start of the match,' reported Casual. 'A huge crowd thronged the popular sides and when a torrential downpour of rain and, at times, hail which accompanied the vivid flashes of lightning and loud claps of thunder came, there was a stampede for the already well-packed shelters. Hundreds of people were soaked to the skin, but it takes more than a soaking to damp the ardour of Chesterfield football supporters, and they stuck it cheerfully, being rewarded by seeing the hard and thrilling game expected between such old rivals as Chesterfield and Bradford Park Avenue.'

Bradford's star opened the scoring, but Casual was more impressed by Chesterfield's attack, 'Shackleton should have scored in the first ten minutes but he made a bad shot. After 15 minutes, however, he scored. His goal looked an easy one, but it was the goal of an opportunist for, as Middleton ran out, Shackleton lobbed over Middleton's head and the ball dropped in the back of the net. After many sparkling efforts in which all the forwards shared, Chesterfield were awarded a penalty. Linacre was cutting across to goal and was brought down. The penalty kick was taken by Booker, who scored with a terrific drive. It was enlightening to see the Chesterfield attack which was hammering away and the crowd were expecting the winning goal at any moment.'

Casual's complimentary view of the Spireites was not unanimously held – 'CHESTERFIELD IN NEED OF IDEAS' was the headline in the *Derby Daily Telegraph* – but the visiting press were also impressed by the home side. 'A point from Chesterfield was a grand start by a Bradford side which would have made it two had it maintained to the end an inspiring first-half vein which deserved a winning lead,' reported the *Bradford Observer*. 'Instead an opportunistic Shackleton goal in 15 minutes was followed by an equaliser only from a strongly disputed penalty-kick two minutes before the interval. In the last half-hour, Chesterfield, despite the loss of outside-left Roberts (injured), compelled Bradford to adopt a defensive role in which Farr, Stephen and Danskin took full marks.'

The *Yorkshire Post and Leeds Intelligencer* scribe concurred with his counterpart from Bradford – and threw in a bit of a dig at Shackleton,

'Bradford were slightly fortunate to draw at Chesterfield, where the home team attacked for most of the second half, though Shackleton might have had more than one goal had he shot instead of keeping the ball.' Around the corner for Shackleton was a big-money move, and spectacular debut, for Newcastle United (see Chapter 4). His mercurial skills continued to split supporters. After another big-money move to Sunderland, the National Football Museum added, Shackleton, who played for Arsenal before the war, upset the Gunners faithful by 'humiliating his old club Arsenal, putting his foot on the ball in the penalty area and pretending to check his watch and comb his hair'.

Park Avenue finished 1946/47 in 16th place, but desperate times lay ahead. They were relegated to Division Three North in 1950. Twenty years later, their fifth successive application for re-election to the league, at the bottom of Division Four, was unsuccessful. They were replaced by Cambridge United who polled 31 votes to Park Avenue's 17.

The Spireites were looking up. The 'successful season envisaged' by the *Derbyshire Times* came to pass and if Mr Rodgers stuck to his boycott of the club, he missed some treats. They ended the 1946/47 fourth in Division Two, the club's highest finish in the Football League. It was an excellent season, including a thrilling 4-3 win over Tottenham at White Hart Lane, which brought great joy to the townsfolk and not least coal miner Ernest Vaughan who had just become a dad for the 23rd time. Mr Vaughan, aged 67 and still working at the coal face at Holmewood Colliery, had fathered 16 children with his first wife, Daisy, and seven with second wife, Gladys.

44

Football League Division Two
Leicester City 0 Manchester City 3 (HT: 0-0)
Scorers – Manchester City: Jackson, McDowall, Walsh
Attendance: 28,159

'A sensational spell of bowling by Walsh, who took five wickets in nine deliveries for two runs, completely routed Notts.'

ENGELBERT HUMPERDINCK and his family moved to Leicester in 1946. The arrival of the great singer-to-be passed largely unnoticed at the time but the arrival of the new football season elicited great excitement. It brought a huge lift to a city which had known its share of suffering in the preceding years. The Luftwaffe targeted Leicester on numerous occasions, notably the night of 19 November 1940, the Leicester Blitz, when 108 people lost their lives. There were frequent air raids, two of which caused damage to the Filbert Street home of Leicester City Football Club.

Much work went into repairing and readying Filbert Street for 31 August 1946, when it was to host its first Football League match for seven years. The anticipation of the city, a microcosm of the mood across the country, was eloquently captured by the *Leicester Chronicle*, 'Football, real, honest-to-goodness stuff, comes back with a bang today. A million voices will send a mighty roar re-echoing around the terraces as the great kick-off plunges a hundred teams into the biggest soccer boom of all time. The synthetic milk and watery substitute of the war has gone for good. Instead, promotion and relegation – survival of the fittest and the devil take the hindmost – will arouse the fans from the boredom of a rationed existence.'

Immediate promotion was the aim for Leicester City and their visitors, Manchester City. The two clubs were desperate to regain glories which each had tasted relatively recently before their fortunes took a decline. In 1929, Leicester finished runners-up in the Football League, just one point behind champions Sheffield Wednesday, but that happy season was followed by a succession of relegation battles culminating in demotion to Division Two in 1935. They went back up in 1937 and back down in 1939.

Manchester City, meanwhile, had been champions less than ten years earlier. In 1937, powered by the goalkeeping of Frank Swift and the goalscoring of Peter Doherty, they finished three points clear of Charlton Athletic to bring the title to the city of Manchester for the first time. It was a wonderful season for the Maine Road club, but the history of the light blues is full of vicissitudes. They kicked off the following campaign as defending champions. They ended it relegated with only West Bromwich Albion below them in the table. The two Citys both felt they belonged in Division One and entered the 1946/47 season on a mission to return there sharpish. For one of them, it would be mission accomplished.

The *Manchester Evening News* was cagey ahead of the opening game, 'City, treading again the hard road back, have got hopes that the introduction of new life into the front line may make their visit to Leicester profitable. Certainly, Harry Jackson and Andy Black come with sharpshooting reputations, but the whole side will have to dovetail well against one of the youngest teams ever fielded at Filbert-street.' Leicester were indeed leaning heavily on youth, partly due to a sluggish transfer market, as explained by the *Leicester Chronicle*, 'Close-season transfers have been few and far between. Ridiculous prices have been demanded for even reserve players who lack big football experience, and anything less than four figures is almost unheard of these days. Clubs are setting a high price not in the hope of pulling off a big deal, but rather to discourage transactions. In this transitional period, anything can happen. The unknown of today is the star of tomorrow, and with so many old-timers retained at an age when they would normally be looking for coaching jobs, managers are not letting anyone slip through their fingers.'

While managers Johnny Duncan and Wilf Wild honed their preparations, work continued at Filbert Street to ready the ground, reported the *Leicester Evening Mail* on the eve of the match, 'All the members of Leicester City's team for tomorrow have reported fit and last-minute arrangements are being completed to have all parts of the Filbert-street ground in a spick and span condition for the visit of Manchester City in the season's opening game. With eight internationals in the two sides, a good game is assured.'

Leicester sports fans who believed in good omens were encouraged by news from Nottingham. Australian left-arm wrist-spinner Jack Walsh was twirling Leicestershire towards victory over arch-rivals Nottinghamshire at Trent Bridge. 'A sensational spell of bowling by Walsh, who took five wickets in nine deliveries for two runs, completely routed Notts and they were all out for 174,' reported the *Mail.* Thanks to Maurice Tompkin's skilful unbeaten 69 in good bowling conditions, Leicestershire closed out a 129-run win. Could the footballers round off a happy weekend?

To judge from the start they made, yes. 'LEICESTER PROVIDE THE FIRST THRILLS' announced the *Leicester Daily Mercury*'s late Saturday edition as Manchester City, in their away kit of 'white shirts and black knickers', were pinned in their own half early on. But the home side came up against greatness in the form of Frank Swift. 'City's opening was highly promising,' reported the *Mercury*. 'In the first minute a free kick led to a smart move on the right, in which Sep Smith pushed through a capital ground pass to Griffiths who cut in to sweep the ball across the goalmouth. King, making a headlong dive, got his head to the ball and only just missed the target. For the first few minutes, Leicester dictated the pace, and Sep Smith was often brilliant with his constructive designs. The football was hard and there was plenty of method in Leicester's play. They were applying the through pass very well and also swinging the ball about at times in a manner that clearly disconcerted the opposition.'

Swift, however, deployed his 1.88m of height and 29.8cm of finger span to great effect. He made brilliant saves to deny Smith, Mel

Griffiths and Charlie Adam while, at the other end, Alick Grant had his cigar out. 'Leicester's goalkeeper was having a really cushy time compared with Swift, who was the central figure in many a dramatic situation,' said the *Mercury*. 'If you don't take your chances' is a truism which has applied to every football match ever played. In 1897. In 1909. In 1982. In 2026. And in 1946. Swift's excellence was the foundation on which his side built an unlikely victory.

'SWIFT BEAT CITY' was the *Leicester Evening Mail* headline, under which Crusader reported, 'After being definitely in command for the first half, Leicester City foolishly allowed Manchester City to score three soft goals at Filbert-street on Saturday, and thus the Lancastrians started their season on a high note with a flattering 3-0 victory. With a crowd of 28,159, it would have been a great send off for Leicester City if they could have turned their midfield superiority into goals. Eight minutes sufficed to transform Manchester City from a struggling side into a commanding force with a three-goal lead in which the speed of Jackson and the luck of Walsh had sealed Leicester's fate with over 30 minutes of the match still to run. In fairness to the City attack, however, the fact must not be lost sight of that Swift played a "blinder" in goal for the winners. This long-limbed English keeper, who skippered the team, had a grand sense of anticipation and his covering was almost uncanny.'

Swift apart, Crusader was not overly impressed, 'All in all, the football was not of a high standard compared with prewar games, and both teams will have to show considerable improvement to avoid a struggling climax.'

While the *Mail* readers digested other headlines from around the noble county of Leicestershire – 'SIX WEEKEND BURGLARIES IN MARKET HARBORO; IMMUNISATION VAN IN BOSWORTH AREA; HINCKLEY BREAD RATIONING SURVEY' – the *Manchester Evening News* reported that, despite the opening-day win, 'CITY WILL IGNORE COST TO REBUILD SIDE', 'Three clubs with great soccer histories have joined the queue of officials with cheques to exchange for football stars – Manchester City, Derby County and Leicester City. Their opening success has not blinded the Maine Road folk to the necessity of infusing still more new blood into the senior side. There is a left-wing problem to be solved, and it is also recognised that Barkas and Sproston cannot continue to outstrip Father Time. City are ready to pay really big money for worthy successors.'

Next up for Wild's side was a home derby against a Bury team which had started the season by thrashing Fulham 7-2 (see Chapter 26). Special Correspondent, writing for the *MEN*, came up with an intriguing wrinkle to the game, 'More than ordinary interest attaches to tomorrow's City v Bury match at Maine Road (kick-off 6.15). Manchester will have a chance of watching a new departure in football strategy by Bury. Bury's "G Man" plan is still in its experimental stage, but when tried out against Fulham, Bury overwhelmed the London team and produced the day's highest score. Spotting the "G Man" will provide an interesting sidelight at the game, but all the spectators will see will be four Bury forwards in the front line with Wyles, the inside-right, playing as an auxiliary half-back.'

City were untroubled by the 'G Man'. They beat Bury 3-1 and four points out of four proved to be a platform for promotion. While Leicester finished the season in ninth place (they would have to wait until 1954 for promotion), Manchester City's momentum grew and grew. They lost just three matches before Christmas, away to West Ham, Newcastle and Birmingham. At home, they were rock solid and particularly destructive against opponents with three words in their name. They hammered Bradford Park Avenue 7-2 and West Bromwich Albion 5-0.

City enjoyed a profitable Christmas. The fixture compiler decreed that the players and supporters of Manchester City and Plymouth – not an easy trip in 2026, never mind 1946 – should mingle on Christmas Day and Boxing Day. They won both games, 4-3 at Maine Road and then 3-2 at Home Park, followed up with a nuggety 1-0 win at home to Leicester on the 28th. The Christmas Day victory was the first of eight in succession that left City strongly placed when the season went into deep freeze. They sealed the Division Two championship with a 2-0 win over West Ham at Maine Road on 24 May before finally concluding their season with a 5-1 home win over Newport County on 14 June. Manchester City finished four points clear of Burnley at the top. Newport finished six points below Swansea Town at the bottom and it was the last-ever league meeting between the clubs.

Their paths were to spectacularly diverge, though they did cross once more, in 1962, when City won a League Cup tie at Somerton Park. 'County fought like Tigers before going down 2-1,' reported the *Manchester Evening News,* though the match report from south Wales was somewhat overshadowed by big news concerning two future knights. 'ALF RAMSEY IS NEW ENGLAND BOSS' was the back-page headline, announcing that the Ipswich Town manager had agreed to succeed Walter Winterbottom in the role. 'This is a tremendous challenge and I shall be sorry to leave Ipswich,' said Ramsey. 'At first, I was unable to make up my mind because I felt my responsibility to Ipswich very keenly. Then I realised I would have to take it.' Ramsey was, the paper revealed, 'the FA's second choice for the job, Burnley skipper Jimmy Adamson turned down the £5,000 a year job for which he did not apply'.

A busy back page also reflected upon the dire position in which Manchester United found themselves. Matt Busby's reign as manager may have started with a victory over Grimsby Town on 31 August 1946 (see Chapter 39) but, in 1962, Old Trafford was consumed by crisis talk. They had just lost 6-2 to Tottenham Hotspur at White Hart Lane, their fifth defeat in six games. 'Manchester United are now rock-bottom of the First Division,' wrote *Manchester Evening News* legend David Meek, 'and today's question is WHAT NOW MR BUSBY?'

45

Football League Division Two
Luton Town 4 Sheffield Wednesday 1 (HT: 2-1)
Scorers – Luton: Daniel (3), Waugh; Sheffield Wednesday: Robinson
Attendance: 20,950

'One of the main difficulties is a shortage of turnstiles and Mr Coley asks me to appeal to supporters, especially those for the 1s 3d part of the ground, to try to bring the correct money.'

FOUR HAT-TRICKS were scored on the opening day of the 1946/47 season, by Jesse Pye (Wolves v Arsenal, see Chapter 2), George Robledo (Barnsley v Nottingham Forest, see Chapter 15), Steve Griffiths (Aldershot v Bristol City, see Chapter 8) and Mel Daniel, for Luton Town. Of that list, only the last-named had to share the spotlight on the following Monday with two chimpanzees. 'WHIPSNADE AGAIN ON THE AIR' was the headline in the *Luton News*, 'Uno and Booboo, two of the Whipsnade chimpanzees, were heard upon the air in the Children's Hour on Saturday, when Uncle Mac (Derek McCulloch) and David Seth Smith, "The Zoo Man", toured Whipsnade Zoo with a transmitting car. It was the second of such visits.'

Exactly what Uno and Booboo discussed live on air was not disclosed, but it may well have been the splendid start made by Luton. Under the shrewd guidance of manager George Martin, they made short work of a Wednesday side whose history sat proudly among the English football elite. *Luton News* correspondent Chiltern had certainly bigged them right up in his pre-match preview, 'The Town could have had few more attractive visitors for the opening of their league programme than the famous Sheffield Wednesday, who, in the course of their glorious past, have won all the main honours which English football has to offer. Luton's team to duty on this match has been chosen, and follows very much the lines indicated by the constitution of the trial teams. The forward line contains no surprises. Daniel was the obvious choice at inside-right, with Eddie Duggan out of the running. Altogether, it looks a nicely balanced team and there seems no reason why it should not meet with a good measure of success. If the Town keep the ball down and play the football of which they are capable, then the odds are that they will start this new era of postwar football with a win.'

George Duke would take his place in goal for Luton, Chiltern added, with some sporting success recently banked, as a boxing champ, 'If ever a footballer played himself into a team it was George Duke. I am almost sure his display on Saturday was the best I have seen him give. If he can keep up this form, then one of the Town's main anxieties will disappear. At any rate he was an automatic choice for this week. There is no one more keen than George, who is still in the army and is likely to be until the end of the season. Recently, he has taken up boxing, and won an army competition in the light-heavyweight division. In the final, he gained a knockout in the second round, so there was no doubt about the decision.'

Turning his attention to Sheffield Wednesday, Chiltern warned, 'The most dangerous number is likely to be Jackie Robinson, who played for England against Finland in 1937, against Germany and Switzerland in 1938, and against Wales in 1939. He and Doug Beach know each other's play, for they were with the same army unit at Colchester for some time.' The threat posed by Robinson was even greater, revealed the *Sheffield Star* 'Green 'Un', now that his corns had cleared up, 'There is every reason to believe that Wednesday will see the best of Jackie Robinson this season. Last season, following his release from the army, he was troubled from corns on the soles of his feet. He had never suffered this way before and they were attributed to his work as a PT instructor in the services, which necessitated rubbers being worn almost continuously in the gym.

'Jackie has now had the corns cut out and hopes to recover his old dash. After all, two years back, he was the fastest player in a short spurt with the ball the game had probably seen since Bob Kelly's days.'

Sheffield Wednesday arrived in Bedfordshire with a team in deep transition. Robinson was the only member of it who played in the opening fixture seven years earlier (which Luton won 3-0). During the war, long-serving secretary Eric Taylor had also taken on the manager's role and enjoyed some success. During the 1942/43 season Wednesday scored more than 100 goals in 39 games, including a 10-2 win at Mansfield and an 8-2 victory over arch-rivals Sheffield United. As the war lengthened, however, they found it difficult to even field a team at times. The squad became thin and inexperienced and the summer of 1946 brought very little transfer activity to reinforce it. Eric England was appointed as assistant to Taylor but, in terms of proven player collateral, the two Erics didn't have a lot to work with.

There was some good news for the visiting fans when the teams ran out. Their team had ditched the unpopular hooped shirts of the previous season – 'Wednesday were wearing their prewar jerseys instead of last season's hoops ones,' reported the 'Green 'Un' – but that was pretty much where the good news ended. Only three minutes elapsed before Luton scored. Frank Soo, an elegant midfielder recently signed from Leicester City, started a slick move which Daniel finished off with a ferocious angled shot which went in off the bar. Robinson equalised from Wednesday's first attack in the 12th minute, but Luton regained the lead five minutes before half-time when Billy Waugh headed home Alan Steen's free kick.

At half-time, the Owls were still in it but, to the delight of Uno, Booboo and the rest of the Luton faithful, Daniel showed his quality. 'The Town began the second half in rip-roaring style,' reported the *Luton News*. 'Even so there was always the possibility that Wednesday, dangerous in the breakaway, might steal another equaliser. That possibility was disposed of completely when Daniel took a pass from Billington, and ignoring appeals to the referee from the Wednesday defenders, slammed the ball into the net. After that it was all Luton and Daniel helped himself to another goal 15 minutes from the end, when Billington provided another opening.'

'DANIEL GOT IN WEDNESDAY'S DEN' was the biblical slant taken by the *Sheffield Star* 'Green 'Un' headline writer, while reporter Taffy Williams lamented, 'The slowness of the carrying out of their movement lost Wednesday a lot of their effectiveness.' Luton had impressed the occupants of the press box. 'Watch Luton as a strong ninety-minute team liable to upset the best,' advised the *Daily Mirror*, adding, 'Advice to Sheffield Wednesday: check up on defence.' The *Sunday Express* reckoned, 'Luton were always better than a moderate Wednesday team whose weakness was in defence. The scheming of Connelly and Soo had much to do with Luton's superiority, which was most pronounced in the second half when Luton were almost run off their feet. Daniel, Luton inside-right, gave a pointer to the Welsh international selectors with a hat-trick on his first appearance in peace-time league football.'

In Monday's *Luton News,* meanwhile, the well-informed Chiltern gave supporters the inside track. Under the headline 'PLAYERS WERE CONFIDENT THEY WOULD WIN', he began with a swipe at certain national media organisations, 'If the world in general, and the London press and the BBC in particular, regarded the Town's win over Sheffield Wednesday as one of the day's surprise results, this view was not shared by the Luton players themselves. Throughout the week before the match they were full of confidence that they would get away to a flying start. Manager George Martin shared in the general optimism – perhaps he did a lot to foster it, for George is an old campaigner and knows the value of players believing in their own ability. Much can be done towards winning a match before the players take the field. Tactics talked over in the dressing room have become a part of modern football, and they helped in the defeat of Wednesday. It was decided beforehand that the Wednesday would concentrate their defensive plan on keeping a close watch on Billington. Obvious answer was to send someone upfield to help him and make use of the gaps which were bound to occur. Daniel was detailed for the job, and made such use of his opportunity that he became the man of the match with three grand goals. So everything came up to expectation, and the biggest league crowd since 18 September 1937, when Tottenham Hotspur were the visitors, went home happy and with a firm belief that their team will be going places this year.'

A happy day for the Hatters, though it brought its pressures off the field. Phil Coley, starting an 18-year tenure as club secretary, and his staff were fully stretched to deal with the big crowd. Chiltern reported, 'The club were faced with certain difficulties in coping with the crowd on Saturday. One of the main difficulties is a shortage of turnstiles and Mr Coley asks me to appeal to supporters, especially those for the 1s 3d part of the ground, to try to bring the correct money. The giving of change holds up the queues and if this is not necessary then much time would be saved. Another point is that if people from the Dallow-road area who wish to go into the grand-stand would use the Maple-road entrance, they will get into the ground more quickly. Everything went off in the most orderly fashion, and although there were rumours that the gates had been closed, they were rumours and nothing more.'

It was a brilliant start for Luton, but they could not fully build on it. They ended the season in 13th, the first of a series of mid-table finishes which gradually improved until they were promoted in 1955. For Wednesday, it was a struggle. Two days after losing to Luton, they shipped another four in a 4-2 defeat at home to Barnsley, during which the crowd was addressed at half-time by England cricketer Freddie Brown. 'Mr F.R. Brown, the Surrey and England cricketer, will be making an appeal during the interval in the match between Wednesday and Barnsley at Hillsborough on Monday, on behalf of the Sheffield Appeal of Boys' Clubs,' revealed the 'Green 'Un'. 'Mr Brown himself was a prisoner in Oflag 79 where the appeal movement started. In Sheffield, it is hoped to raise £30,000 to meet the local commitments.'

The Owls finished with only the two relegated clubs – Swansea and Newport – below them. It didn't help that Robinson left in October when he joined Sunderland for a club-record £6,800. His departure was a big blow to the team but represented a decent bit of business. In October 1934, Wednesday had bought him from Shiremoor for £20.

There was no big-money move for the hat-trick hero. The versatile Daniel, a qualified carpenter, stayed with Luton, playing up front, at half-back or full-back, until 1949. Spells with Aldershot Town and Newport County followed before his skills finally landed in the Kent League with Betteshanger CW.

Back in Bedfordshire, meanwhile, Chiltern found space among his salutations of Luton's fine win to also report 'A HOUGHTON REGIS GRUMBLE'. The story chronicled an instalment of an eternal conflict which many sports clubs up and down the country will recognise: football v cricket, 'My old friends in the Houghton Regis Cricket Club are up in arms, so some of Luton Town's players who were over there on Sunday tell me. The trouble is that the village football club has received permission to play on the green, and that part of the pitch which has been marked out takes in the wicket. Now Houghton Regis have spent a number of years in bringing this wicket to something near perfection, and if the football arrangement stands, then it seems that all this labour will be lost. I understand that it is possible to mark out a football pitch without touching the wicket, and that this has been done previously. Surely the footballers could go this far to meet the cricketers.'

46

Scottish League A
Motherwell 2 Hibernian 1 (HT: 0-0)
Scorers – Motherwell: Kerr, Brown; Hibernian: Peat
Attendance: 10,000

'A strident voice repeatedly pointed out to all concerned that the object of pursuit was "a baw, no' a dumplin".'

BAILIE WELCH was a compassionate man. Presiding at Motherwell Police Court on Monday, 26 August 1946, the dispenser of justice displayed considerable humanity after he heard an unusual and emotive case – 'DENTAL MECHANIC IS BITTEN ... THE DISCRIMINATING DOG'. The canine in question had raced wildly out of a garden and wrapped its jaws around the thigh of a passing dentist. It survived the subsequent legal proceedings by the skin of its teeth, thanks to the kindness of Mr Welch.

The *Motherwell Times* reported the story with a whopping 61-word intro and a strange slant, implying that the dog had attacked the passer-by because it had information that he worked in the dentistry business, 'A remarkable story of a Motherwell dog which gave right of passage to painters working about the house but was so absolutely prejudiced against a dental mechanic that it jumped on him as he was passing along the street and bit him on the left thigh, causing a punctured wound, was heard at Motherwell Police Court on Monday before Bailie Welch. The dog's attitude may have been due to some curious instinct that the passer-by had something to do with teeth and might not be averse to being himself the object of a demonstration. The dog is a cairn terrier, and the owner is a school teacher.

'The case was called at the court on Monday, when the owner appeared in person and answered the charge which was that, being the owner of a dog which was dangerous, he had failed to keep it under control, whereby it attacked and bit the pedestrian already described. The respondent admitted he had previously been warned to keep the dog under control. He felt that the dog was not really so dangerous as one would imagine. On this particular day, he was working in the garden and he allowed the dog to run about inside the garden grounds. He heard the dog barking and brought him in, but he didn't see the attack on the pedestrian.

'The Fiscal (Mr John Ford) said the pedestrian was simply passing along the roadway in front of the house when the dog ran out of the gate, jumped up on him and bit him. The owner explained to the court that, after being warned on the last occasion, he endeavoured to find means of exercising the necessary control over the dog. He tried to get a muzzle, but the required article had gone out of stock during the war and was not obtainable at the moment. Failing this, he sought to restrict the dog to its own habitation, which was the house and the garden grounds, feeling sure it would be perfectly safe there. He had not bargained for the dog making a bolt out of the gate and attacking someone. Still, he thought the dog would come round and he was rather unwilling to have him destroyed. Bailie ordered the owner to see that the dog was kept under proper control, for if there was any further complaint, an order would be given to have it destroyed.'

Three weeks into the Scottish League season, Motherwell supporters wanted their team to start showing their teeth. It was truly a new era at Fir Park, the first campaign since 1911 which the team did not enter under the management of John 'Sailor' Hunter. After 35 years, the 67-year-old had relinquished team responsibilities to concentrate fully on the role of secretary. The managerial reins passed from one Well legend to another – George Stevenson. The 'Prince of Inside-Forwards', Stevenson made 510 appearances for Motherwell between 1923 and 1939. The first player to be awarded a benefit game by the club (against Huddersfield Town in September

1929), he played a huge part in their championship triumph in 1932, the first time since 1904 that the title was won by someone other than Celtic or Rangers.

As manager, Stevenson had a huge rebuilding job to do with a squad which contained none of the prewar playing staff. His side had started the season slowly with just one win from six games, and none from three at Fir Park, so for the visit of high-flying Hibernian the new boss shuffled the pack. 'Motherwell make revolutionary changes in their side to face Hibernian at Fir Park tomorrow,' reported the *Glasgow Evening Citizen*. 'A new centre-half makes his debut; Watson, now fit, takes over at inside-right; and Humphries comes in at inside-left to the exclusion of Gordon Bremner. The new Fir Park pivot, a well-built lad named Kerr, was demobbed recently, and played with St Bernard's before the war. He has figured in the reserve side in recent games and has now been signed. Watson's return will be well-received. He has been out of the game for several months. He and Humphries should give Motherwell speed and virility in the inside positions.'

Hibernian arrived at Fir Park top of Division A, but having just lost their 100 per cent record with a defeat at Aberdeen. They had started the campaign in sensational style by beating Queen of the South 9-1. 'Hibernian's thumping success over Queen of the South should put thousands on to the "gate" at Ibrox on Wednesday night,' reported the *Edinburgh Evening News*. 'This match against the Rangers will give an immediate pointer to the championship prospects of the Easter Road side.' Hibs won that one too, 2-1, and then beat Queen's Park, Clyde and Hamilton Academical before losing at Pittodrie in a Wednesday-night match that left a difficult legacy of injuries. 'The stiff games in midweek exacted a pretty heavy toll on players, and the prospects for tomorrow's games are overshadowed by uncertainties regarding the composition of the teams,' the *Evening News* revealed. 'This is specially reflected in the case of the Hibernians: and while the defence will be on the usual lines for the visit to Motherwell, the line-up forward will not be decided upon until after tonight's Reserve Cup Final replay with the Rangers at Easter Road. It will be good news for supporters of the Greens that the X-ray examinations yesterday of Smith and Weir revealed no breaks. The outside-right, however, is suffering from torn ligaments. Cuthbertson's leg injury is responding to treatment, but it is unlikely that any of the three will strip at Fir Park.'

Hibs appeared to be coping adequately with the disruption when, in a tight game, Willie Peat fired a 20-yard free kick through a dodgy wall to give them a 52nd-minute lead. However, the home side quickly turned it around with two goals in four minutes. They equalised when John Kerr finished off a 'grand passing movement' then added a winner which had nothing to do with grandeur, Jimmy 'Buster' Brown netting one very much from the old school. 'Over came a high ball from the left,' reported the *Sunday Post*, 'Kerr pulled it down in front of the onrushing Brown. Everyone – and the ball – landed in the net.' The referee, William Crawford of Glasgow, saw nothing wrong, Motherwell had their first home win under Stevenson, and Hibs, after their flying start, were nursing back-to-back defeats.

The scorer of the first and creator of the second, Kerr – who was included in midfield only due to an injury to Andy Paton – was headlined in the *Post* as '"FORGOTTEN" MAN THE INSPIRATION': 'Away back in the good old days of 1938, St Bernard's sensationally knocked Motherwell out of the Scottish Cup. A young man named John Kerr was Saints' hero. Yesterday that same John Kerr, forgotten by everyone but Motherwell, walked off Fir Park with the cheers of the crowd ringing in his ears. When Hibernian were in the lead, they had chances to put the result well beyond doubt. They just frittered them away. I can recall Weir, in the first minute, Arthur Milne in the 21st, and Peat near the end, all doing amazing things with the ball when it seemed much easier to plonk it into the net. When Peat's free kick from 25 yards slithered its way somehow or other into the net, up went the Motherwell sleeves. In a twinkling they were storming around Kerr.'

While Kerr made the headlines on the *Post*'s back page, the front brought hot vegetable news. 'YOU CAN'T EAT SMALL CARROTS', 'Carrots which will pass through a screen of three-quarters of an inch mesh may not be sold for human consumption. So says a Food Ministry Order. The use of the screen will exclude very small carrots and excessive soil.'

This revelation must have tempted *Glasgow Evening Citizen* columnist Harry Young to offer his thoughts on it. However, in light of a second successive defeat for Hibs, he instead delivered a frank appraisal of their title prospects, 'Hibernian, who are reckoned to be Rangers' most serious challengers, have already had a weakness exposed. The absence of Gordon Smith and Cuthbertson from their attack made them a moderate company at Fir Park and it looks as if Hibernian are relying too much on individual stars. I was also surprised that a team with a reputedly good reserve string should find it necessary to field an injured man at outside-right. Weir, who deputised for Gordon Smith, had his left shoulder strapped up as a result of a knock at Aberdeen and was unable to do himself, or his team, justice.

'Motherwell are not yet back to their best, and this was their first home win of the season. But they are beginning to see daylight. Kerr, who came into the side at centre-half in place of Paton, gave a most steady display, and the ex-St Bernard left-back showed that his experiences in top-class services football on the continent have given him a flair for leadership.'

The *Motherwell Times* saluted the spirit of Stevenson's men, 'It was not an easy victory, for the Easter Road side were a convincing company, but a better and brighter Well, after being a goal down, overcame their opponents' defence and got two goals to win the game.' The paper also passed on a most courteous invitation to travel with the supporters to Clyde in two weeks' time, 'All members wishing to travel to Shawfield on Saturday, 14 September 1946, please hand in names to secretary at the British Legion Hall, Motherwell, on Sunday, 8 September 1946, at 6.30pm. Also anyone desirous of joining cordially invited.'

Those fans who took up the gracious invitation were not rewarded with a match to remember. 'A greasy ball and a slippery pitch made this league game at Shawfield on Saturday one of the less skilful exhibitions of football' was the *Motherwell Times*'s verdict on Clyde's 3-1 win. More rewarding was the experience of spectators who watched Raith Rovers' 3-1 win over Cowdenbeath in Division B. These fortunate individuals, reported the *Dundee Evening Telegraph*, were treated to an entertaining game on the field – 'Wee Jackie Stewart played a blinder on Rovers' right wing' – and some wise words off it – 'A premature festive note was struck at Stark's Park on Saturday, as a strident voice repeatedly pointed out to all concerned that the object of pursuit was "a baw, no' a dumplin".'

47

Football League Division Three South
Notts County 1 Bournemouth 0 (HT: 0-0)
Scorers – Notts County: Brown
Attendance: 39,200

'A bright and happy announcement will always have more effect than the doleful and funereal-toned appeal for clothing coupons heard on Saturday which ended "do your best please", as if the speaker was already impressed with the hopelessness of dressing the modern footballer in these days of clothes rationing.'

BOURNEMOUTH'S SUPPORTERS travelled to Nottingham on 31 August 1946 still needled by the injustices of 6 February 1937. On that chilly late-winter afternoon nine years earlier, Meadow Lane hosted a thriller in which Notts County, powered by a Billy Chalmers hat-trick, fought back from behind to beat the Cherries 4-3 to leapfrog Brighton to the top of the Division Three South table.

The *Nottingham Journal* saluted Chalmers, a former Rangers, Newcastle United and Bury inside-right who would one day manage Juventus, whose famous black-and-white-striped kit was inspired by Notts County's, 'Apart from his three goals, Chalmers was the County's best forward, putting in a lot of work in midfield and showing a wise discretion in the way he distributed the ball.' A happy day for County was completed by the news that Brighton had lost to Northampton Town courtesy of Syd Rawlings's double at the County Ground. What the *Journal* scribe omitted to mention was the strident view of the Bournemouth camp that all four Notts goals were offside.

'Some dispute was caused by the four goals, appeals being made by the visiting side for disallowances on the grounds of offside,' reported A Special Correspondent for the *Bournemouth Weekly Post and Graphic*, before adding, with a touch of Corinthian spirit, 'While I am prepared to share Boscombe's doubt about the second goal and to admit that the other three were "benefits of the doubt", so far as Notts were concerned, nevertheless the visitors had been clearly outplayed in the movements that led up to them.'

All associated with the Cherries (A Special Correspondent stuck with Boscombe even though the club's original name, Boscombe St John's Institute, was changed to Bournemouth & Boscombe Athletic in 1923) no doubt felt that justice was done two months later when Notts were pipped to promotion by Luton Town.

Having tasted the frustration of missing promotion by just two points, County then went backwards. They finished 11th in the following two seasons, the last before the war. Eleventh in Division Three South was a considerable fall for the biggest club in Nottingham at the time, FA Cup winners in 1896 and a Division One side as recently as the mid-1920s. In 1946/47, a serious tilt at promotion was expected and, against a Bournemouth side which had bobbed along unspectacularly in Division Three South since joining the Football League in 1923, a winning start was expected.

A big crowd was anticipated, with Meadow Lane, damaged by wartime bombing, having passed all the relevant safety inspections. 'With memories of the Bolton disaster still fresh, clubs, police and local authorities have co-operated during the close season in an effort to make the watching of football as safe as possible,' reported the *Nottingham Journal*. 'Crowd limits have been set for many grounds, and repairs carried out to stands, terraces and equipment. Mr C.G. Barnes, chairman of Notts County FC, announced that Mr G.W. Downs (assistant chief constable of Nottingham) and Supt. Coates (Southern Division) inspected the Meadow-lane ground yesterday and fixed a maximum holding capacity at 50,000. This makes the Notts ground one of the biggest in the Midlands.'

Turning to on-field matters, the *Journal* highlighted the debut of Canadian striker Fred Whittaker. The 23-year-old was a quirky pick-up by County manager Arthur Stollery. Having served with the Royal Canadian Artillery and Canadian Infantry Corps during the war, Whittaker was in the midst of a prolific career in his native country and had been leading scorer in the Pacific Coast League in the 1945/46 season. Stollery, formerly trainer at Dulwich Hamlet, Chelsea and with the England amateur side, decided to take a punt. The *Journal* wrote, 'The big kick-off on Saturday finds Notts County fielding several newcomers in their Div III League match against Bournemouth at Meadow Lane. Notts supporters will naturally centre most attention on tall 23-year-old Canadian, Fred Whittaker, who is making his debut in English League football. There should be better and faster soccer this season. Not only is the incentive present again but players for the first time for seven years have been able to train seriously and regularly under almost normal conditions.'

Bournemouth arrived in Nottinghamshire with the unusual incentive of looking to complete back-to-back 10-0 Football League wins. They had signed off before the war by drubbing Northampton Town by that margin, but seven years later, on the eve of the big kick-off, the *Bournemouth Times* made no mention of that result. Instead, the paper focused on the previous Saturday's internal trial game, the reporter clearly sharing the timeless frustrations of onlookers at pre-season warm-up matches, 'Puzzled watchers were confused in the second half as both teams had been turned inside out to give the largest number possible the chance of a game. Goalscorers were Kirkham, Marsden, Burke, Rose (2), Ames, Morris and Tunnicliffe. Owing to the switchover of players at half-time, no result can be given.'

The reporter was enthused by the antics of hardy Scottish midfielder Tommy Paton, less so by the monotone of the morose chap on the newly installed public address system, 'Some 2,000 cold spectators braved the weather to watch Boscombe's trial match – in aid of charities – which culminated in 30 players giving a rain-soaked display throughout the afternoon on a pitch which Paton, for one, embraced many times as he cheerily slipped, skidded and fell while giving the crowd a laugh and a chance to appreciate his hardworking game at inside-right.

'Tail note: the expensively installed public address system worked perfectly and favourable comments were heard in the stands regarding the brighter music, but the suggestion that the announcer should brighten his voice is a good one. Come along, Boscombe! A bright and happy announcement will always have more effect than the doleful and funereal-toned appeal for clothing coupons heard on Saturday which ended "do your best please", as if the speaker was already impressed with the hopelessness of dressing the modern footballer in these days of clothes rationing.'

The paper's only reference to the Cherries' visit to Notts County the following day was the listing of the likely XI, but there was plenty of other sports news, including success for an up-and-coming local golfer, 'Peter Alliss, son of the Ferndown professional Percy Alliss, is doing well in the boys' golf championship at Edinburgh this week, beating DS Blair by two and one in the third round yesterday.' There were also full details from the Town Hall where poultry aficionados clamoured for glory and 'MR CAFFYN'S BIRD WAS THE BEST', 'Bournemouth and District Domestic Poultry Club's first show at the Town Hall brought 55 entries of birds and a good show of eggs. All the later exhibited were sent to Boscombe Hospital. Mr G.A. Kent, E. Boldre was judge. Mr Caffyn has the best bird in the show and Mrs King's was the best dish of eggs. Other results: Light breed hen or pullet: 1 and 3, Mr Benbow, 2, Mr Heath. Heavy breed hen or pullet: 1 and 3, Mr Caffyn, 2, Mr Daly. Any breed cock or cockerel: 1, Mr Benbow, 2, Mr Dowell, 3, Mr Daly. Cross breed hen or pullet: 1 and 2, Mrs King, 3, Mrs Sutton. Bantams: 1, 2 and 3, Mr Best. Eggs – Brown: 1, Mrs King, 2, Mr Dowell, 3, Mr Plant. White: 1, Mr Dowell, 2, Mr Heath. Tinted: 1, Mr Dowell, 2, Mr Curtis, 3, Mr Tappenden.'

Disappointment awaited Mr Caffyn and his challengers when news arrived from beside the Trent that the Cherries had opened their season with a narrow defeat. Whittaker took time to settle into the home attack but County grabbed the decisive goal in the second half when Willie Fallon's cross was netted by Cyril Brown. The home side hung on for victory despite effectively ending the game with ten men after Fallon was crocked and returned to the field able to do little more than hobble around the wing.

There was plenty to please County chairman Charles Barnes: two points in the bank, along with plenty of lovely revenue from a big crowd: '39,000 SEE NOTTS OPEN WITH A VICTORY' was the *Journal* headline with 'WHITTAKER NEEDS TIME TO SETTLE DOWN' as a subheading in defence of the Canadian who had only landed in England seven days earlier so had little time to gel with his new team-mates. 'Biggest surprise at Meadow-lane was not Notts County's merited opening victory over Bournemouth – one of the sides fancied to make a bold promotion bid this season – but the size of the attendance, officially returned at 39,200,' reported A.E. Botting. 'This is indicative of the big football boom Nottingham is experiencing and it also points to the fact that if Notts can find a winning team, they will not lack support. Saturday's huge crowd saw a game of contrasts. Play was good in some phases, indifferent in others. Men of the match were the rival goalkeepers. Harry Brown made never the semblance of a mistake and gave his defence ample confidence by his clean handling, while Bournemouth, well-served in defence by Marsden and Wilson, owed it to the agile Bird that they were not in arrears at the interval. Taking the match all through, Notts earned their bonus money.

'The afternoon's centre of attention was, of course, strongly built, tall, Canadian centre-forward Fred Whittaker, making his English football debut, exactly a week after landing at Southampton. It was a big ordeal for the 23-year-old to play his initial match before such a big crowd, and supporters will realise that he needs time to settle down before one can judge his play by league standards. When he sharpens up a little, he may well be an outstanding performer.'

Whittaker's stay with Notts was to be brief. Troubled by a sciatic nerve problem, he played just ten games, scoring two goals, but he earned the admiration of County's fans for giving it a go, very capably, in goal when the team was hit by a goalkeeper crisis in the spring. In two games between the sticks, Whittaker conceded just once, in a 1-1 draw at Bristol City, before keeping a clean sheet in a 1-0 home win over Reading.

That punt by Stollery did not come off but another he was to make certainly did. In November the following year, he persuaded Tommy Lawton, a friend from their time together at Stamford Bridge, to drop down from Chelsea, in Division One, to the Third Division South.

Six days after the season opener, the *Bournemouth Times* made no mention of the Cherries' game at Notts County. With limited space at its disposal, the paper concentrated instead on the team's opening of their points account with a midweek 1-1 draw with Queens Park Rangers, 'A crowd of 5,000 saw Boscombe and Queens Park Rangers share the points at their first home game at Dean Court on Wednesday. They also shared the wind, mud and rain.' Bournemouth were to enjoy a solid season, finishing seventh, four points and five places above County, whose season of under-achievement also brought a 6-0 defeat to Luton Town in the FA Cup third round.

At the start of September, all that lay ahead. And while County's supporters pondered what lay ahead for their team and who Stollery might bring in next, the big question in the city was revealed by *Nottingham Evening Post.* Where is Elsie?

'Because she decided to go for her holidays at Skegness this week instead of attending the Nottingham Guildhall Court to answer two allegations of receiving a number of pullovers, vests and other stolen goods, the magistrates today issued a warrant for the arrest of Elsie Hickling, of 17 James-street, Hucknall.'

48

Football League Division Three North
Tranmere Rovers 1 Rotherham United 4 (HT: 1-2)
Scorers – Tranmere Rovers: Atkinson; Rotherham United: McLean, Ardron, Wilson, Guest
Attendance: 7,000

'All just cannot afford to give the missus her money and have enough left to go fishing.'

FOOTBALL PLAYERS and supporters had many complications to confront with the plethora of postwar restrictions and shortages, but if they thought they had it bad, they needed to spare a thought for anglers. The rocketing price of maggots was just the tip of an iceberg of adversity faced by the nation's fishermen. On 31 August, news of the dismantling of Tranmere Rovers' defence by Rotherham United's Wally Ardron, in the *Sheffield Star* 'Green 'Un', sat alongside a plangent plea to politicians by angling columnist Plebeian, 'I am certain I do not have to make any apology, rather do I think I have wholehearted backing, when I keep writing about the extremely heavy expense local anglers are under to get a bit of fishing. We are under a terrible expense with rail fares as the major item. These alone kill the thoughts many have of a day's fishing and, as there's supposed to be no shame in poverty, then let's face the facts. Things in general are not what they were, and far from being what they should be. All just cannot afford to give the missus her money and have enough left to go fishing.

'I've tried, even to the tune of cornering some of our MPs on this matter and asked for their support to the application made for the restoration of anglers' privileges with rail travel. They were, as one could expect, very polite, attentive and supportive (verbally) but without exception stated the matter was not one for them, but for the Railway Rates Tribunal. One said, "Until we nationalise the railways, the government cannot do anything." Cannot do anything, eh? That's a nice kettle of fish. They could do something when they raised the fares, when they took off trains without apology, when they made it so very awkward to get away even for an annual holiday, when they asked all to be patriotic and spend holidays at home. Oh yes, they didn't say they couldn't do things then. They did them.

'Tackle, maggots too, have gone sky high in price, whilst replacing a decent rod needs a cheque book instead of a few shillings. Try to buy a fishing basket or even a bit of good line and you are either laughed at or stared at with amazement. Somebody mentioned golf was the most expensive game for the working man to try – the man who thinks that is barking up the wrong tree. Let him try fishing.'

To add to the anglers' woes, 31 August brought weather so wet they were drenched through after ten minutes beside the water. The Leeds and Liverpool Canal (which took 46 years to build and cost five times the original budget – a template for HS2) was filled to the brim by the incessant rain, its towpath flooded. The deluge was also less than ideal for the footballers at Prenton Park, but when it came to inclement weather, Wally Ardron had experienced worse.

Swinton-born Ardron's first and second Football League appearances for Rotherham were separated by seven and a half years. He made his debut on 14 January 1939, as a 20-year-old inside-left, in a 2-0 defeat at Wrexham amid a cocktail of hostile conditions. 'The ground was coated in frozen snow,' reported the 'Green 'Un', but it was later in the game, as Wrexham doggedly protected their two-goal half-time lead, that the weather really closed in. 'The services of the trainers were often required at this period of the game, slight injuries calling for their aid. It was the state of the ground that was mostly responsible for this. The light was beginning to fade and fog threatening and this made matters worse for all concerned.'

It was a dark, cold debut for Ardron, but he did enough to earn the offer of a full-time contract. He declined it, to retain his job as a fireman on the railways, so Rotherham let him go and he joined

Midland League side Denaby United. Two years later, the Millers bought him back for £750 and he repaid them with 122 goals in four wartime seasons, warming up nicely for his second Football League appearance, at Prenton Park, which would bring his first Football League goal.

Rotherham entered the new era on a roll, having won the Third Division Cup and the Division Three (East) league trophy in the 1945/46 season. Tranmere had excelled in 1938, when they won the Division Three North title, but their inaugural season in Division Two was an isolated one. Out of their depth, Rovers trailed in bottom, 14 points adrift of the rest. In 42 league games they scored just 39 goals, a desperately thin return which caused supporters to wistfully recall Boxing Day 1935 when Rovers scored a third of that number in one game – a 13-4 victory over Oldham Athletic. Oldham had beaten Rovers 4-1 at Boundary Park on Christmas Day but revenge was swift and hefty 24 hours later, as Robert 'Bunny' Bell scored nine – and then the following day was back at his day job. 'A young man who is the talk of England walked quietly into a Liverpool shipping office this morning, opened his ledgers and settled down to work,' reported the *Liverpool Evening Express*. 'It was a grand feeling when I got the eighth but the greatest pleasure was the manner in which all my colleagues helped me to get the necessary goals,' Bell told *Express* reporter The Watcher, who added, 'There was an unforgettable scene at the end of the match. The crowd broke down the barriers, rushed on to the field, and carried Bell shoulder-high to the dressing room.'

Eleven years on, with Bell having just left Everton after a decade spent in the shadow of Dixie Dean and Tommy Lawton at Goodison Park, another 13-4 scoreline was unlikely against a Rotherham side viewed as strong promotion contenders. 'Last season, Rotherham won the Eastern Region championship for the first half of the season from Darlington, and then went on to the final of the Northern Section Cup competition in which they defeated Chester on aggregate 5-4,' observed the *Liverpool Evening Express*. 'Clearly, Rovers will have to go all out to collect full points.'

The city's other two papers were more positive about Tranmere's prospects. 'Tranmere Rovers receive Rotherham United at Prenton

Park, a side the Rovers always find difficult to overcome,' reported the *Daily Post,* 'but with experienced players like Anderson, Hodgson, Price, Ashcroft, Rosenthal and Bridges, they should be strong enough to succeed on this occasion.' The *Echo* commented, 'Tranmere tackle Rotherham at Prenton (3.15) with an 11 which is well known. There are no newcomers, but that is not to say Tranmere's prospects are not bright. They have plenty of useful youngsters, a new management and a right wing which is outstanding. Rotherham are among the sides who always fare well at Prenton but Tranmere should start with a win.'

The *Post* and *Echo* correspondents had reckoned without the artistry of Ardron. Come 3.15pm, however, first to catch the eye of the press box was not Ardron but another proud son of Swinton – referee Percy Snape. 'Mr Snape claimed all the early limelight for his sensible attire,' reported the *Evening Express.* 'He appeared in a maroon battle-dress shirt, with white collar and dark blue shorts.' After Snape, blinking away the raindrops, started the season with a firm blow on his whistle, it was not long before Ardron, on his long-awaited second Football League outing, was making up for lost time. 'ARDRON'S ROVING TACTICS UPSET TRANMERE' announced the 'Green 'Un', 'The United always do well at Tranmere, where they hold a good record of away wins, and they received a hearty welcome from a crowd of about 5,000. Rovers included no newcomers, the directors having great faith in their wartime personnel. Tranmere won the toss. From some close dribbling by Guest, Ardron received the ball and made ground goalwards, until he was deprived of the ball by Tranmere's right-back. A smart tackle by Ardron found Anderson, their home team skipper and right full-back, unawares and compelled him to clear over the line for a fruitless corner.'

Tranmere took the lead in the 25th minute, against the run of play, when Llew Ashcroft's cross was headed home by Harold Atkinson. But then, as the 'Green 'Un' described, 'After 28 minutes, Ardron took the ball on to the left wing and shot. Lloyd gathered the ball but dropped it at the feet of McLean who placed it into the empty net. With the score equal, play settled down and for a while was concentrated in midfield. Tranmere were awarded a free kick for an offence against Bridges, but Williams (H.) saved a dangerous situation with a cool clearance in the penalty area. Following a cleared centre made by McLean, Edwards essayed a long drive which was deflected by a home defender. This was repeated almost immediately when Ardron was through. The roving tactics of Ardron were severely upsetting the Tranmere defence. Just before the interval, Edwards centred for McLean to collect and pass to Ardron who had no difficulty in scoring.'

Rotherham showed their strength in the second half. They added further goals by Albert Wilson and Gladstone Guest to wrap up their third successive win at Prenton Park and extend their unbeaten run there to six matches. 'Tranmere Rovers crashed at home against their bogey opponents, Rotherham United, who well deserved their victory,' reported the *Liverpool Daily Post*. 'Though the visitors were a goal down in 20 minutes, they were always the more impressive side, being faster and more methodical. The Rovers lacked balance and concerted effort. Lloyd had a hectic second half in goal, and but for him the visitors would have won by an even bigger margin.'

It was an impressive performance from Ardron and his team-mates, though few people would have expected Rotherham to be back-page material for the Sunday papers. However, *Sunday Mirror* writer Stanley Russell had conducted an interview with Millers secretary Billy Heald, and on to the back page it went, under the headline 'A CLUB TO BE ENVIED', 'I spoke to secretary W. Heald of Rotherham United in the Third Division North, a man who, in a long lifetime devoted to football, has suffered all the ups and downs of the league game. Rotherham were lucky in being able to keep a team together through the war; being in a highly industrialised area, most of their players stayed at home. Mr Heald thinks this will still be a transitional era, as so many men still have to get Service leave. But with no guests allowed, clubs will be thrown on their own resources – "a fair test of their work in previous seasons," he says. "On the whole, the Third Division clubs stood up very well to the strains of wartime football. The conditions brought about a great levelling up. For the first time for years, we all start level. We're all enthusiastic about our chances and we all really believe we shall win the league. Nearly all of us are booked for a disappointment but it will take a little while to find that out."'

For Rotherham, a fine season would end in disappointment. They scored 114 goals (Ardron contributing 38) but finished in second place behind Doncaster – and only one team was promoted. Similar frustration followed in each of the next two seasons when they were again runners-up, to Lincoln City and Hull City. The richly deserved promotion finally arrived in 1951 when they topped the division by seven points, ahead of Mansfield. At last, up to Division Two went Rotherham as champions of Division Three North while up at the same time from Division Three South went Nottingham Forest, powered by 36 goals from a gentleman they had signed for £10,000 in the summer of 1949 – Wally Ardron.

49

Football League Division Three North
Oldham Athletic 0 Carlisle United 2 (HT: 0-1)
Scorers – Carlisle United: Moir, Broadis
Attendance: 7,696

'Hayes is at present on holiday at Blackpool, but Mr Womack caught up with him by the glad sea waves, and the player signed on the dotted line there and then.'

THE BOURNEMOUTH public address announcer's mournful plea to spectators for clothing coupons (see Chapter 47) was not replicated at Oldham. Around the country, clubs and managers at all levels, including Matt Busby at Manchester United (see Chapter 39) were trying to cobble together kit for their players, but in Oldham it was not a problem. The town's football and rugby teams were smartly attired thanks to the generosity of Alderman Stirling T. Marron. 'The mayor (Alderman S.T. Marron) has made many gifts during his year of office, but none more appreciated than that he is making to Oldham Football Club and at Athletic,' reported the *Oldham Chronicle*. 'To each he is giving a set of jerseys – a particularly valuable gift in these days of clothing coupons which make the provision of players' outfits a persistent headache for club managers.'

The mayor's largesse added to the air of positivity around Boundary Park as the big kick-off approached. Oldham faced an interesting opening-day fixture, at home to a Carlisle United side led by 23-year-old Ivor Broadis, the youngest player-manager in Football League history. After attending the club's final pre-season trial game, seven days before the competitive fixtures began, the *Chronicle* correspondent was as optimistic as could be, 'There was a promotion drive atmosphere about Boundary Park on Saturday when a crowd of over 2,000 saw Athletic's final practice match before the curtain goes up on a season which it is hoped will carry them into the Second Division. Among directors, officials, players and supporters, there was a feeling of confidence, a firmly implanted belief that it will be a notable season for the club. For the first time since 1939, Athletic have had season cards printed, and such has been the demand that it is expected that by tomorrow all those for the ground will have been sold. Enclosure and centre stand cards are still available, but already more have been sold than during the 1939/40 season. After watching a potential first team, which included the close-season captures, play against a reserve team, I felt that confidence was not misplaced. That the match ended in a draw of 2-2 meant very little. What did matter was the way the Blues (first team) played together as a team.'

The *Chronicle* also brought good news on the eve of the match: Athletic manager Frank Womack had enjoyed a productive hunting expedition to Blackpool, 'After a chase round the country, Mr Frank Womack, Athletic's manager, rang me up from Blackpool this morning with the good news that he had re-signed Bill Hayes, the half-back. Hayes lives and works at Runcorn, and his employer was not very keen on releasing him from work to play football. Mr Womack interviewed the employer yesterday and came to a satisfactory arrangement with him. Hayes is at present on holiday at Blackpool, but Mr Womack caught up with him by the glad sea waves, and the player signed on the dotted line there and then. Hayes, who played centre-half for the Blues in last Saturday's final practice, will be among the men from whom the Athletic will pick the team to oppose Carlisle United at Boundary Park this weekend in the first league game of the season.'

On the morning of Saturday, 31 August, Oldham's players rose at their leisure, enjoyed a nice cup of tea and looked forward to donning their smart new jerseys. Carlisle's, meanwhile, were on a draughty bus trundling slowly south from their home nine miles south of the Scottish border. The team coach took five hours to complete the 120-mile journey to the Pennine foothills. That remoteness, far up in beautiful Cumbria, had come at a high cost for United's supporters during the war. After the abandonment of the 1939/40 season, Carlisle took part in the regional competitions that were hastily organised to fill the rest of that campaign. With wartime restrictions, travelling from such an isolated location was extremely difficult and expensive, however, so the club had little choice but to withdraw from senior football for the rest of the conflict. From 1940, Carlisle's football lovers had to make do with the passionate but less illustrious fare of the Carlisle and District League.

United's fans got their team back in August 1945 when Carlisle rejoined Division Three North (East). The club also re-entered the FA Cup, triumphantly at first with an 8-3 aggregate victory over North Shields in the first round, before losing 8-5 to Barrow over two legs in the second. As the club prepared for the return of the Football League, there was also a gradual influx of players returning from the armed forces. Much the most significant arrival was Broadis.

A Londoner, Broadis joined the Royal Air Force and ended the war as a flight lieutenant, serving as a navigator in Transport Command. He was also a very accomplished footballer. A clever and creative inside-forward, during the war he played regularly as an amateur for Tottenham Hotspur and also guested for Millwall, Manchester United and Bradford Park Avenue. After the conflict ended, he was posted to Crosby Aerodrome, just outside Carlisle, and soon began to play for United. Up to Christmas 1945 he continued to play occasionally for Spurs, but thereafter his football loyalties lay with Carlisle. In the summer of 1946, freshly demobbed, he was appointed player-manager. 'Ivor Broadis, now released from the RAF, has been putting the players through the intricacies of ball movement at Brunton Park this week,' reported the *Cumberland News*. 'Ivor has several new moves up his sleeve, and the players are all keenly interested in them. It was grand to watch him demonstrate his "backroom" secrets. There is no question about it, Ivor has got his heart and soul in this manager's job, and he is not lacking in public support, because the Football public are with him 100 per cent.'

The manager was actually the youngest member of the 11 which he selected to face Oldham in his first game. Among the challenges of his first assignment: to shackle a home attack containing four new prongs. Womack had been busy. 'Six new signings figure in Oldham Athletic's team to meet Carlisle United at Boundary Park,' reported the *Manchester Evening News*. 'Four will be in attack. Fred Howe, ex-Grimsby and one-time Maine Road favourite, is to lead the forwards, Blackshaw, another with Manchester City experience, and Butler, signed 12 days ago from Middlesbrough, form the right wing with Ormandy (Southend) on the extreme left.' The *MEN*'s Eric Thornton added, 'I like the strong, all-round look of Oldham Athletic who will surprise most folk if they fail to account for Carlisle at Boundary Park.'

Oldham began the match in a fashion to suggest that all the positivity surrounding the club was justified. 'Athletic were playing well together as a side and their passing was accurate and purposeful,' reported the *Chronicle*. 'It was only sheer bad luck which prevented their taking the lead in the first quarter of an hour. Corner after corner fell to Athletic and once, when the ball was coming in to him at great speed, Jones tipped it over the bar with a brilliant save.'

If you don't take your chances, however, 'Then, at the end of 30 minutes' play, when all against the run of play so far, Carlisle took the lead. This followed a free kick awarded to the visitors a few yards over the halfway line for an infringement by Williamson, who brought down one of the Carlisle forwards. The ball went out to Dellow who returned it smartly to Moir who scored from a yard or two out. This was only the third occasion on which Carlisle had penetrated the home defence.'

If that goal applied a slow puncture to Oldham's momentum, another, two minutes after half-time, deflated it completely. Vastly experienced right-winger Ronnie Dellow, who had made his league debut for Mansfield Town back in 1934, was again the creator. It was from his cross that Jimmy Moir's shot was parried by Bill Harris before Broadis pounced on the rebound to net a decisive debut goal. From that point, Oldham went out like a light. Carlisle controlled the rest of the match to seal the perfect launch to Broadis's reign and a disappointing start to Wakes Week (the annual holiday for workers at the town's mills and factories) for the Oldham fans. The immensely supportive *Chronicle* reporter, however, remained upbeat, suggesting that a more appropriate scoreline would have been a 4-0 win, rather than a 2-0 defeat, 'A Wakes holiday crowd of over eight thousand people who paid £522 at Boundary Park on Saturday were disappointed to see Athletic beaten 2-0 by Carlisle United in the opening game of postwar football. That disappointment was increased by the fact that on the run of play the result should have been at least 4-0 for Athletic. It was just the right setting for the opening of a season which we are all hoping will be a promotion one for Athletic. The crowd was in holiday mood, loud speakers around the ground were cheering them with gay music, and when the teams turned out, one felt that the club's enthusiastic followers were saying to themselves, "Now we shall see an Athletic side that can play football as it should be played."

'The general inference to be drawn was that here was a side that should be persevered with to give them a chance to settle down and blend thoroughly. After all, it was not all bad finishing that left Athletic with a blank card. Luck was dead against them. On many occasions, Harris and his colleagues scraped the ball away in the nick of time when in nine cases out of ten, goals would have resulted. I hope Athletic will not be discouraged by this reverse. Luck will not always be against them, and a little more punch in finishing will swing the odds in their favour.'

Oldham did have better luck in the next three games, taking five points out of six from Halifax Town, Accrington Stanley and Rochdale, but they struggled badly as the season deepened. Eight defeats in nine games between 8 February and 12 April left them in the bottom four and there they finished, in 19th position. Their final game brought a rout at Rotherham. The season which began with such high hopes ended with an 8-0 defeat at Millmoor. 'Athletic were cut to ribbons,' lamented the *Chronicle*. 'The wonder is the score was not doubled. Comparison between the teams beggars description. It cannot be said, however, that Rotherham owed their pronounced success to a scintillating display of polished football. They do not believe in sparkle at Millmoor. Experience has taught them the reverse. Power football is their motto, and it has been justified by results.'

Carlisle's season also failed to hit the heights. The defence that rode its luck at Boundary Park was less fortunate elsewhere, conceding nine at Doncaster and six at Rochdale as well as a five and four fours.

They finished in 16th place and were to spend the rest of the 1940s hovering around mid-table. The talents of Broadis as a player could not be contained in Division Three North. In January 1949, he joined Sunderland for a fee of £18,000, but his bond with Carlisle United was to remain lifelong. His playing career was stellar. After two years at Roker Park, he moved to Manchester City where he rose into the England team. He became the first England player ever to score twice in a World Cup match when he did so in a 4-4 draw with Belgium in Basel in the group stage of the 1954 finals in Switzerland.

The following summer, after a short spell at Newcastle United, Broadis returned to Brunton Park as player-coach. He ended his playing days in Scotland, at Queen of the South, but still hadn't finished with his beloved Carlisle. He became a well-respected sports reporter and, for many years, wrote for the *Newcastle Journal* and *Sunday Sun* before, appropriately, a final spell at the *Carlisle Evening News*.

50

Football League Division One
Preston North End 3 Leeds United 2 (HT: 2-1)
Scorers – Preston North End: McIntosh, Finney, Dougal; Leeds United: Grainger (2)
Attendance: 25,000

'He took Milburn to the line then with a quick turn and side flick, sent his opponent stumbling and reeling off his balance into space. He left himself with a clear opening and planted a beautiful shot just inside the far post.'

FOR SUPPORTERS of Doncaster Rovers, the 1946/47 season was a wonderful journey, filled with excitement and joy, culminating in glory (see Chapter 29). They didn't want it to end. Thirty-five miles away, the fans of Leeds United endured the polar opposite. They couldn't wait for it to end. Leeds collected only 18 points, a record low for Division One, as an ageing side, which manager Billy Hampson had no money to strengthen, suffered 30 defeats in 42 league games.

The first of those defeats, away to Preston North End on the opening day, gave no indication of the nightmare ahead for United. It was a tight, hard-fought, competitive match. They just happened to run into a masterclass from a player on his way to becoming one of England's all-time greats. For Preston-born Tom Finney, freshly demobbed, it was a belated Football League debut. A fiendishly fast, skilful and tricky winger, the 24-year-old had fledged in the North End team during the wartime years and was a month away from making the first of his 76 appearances for England. Already he was widely regarded as the natural successor to Stanley Matthews on England's right flank.

Finney clearly presented the biggest danger to Leeds, though if Hampson and his team leafed through the pages of the *Lancashire Evening Post* on the way to Deepdale, they discovered plenty of evidence that Preston, as a whole, was a dangerous place.

'PRESTON ACCIDENTS' was the simple headline, 'Preston Ambulance was kept busy today, dealing with a succession of accidents. Elizabeth Hacking, aged 62, of 6 Harold-street, Bolton, fell at the Ribble bus station, Preston, and injured her arm. Seven-year-old Victor McLaren, of 3 Worden-road, Preston, suffered injury when a fishhook penetrated his left hand. George Moore, aged 48, of 10 Moor-avenue, Penwortham, was knocked from his cycle at Howick Cross, near Preston, in a collision with a motor lorry and John Graham, of 10 Eversleigh-street, Preston, received injuries to his back when he fell 12ft from a scaffold at the Ribble power station. They were all taken to Preston Royal Infirmary.'

As if the infirmary staff didn't have enough on their plate, they were also required to deal with a self-imposed casualty – 'SWALLOWED SPOON', 'Francis Henry Albert Voisey (32), of no fixed address, who swallowed his teeth at Fulwood, Preston, police station, while in custody on a charge of housebreaking, was again taken to Preston Royal Infirmary this morning. This time he had swallowed part of a spoon.'

Leeds arrived at Deepdale with a solid league record over the previous two decades. They had spent 13 of 15 seasons up to the war in Division One, but the last five brought only one top-ten finish, so it was a difficult start for them, against one of the great clubs of world football. Preston North End were founder members of the Football League in 1888 and won the title in its first two seasons. They continued to challenge hard, finishing second for the next three years, two points behind Everton in 1891, five behind Sunderland in 1892 and 11 behind Sunderland in 1893, but then lost power and, in 1946, were still waiting to complete the hat-trick of titles. They suffered occasional dips into Division Two but returned to the top level in 1934 and re-established themselves there. In 1938, the glory days returned when they lifted the FA Cup, George Mutch's last-minute penalty seeing off Huddersfield Town 1-0 in the first final to be broadcast live on television. Good times were back at Deepdale and the war interrupted a rising belief that it was time to complete that title hat-trick. With Finney in the ranks, along with the Scottish powerhouse Bill Shankly and newly signed striker Billy McIntosh, they went into the 1946/47 season as realistic title contenders.

The *Yorkshire Evening Post*'s match preview was brief, 'Leeds United visit Preston, where they drew 0-0 on the opening day in 1939. Ainsley is unfit with an injured shoulder, and Henry will play at centre-forward.' Greater space was allocated to an opinion piece from the paper's United correspondent Will Watch whose style was less rooted in brevity, 'Football form, so difficult to estimate at the best of times, was never more of a mystery than today. One difficulty is to imagine how nearly the standard of play in the regional competitions last season approximates to the ability and staying power necessary this season when teams will be all out, and when much more thorough training has been possible. Another incalculable factor is the effect of the war years on older players. How many of them will be able to reproduce the form of which they were capable in 1939?

'Supporters all over the country have been lamenting that their own particular club has been lacking in enterprise and prophesying serious deficiencies, but it is astonishing how prone the followers of a club often are to belittle their own team, though they get enthusiastic enough when the game is on. At various times there have been some Dismal Jimmies at Elland Road, but looking through some old programmes a day or two ago, it was cheering to find references to Leeds United which were as complimentary as anyone could wish for.'

The *Evening Post* also brought the latest on the nation's collective desire to fill in and post off their coupons – 'POOLS RUSH BEGINS', 'The football pools "rush" at Leeds post offices has already started, and by next weekend, in the words of a postal official, "It will have warmed up considerably." Most of the additional customers in the last few days have been stamp purchasers. Yesterday, the automatic stamping-machine at the GPO showed a turnover of 15,000 above normal, though there is no proof that all the envelopes were for pools firms. Next week, when all the unlucky forecasters will be owing money, a big demand for postal orders is anticipated.'

As a grey Saturday morning gave way to an even greyer afternoon and kick-off approached, Leeds took the first plaudits. 'The turnstiles were clicking merrily at Deepdale half an hour before the start of the big kick-off in league football after seven years of the ersatz variety,' reported Viator in the *Lancashire Evening Post*. 'Leeds United, as in the opening of the ill-starred 1939/40 season, were the visitors and looked very spruce; a smart, colourful turnout with numbers distinctive, easy to read, and an example to many other clubs. Chief North End interest lay in the debut of the versatile Scottish forward, McIntosh, the long-waited return of Tom Finney, and the experiment of playing energetic Shankly at centre-half.'

McIntosh had just arrived after scoring a lot of goals in his native Scotland for Rangers in wartime competition. He quickly opened his Deepdale account, with an assist from Finney. 'With four minutes gone, North End gave the crowd a real tonic with a beautiful goal, as well-executed as it was begun,' reported Viator. 'Leeds were bewildered by the speed and accuracy of the perfect forward move in which Finney, found unmarked by Horton's pass, slipped a deadly pass inside for McIntosh to take it in his stride and score with an excellent shot across the face of goal, well out of Hodgson's reach. Thus the Scot made an auspicious start with his new club and could not have wished for a bonnier goal.'

After 18 minutes came a moment which brought the crowd to its feet, 'It had class all over it and Finney, the schemer and scorer alike, showed this early he is going to be a tremendous force in North End football. Twice already he had been fouled when sliding and shuffling his tricky way goalwards but the free kicks came to nothing. Now he had Milburn baffled and staring leg-locked and deceived by a slow, fascinating dribble reminiscent of Matthews' finesse of last week. He took Milburn to the line then with a quick turn and side flick, sent his opponent stumbling and reeling off his balance into space. He left himself with a clear opening and planted a beautiful shot just inside the far post. Storming applause greeted this brilliant solo effort.'

Leeds' response was swift and strong. Seven minutes later, they pulled a goal back when Dennis Grainger's shot slithered through the hands of goalkeeper Jack Fairbrother. 'Fairbrother looked somewhat chagrined and it was a surprise he did not get it,' continued Viator. The keeper was beaten again in the second half, again by Grainger, a £1,000 signing from Southport early the previous season, but North End took the points thanks to a goal from Jimmy 'The Galloping Ghost' Dougal.

The *Yorkshire Post and Leeds Intelligencer* saluted the brilliance of Finney but also had encouraging words for his opening-day victims, 'Leeds United learned what many services people have been thinking for a long time – that Finney, of Preston North End, will be in England's team if Matthews loses his form. He scored one of the three goals by which United were defeated in a hard and fairly even match. Milburn was given a trying time attempting to stop him but there was little wrong with the Leeds team. The right wing of Cochrane and Powell did not quite attain its expected high standard and Short and Grainger were the best forwards. But the impression was gained that when the right wing settles down – as it may have done by Wednesday when the cup finalists, Charlton, play at Elland Road, Leeds United's team will be difficult to beat.'

They weren't. Charlton won the midweek match 2-0 and completed the double with a 5-0 victory at The Valley three weeks later. Leeds took three points from the first eight games and were soon adrift at the foot of the table. Their form deteriorated further the longer the season went. They lost 20 of their last 24 games and ended with an away record of won none, drew one (1-1 at Brentford at the end of November) and lost 20. It took them time to recover from such a humiliating relegation but nine years later, managed by Raich Carter, powered by John Charles up front and with a callow Jackie Charlton settling into defence, they returned to Division One.

In the *Lancashire Evening Post*, Viator vaunted Finney but voiced reservations about Preston's team, 'The team's 3-2 win against Leeds was encouraging, if not satisfying; the side can and will play better with improved blend and directness substituted for over-deliberation. The opening performance was too much a one-man show, with Finney excelling in his first game since being demobilised. His composure, mastery artifice and tantalising finesse made his match-winning scheming the talk of the town, and established him as a ready-made successor to Matthews when one is needed.'

The reporter, clearly decades ahead of time in his passion for the collection of data, added, 'The season is young, and early scrappiness can be understood. Sixteen corner kicks (12 to North End) were futile. There were 45 throw-ins, ten offside decisions, 21 saves and clearances by goalkeepers, and 12 free kicks for fouls.'

Forty-two miles to the south, in Runcorn, meanwhile, the number of throw-ins was unrecorded (probably 75 – see Chapter 13) but the home side emulated Preston's result. 'OFF TO A WINNING START. RUNCORN ACCOUNT FOR WIGAN ATHLETIC' was the headline in the *Runcorn Weekly News* after the home side fought back from 2-1 behind to win with two late goals. 'Generally speaking, the Runcorn club has never been one of Dame Fortune's darlings,' the paper reflected. 'If that last-minute incident on Saturday is an indication of the favour she is to bestow this season, then Runcorn can look forward to a successful time.'

Never mind Billy Wright, Jackie Milburn, Len Shackleton, Nat Lofthouse, Tommy Lawton, Willie Waddell, George Robledo, Sam Bartam, Stanley Matthews, Ted Ditchburn, Gil Merrick, Raich Carter, Bill Shankly, Wilf Mannion, Stan Mortensen, Frank Swift, Ivor Broadis, Tommy Lawton and all the other great footballers, if there's one player that any team wants on its side, it's Dame Fortune.

Acknowledgements

SO MANY people have been so helpful towards the writing of this book. It simply would not have been possible without the kindness of those who contributed their time, knowledge and expertise. Friends I knew well were as great as I expected them to be. People I knew slightly delivered big style. People who had never heard of me until they received a random email or text were amazingly helpful. I could pick out examples of where the generosity of time and spirit was exceptional, but where would I stop?

At the heart of the project was the brilliant British Newspaper Archive. For the vast majority of their existence, newspapers were crucial to their communities. They reflected, with total immediacy and authenticity, exactly what was happening in their locality and their time, so the BNA is an unbelievably precious resource. Every newspaper from 1946, for example, is like a small history book – my word, they packed in so much info!

It is very sad that the newspaper industry is so spectacularly diminished. If, 80 years from now, a writer wishes to research 2026, newspapers will be of some use, but will nowhere near tell the story of their age in such magnificently descriptive, detailed and engaging fashion.

For every chapter, I plundered the pages of the relevant newspapers, mainly from August and September 1946, but occasionally also other years. My deepest thanks and respect go to all the reporters from across the UK, from Aberdeen to Torquay and from Swansea to Norwich, who filled the papers with such colourful and passionate accounts of what was happening around them. Some of the writing is just wonderful: bold, quirky, informative, funny.

Thanks to Duncan Olner for the cover design and to Andrea Dunn for proofreading. Heartfelt thanks also to: Wayne and Sarah for telling me to stop talking about the project and get on with it; to Phil, Jo and Jack for the invaluable feedback and encouragement; to wonderful Anele for all the support (darling, this project would not have happened without you!); and to wonderful Mary for the strength and inspiration to carry on.

Thanks too to Neil Allen, Ash Ball, Mike Berry, David Blair, Richard Bland, Jess Blower, Jim Brown, Lionel Clauzon, Marion and Richard Clemons, John Cole, John Coyle, Julia Davison, Jenny Driver, Neil Duggan, Matt Epps, Dave Fletcher, Henri Griessel, Molly Griessel, Roger and Lesley Halford, Boeta Kemp, Rebecca Marsh, Ian Mathews, Frank McCrossan, Dr Kirsty McGill, Johnny Meynell, Dan Nice, Gary Nickolls, Phil O'Farrell, Ben Parham, Kevin Plant, Max Saunders, Sara Steel, David Steele, Mark Taylor, Doug Thomson, Norman Turpin, Samantha Wadsworth, Katherine Williamson and to the staff at Basildon Borough Heritage, the Royal Berkshire Archives and the libraries in Accrington, Bolton, Bristol, Chesterfield, Glasgow (Mitchell Library), Ipswich (Queensland, Australia), Mansfield, Newport, Oldham, Rochdale, Southend, Stratford-upon-Avon, Swindon and Wrexham.

There were occasions when highly respected sources differed on matters of fact. I have done my best to check and ratify and, as far as possible, consult experts. Apologies if any errors or inaccuracies have slipped through.

Offices

APARTMENT 135, Fairways Drakensberg Resort; Bake180, Middleton Hall; Birmingham International Airport; Bread & Co, Warwick; Broadwalk Shopping Centre, Edgware; Brooks Building, Manchester Metropolitan University; 15.32pm train from London Marylebone to Warwick; Caffè Nero, Holborn; Coffee Junction, Warwick; Coffee on the Corner, Kenilworth; Costa, Balsall Common and Tesco, Warwick; The Creative Café, Kenilworth; Devil's Punch Bowl Café, Surrey; Driffield Library; Ellamia, St Martin's Lane, London; Fantaste, Oxford; Freben and Marissa's living room, West Meon; Frensham Pond Hotel; Gateway Café, Southam; Greenhouse at Ardingly Crescent; Hatton Arms; Hatton Locks Café, Warwick; High Peak Bookstore and Café, Buxton; High Wycombe railway station; Hotel Verde, Cape Town; Hyatt Hotel, Manchester; Ice Station Zebra; Kyndfolk, Worcester; Lamb and Flag, Abergavenny; Lina's Place, Warwick; Little Treat Café, Abergavenny; Love Coffee Co, Oxford; Morrisons car park, Solihull; Mulberry Café, Hereford; Norse Airways flight between Gatwick and Cape Town; Nuffield Hospital, Leamington; Pool Close Farm, Fenny Bentley; Premier Inn, Gatwick; Pret, Holborn; Red Rose Tea Room, Grayshott; Ryanair flight 9935 between Birmingham and Budapest; Safair flight FA171 from Cape Town to Durban; Starbucks, Stratford-upon-Avon; St Borromeo Church, Hampton-on-the-Hill; Sue's Place, Stratford-upon-Avon; The Village Café, Grayshott; Voco Hotel, Marylebone; Warwick Arms; Waterstones café, Birmingham city centre; New Road, Worcestershire County Cricket Club.

Bibliography

Books

Allan, J., *Rangers' Eventful Years 1934–1951*
Barclay, P., *Sir Matt Busby: The Man Who Made A Football Club*
Bonner, M., & Halford, B., *Past Imperfect*
Brodie, J., & Dickinson, J. *Sheffield Wednesday: The Complete Record*
McColl, G., *The Official Biography of Celtic*
Peskett, R., *The Crystal Palace Story*
Peterson, M., *A Century of City – The Centenary History of Hull City AFC*
Robertson, F., *The Men with the Educated Feet – A Statistical and Pictorial History of Queen's Park FC*
Rollin. J., *Soccer at War: 1939–1945*
Sands, Rev N., *Crystal Palace: The History of the Club 1905–1997*
Searl S., *Mansfield Town: A Complete Record 1910–1990*

Websites

afcheritage.org
aftn.co.uk
arsenal.com
avfc.co.uk
barrowafc.com
bcfc.co.uk
beesunited.org.uk
brentford.com
brightonandhovealbion.com
bristolrovers.co.uk
bristolroverssc.co.uk
brownhillsbob.com
bwfc.co.uk

canadasoccer.com
canaries.co.uk
cardiffcityfc.co.uk
chelseafc.com
clydefc.co.uk
cobboldfht.com
crewealex.net
dcfc.co.uk
doncasterroversfcprogrammes.com
eastfifefc.co.uk
englandfootballonline.com
englishfootballstats.co.uk
everton.com
ewegottalove.com
footballheritage.co.uk
friendsofthealdershotmilitarymuseum.org.uk
fulhamfc.com
gateshead-fc.com
grecianarchive.exeter.ac.uk
greensonscreen.co.uk
gtfcheritage.co.uk
hartlepoolunited.co.uk
haslemeresociety.org
hattersheritage.co.uk
itfc.co.uk
kingsteigntonhistorysociety.org
lcfc.com
leytonorient.com
liverpoolfc.com
mancity.com
manutd.com
mfc.co.uk
mightyLeeds.co.uk
millwallfc.co.uk
millwall-history.org
mselliott.plus.com

nationalfootballmuseum.com
newcastleunited.com
new-brighton-afc.co.uk
newport-county.co.uk
ntfc.co.uk
nufc-history.co.uk
oncloudseven.com
penninewaterways.co.uk
plymouth.gov.uk
port-vale.co.uk
portsmouth.co.uk
portvalenostalgia.co.uk
prideofanglia.com
qpr.co.uk
queensparkfc.co.uk
readingfc.co.uk
rochdaleafc.co.uk
saddlers.co.uk
safc.com
scottishfa.co.uk
scottishsporthistory.com
sheffieldhomeoffootball.org
snooker.org
southendunited.co.uk
southendtimeline.co.uk
southportcentral.co.uk
spartacus-educational.com
stagsnet.net
stmirren.info
sunderlandafc.news
swanseacity.com
swindontownfc.co.uk
sufc.com
tranmererovers.co.uk
thecelticwiki.com
thelinnets.co.uk

themillers.co.uk
thisisanfield.com
wakefieldfhs.org.uk
watfordfc.com
whufc.com
wikipedia
wolves.co.uk
wolvesheroes.com
wpbsa.com
wrexhamafc.co.uk
wrexhamafcarchive.co.uk
yorkcityfootballclub.co.uk

Newspapers and magazines

Acton Gazette
Aldershot News
BackPass
Barnsley Chronicle
Barrow News
Berkshire Chronicle
Birmingham Daily Gazette
Bolton Evening News
Bury News
Croydon Times
Daily Herald
Daily News (London)
Daily Record
East End News and London Shipping Chronicle
Eastern Football News 'Pink 'Un'
Evening Despatch
Evening News (London)
Glasgow Evening Times
Grimsby Daily Telegraph
Halifax Daily Courier and Guardian
Hamlet Historian
Hampshire Telegraph

Hartlepool Northern Daily Mail
John O'Groat Journal
Liverpool Daily Post
Liverpool Echo
Liverpool Evening Express
Manchester Evening News
Mansfield Chronicle
Newcastle Evening Chronicle
Newcastle Journal
Northamptonshire Chronicle
Nottingham Evening Post
Nottingham Journal
Oldham Evening Chronicle
Reading Mercury
Reading Standard
South London Observer
South London Press
South Wales Daily Post
Southend Pictorial
Southend Standard
Stockport County Express
Sunday Dispatch (London)
Sunday Post
Swindon Advertiser
The Cricketer
The Guardian
The Independent
The People
Weekly Dispatch (London)
Western Daily Press
Western Mail
Western Morning News
Western Morning Press
Wolverhampton Express & Star
Wrexham Leader